Public information films

Manchester University Press

Public information films

British government film units, 1930–52

Alan J. Harding

MANCHESTER UNIVERSITY PRESS

Copyright © Alan J. Harding 2024

The right of Alan J. Harding to be identified as the author of this work has been asserted in accordance with the Copyright, Designs and Patents Act 1988.

Published by Manchester University Press
Oxford Road, Manchester, M13 9PL

www.manchesteruniversitypress.co.uk

British Library Cataloguing-in-Publication Data
A catalogue record for this book is available from the British Library

ISBN 978 1 5261 5478 1 hardback

First published 2024

The publisher has no responsibility for the persistence or accuracy of URLs for any external or third-party internet websites referred to in this book, and does not guarantee that any content on such websites is, or will remain, accurate or appropriate.

Typeset by Newgen Publishing UK

Contents

List of figures	*page* vi
List of tables	viii
Preface	ix
Introduction	1
1 A shaky start – the British government and film, 1900–30	28
2 The Empire Marketing Board Film Unit: Tallents, Grierson, documentaries and the revival of government interest, 1930–33	43
3 The General Post Office Film Unit in peacetime, 1933–37	69
4 Rumours of war and the creation of the Crown Film Unit, 1938–40	90
5 The Crown Film Unit's wartime productions, 1940–45	109
6 The Crown Film Unit's post-war productions, 1946–52	141
7 Non-theatrical exhibition and audiences	179
8 Commercial and theatrical exhibition	200
9 The end of government filmmaking, 1951–52	221
10 Legacy	238
Appendix: A note on film listing	265
Bibliography	302
Index	321

List of figures

1.1 In *Shelling the Red Cross* (1900), an early propaganda film, the Boers target a hospital tent with inevitable results   *page* 30

1.2 An animated propaganda film showing the German High Seas Fleet shelling the UK's east coast towns in December 1914   37

2.1 *O'er Hill and Dale* (1932) showed the tough existence of hill farmers   58

2.2 *Plums That Please* (1931): one of the EMB Film Unit's simple advertisements   61

2.3 *Close Quarters* (1943) with Jack Lee (director) and Jonah Jones behind the camera. Note the wooden rig on the submarine's conning tower   65

3.1 Evelyn Spice's *Calendar of the Year* (1936) was an annual review of the many tasks carried out by the General Post Office   77

3.2 In *Night Mail* (1936), the travelling post office was a studio set   80

3.3 Post Office staff count daily savings slips in *John Atkins Saves Up* (1934)   83

4.1 The kazoo band in Humphrey Jennings' *Spare Time* (1939)   96

4.2 In preparation for the imminent conflict, the threat of gas attack loomed large, as shown in *If War Should Come* (1939)   98

4.3 The deployment of anti-aircraft balloons in *Squadron 992* (1940)   103

List of figures

5.1	There was a price for authenticity: none of the aircrew of F-Freddie in *Target for Tonight* (1941) survived the war	117
5.2	Sometimes authenticity was staged: a production shot from *Coastal Command* (1942)	118
6.1	A British soldier manhandles an elderly German in *A Defeated People* (1946)	153
6.2	An example of an early campaign against drinking and driving in *Mr Jones Takes the Air* (1946)	165
6.3	Gwen Mercer telling her husband that she expects a nuclear attack in *The Waking Point* (1951)	172
7.1	An early cinema van	186
7.2	Mobile film show car leaving London's Senate House (c. 1943)	187
7.3	A Ministry of Information film show in a works canteen (1944)	198
8.1	*Target for Tonight* (1941), US cinema poster	209
10.1	In *Hole in the Ground* (1962) a telephonist is told that, above ground, her family has been obliterated in a Soviet nuclear attack	258

List of tables

7.1 Categories of COI Film Library borrowers,
   1 September 1946 to 17 April 1947   *page* 183
7.2 MoI film audiences, 1940–44   188
A.1 Government film units' production listing, 1930–52   268

Preface

The original idea behind this book goes back several decades and is a result of a coincidence of both my academic interests and personal circumstances. During my master's course at Queen Mary University of London, my supervisor was the late Professor John Ramsden. John was an early advocate of film as a valuable historical resource and introduced his students to such seminal works as Leni Riefenstahl's *Triumph of the Will* (1935) and Sergei Eisenstein's *Battleship Potemkin* (1925). I now understand that at the time this was seen as both quite subversive by the senior management of the department of history at Queen Mary and contrary to departmental policy. It is difficult to believe, forty years later, that there is not a history course from GCSE to postgraduate level which does not include at least a reference to Riefenstahl's film when discussing Nazi Germany. The moving visual image gives reality, however vicarious, to events and personalities.

My academic interest coincided with a piece of family history which began my particular interest in the General Post Office and Crown film units. My wife's uncle was Frank (Jonah) Jones who, along with H. E. 'Chick' Fowle and Fred Gamage, was a senior unit cameraman from the mid-1930s until Crown closed in 1952. Sadly Jonah died in 1973, but occasionally his younger sister Iris (my mother-in-law) had been included in visits to studios and locations where she met some of the luminaries of the time, such as Humphrey Jennings, Harry Watt and J. B. (Jack) Holmes, and was happy to relate her experience.

What piqued my interest further was both the relative lack of academic discussion about the production of the units' quite extensive catalogue and the general concentration upon a very few of their films. Around the millennium I had the opportunity to discuss this with John Ramsden and he suggested that the government film units would be a valuable area to research. Perhaps inevitably life and employment interrupted the smooth completion of the research, but it is important for me to recognise those others who gave their time and expertise in helping me both complete my doctoral studies and the development of these into this book. Obviously, I must thank all those archivists and librarians in many establishments who helped me with good grace and interminable patience. Also, the technicians at the British Film Institute (BFI) and elsewhere who good-naturedly endured my incompetence with the Steenbeck and rescued me (and the films) on several occasions.

Over the years I have attended a number of conferences and meetings and had the good fortune to discuss my ideas with many scholars. However, there are a few whom I need to identify, as without their support and advice I would have been completely at sea. I've already mentioned the debt I owe to John Ramsden, but Mark Glancy, his colleague at Queen Mary University of London, helped me immensely in developing the research. After a somewhat lengthy hiatus I was encouraged to recommence my study by Karen Randell, then of Southampton Solent University, and I must especially thank my PhD supervisors there, Mark Aldridge and Claire Hines.

I appreciate that in these circumstances it is expected that one thanks one's family but, in my case, it is particularly true. Without the support and occasional prompting of my wife, Mo, then I'm sure this book would have never seen the light of day!

Introduction

Following the general election of 25 October 1951, one of the first actions of the new Conservative administration was to shut down the government's main film production facility. The Crown Film Unit (CFU), with its direct antecedents the Empire Marketing Film Unit (EMBFU) and the General Post Office Film Unit (GPOFU), had completed more than two decades of filmmaking. The units were dismissed in a Central Office of Information (COI) circular which was both brutal and to the point: 'The Crown Film Unit will be disbanded and the mobile projection service abolished. There will be no more home theatrical distribution and narrow limits placed on home film production' (The National Archives, Kew (hereafter TNA): COI 352, 29 January 1952). The unit's political executioner, John Boyd-Carpenter, the financial secretary to the Treasury, later managed to spare it a couple of lines in his autobiography, commenting:

> The CFU made, at Government expense, beautiful films often of high artistic merit. They were also films which no commercial producer would make because they would not pay. So, regrettably, I came to the conclusion that this was not a necessary function of Government. (Boyd-Carpenter, 1980, p. 100)

In 1952 Boyd-Carpenter disregarded the fact that these 'beautiful films' had only recently been internationally endorsed by the Academy Award Oscar for best documentary feature for *Daybreak in Udi*, a film about modernisation in Nigeria. The CFU, EMBFU and GPOFU had produced around 375 films between 1930 and 1952, ranging from short animations to feature-length movies.

A very few of these films, such as *Industrial Britain* (1932) and *Night Mail* (1936), are regarded as almost iconic representations of both the time they were created as well as of the documentary genre. The popularity of others like *Target for Tonight* (1941) and *Fires Were Started* (1943) were based upon their reflection of the British experience during the Second World War. These two wartime films were directed, respectively, by Harry Watt and Humphrey Jennings, who were both regarded as key figures within the British documentary movement. The roll call of the EMBFU, GPOFU and CFU included many who either were, or went on to become, highly successful in the British film and television industries, including John Grierson, J. B. (Jack) Holmes, Pat Jackson, Philip Leacock, Jack Lee, John Mortimer and many more.

From the very beginning the films produced by these luminaries were not usually feature-length cinema-exhibited films, but rather short public information films (PIFs) of between five and twenty minutes. These films were sponsored by the Empire Marketing Board, the General Post Office (GPO) and later, during the Second World War, by the Ministry of Information (MoI). Although the units had never shied away from seeking commissions from departments other than their own sponsoring ministry, after the war ended survival depended upon pitching to individual government departments through the COI. Topics had always ranged widely, from the obviously GPO-sponsored *Introducing the Dial* (1935), to *Malta G.C.* (1943), a film celebrating the heroic defence of the island in the face of massive aerial bombardment, *Breeding for Milk* (1947), a specialist film for those in the dairy industry, and, towards the end, *Festival in London* (1951) which, unsurprisingly, commemorated the Festival of Britain.

The units' films, particularly after 1940, were shown extensively on the commercial cinema exhibition circuits, but also equally widely through non-theatrical venues such as military bases, factory canteens, church and village halls and even in the West African bush. Consequently, millions of people in the UK and overseas, in both colonies and independent countries, saw their productions. The closure of the CFU certainly deprived the country of a major production unit of international reputation, but in doing so it enabled and encouraged the careers of many eminent film directors, cameramen, sound and ancillary technicians who became the backbone of much of the British film and later television industries of the 1950s and 1960s.

A great deal has been written about aspects of these three linked film units although this has usually been of the cherry-picking variety; their overall film catalogue has, as yet, to be considered in its entirety. Those who have approached the films from an auteur perspective, such as Brian Winston (1999), have perhaps unsurprisingly concentrated on the major feature-length films. Yet Humphrey Jennings, probably the CFU's most famous director, not only directed *The Silent Village* (1943) but also *Post Haste* (1934); producer Ian Dalrymple not only produced the Jennings-directed *Fires Were Started* but a year earlier *Builders* (1942), and cameraman Jonah Jones not only shot *Target for Tonight* but also *Roadways* (1937). A small group of people, admittedly a fluctuating membership, produced a variety of films from 1930 until 1952, but there has as yet been no significant attempt to consider the units as a coherent linked structure. A critical review of the three units and their complete production canon informed by original archival research is the primary purpose behind this book.

The closure announcement in 1952 was met with some limited opposition, sufficient to show that the CFU was regarded contemporaneously as an important production house not only in terms of the dissemination of government policies, but also one with an international reputation and model upon which others, such as those film units in colonies like Jamaica and Malaya, were configured. Yet subsequently the standing of the three film units seems to have suffered and their importance and successes mostly ignored. Perhaps this was because the majority of the productions were not major feature films directed by famous individuals with gala premieres and massive audiences but shorts, often with unattractive titles, and were therefore deemed as undeserving of study. Perhaps, too, even though the units were clearly important parts of the British documentary movement, their instrumental and sometimes propagandist output was thought unworthy.

Consequently, this book will endeavour to place the units within their historical, political, social and filmic contexts. It will be especially concerned with explaining why, from the early 1930s to the early 1950s, the units had developed a substantial reputation for producing what became essentially templates for government PIFs.

As far as reception of the films was concerned, it will consider whether the units' output contributed to the British self-image, especially during wartime but also in the subsequent, and less well-studied, post-war years of austerity.

Overall, this book seeks to explore the valuable and overlooked film canon of the main British government film units. It will assess their importance both as film production facilities and as a significant and underutilised resource for the study of Britain from the 1930s through to the early 1950s.

A review of sources

It is perhaps a little surprising, given that the film units became, almost by default, the government's own production facility during the often turbulent pre-war, wartime and post-war worlds, that they have failed to substantially trouble academic discourse except in very narrow ways. The British Film Institute (BFI) has done something to remedy this omission with the collections of essays in Patrick Russell and James Piers Taylor's *Shadows of Progress: Documentary Film in Post-War Britain* (2010) and the next year Scott Anthony and James Mansell's *The Projection of Britain: A History of the GPO Film Unit* (2011). Although both volumes are excellent in their own ways, the essay format does not really promote a coherent, complete and chronological analysis.

It is certainly true that in many of the biographies or autobiographies of John Grierson (1966, 1978, 1979, 1990, 2000), Laurie Lee (2000, 2014) and even John Mortimer (1982, 2005), to name a few, the film units made cameo appearances but, in the main, they were seen as either transitory or, at best, marginally transformative. Mortimer, for example, a young scriptwriter who was exempted military service in the Second World War on health grounds, was somewhat scathing in his retrospective account of the films: 'though efficient at showing the herring fleet putting out to sea, or bombers rising into the air to the accompaniment of symphonic music by Vaughan Williams, they were poor at dealing with human motives and dilemmas' (Mortimer, 1979, p. 6). This judgement at forty-five years' distance does not seem to reflect that of the contemporary reviewers, as will be seen.

For the later years under study there is one contemporary source that does address the CFU and other production houses' films. The Dartington Hall Trust sponsored a survey which was eventually published by Oxford University Press on behalf of the Arts Enquiry and entitled *The Factual Film* (Arts Enquiry, 1947).[1] Essentially this was a review of documentaries and documentary-type films produced during the Second World War. It is valuable in that it not only reviewed the essential themes covered but also looked at the distribution and exhibition of these films. It certainly confirms that there was a ready audience for them as, 'in the ordinary cinema over 25 million attendances are being recorded each week' (Arts Enquiry, 1947, p. 151). The conclusions were quite upbeat and optimistic as the review argued that 'the success of the MoI's non-theatrical film service during the war [in particular] and the development of film for educational, social and cultural purposes shows an increasing interest in the wider use of film' (Arts Enquiry, 1947, p. 153).

Yet within four years the newly elected Conservative government had announced the dissolution of the CFU and this engendered perhaps the most disputatious and widely circulated of all the published material. Much of this appeared inevitably in the trade and popular press in the early 1950s. The speed and apparent remorselessness of the decision to close the CFU did cause some shock and, as such, claims that it was a political vendetta.[2] As the *Manchester Guardian* reported:

> Mr J A Boyd-Carpenter, Financial Secretary to the Treasury, amplifying the Chancellor's statement that expenditure on Government information services in 1952–3 would be reduced by at least £1.2m below the 1951–2 figure, [announced] that production of the films by the Central Office of Information would cease. (*Manchester Guardian*, 30 January 1952)

This announcement not only terminated the activities of the CFU but also closed its new studios at Beaconsfield and ended the exhibition of COI films using mobile cinema vans. At the stroke of a pen, more than twenty years of film production on behalf of the government was ended. As has been seen, the opposition to the closure did not just come from the documentarists themselves but also included representatives of the relevant trades unions and others on the left of British politics. Perhaps surprisingly, there was even some reservation from the commercial sector of the industry, not natural opponents of a Conservative government. The wartime agreements made with the Cinema Exhibitors Association (CEA) and the Kinematograph Renters Society had continued beyond 1945. These arrangements permitted the free distribution of twelve official short films and thirty trailers a year on commercial circuits, giving access to some 4,700 cinemas. It has been estimated that 'one short could be seen by as many as 6 million, and it was theoretically possible for the "flashes" to be shown 47,000 times over a three-week period' (Wildy, 1988, p. 195). The exhibitors were thus assured of something 'new' and free for their programmes and this also enabled the government to spread appropriate informational messages. Although by 1951 many cinema owners and managers had become less than sympathetic towards these government film shorts, their trade journal, *Kinematograph Weekly*, reacted to the closure of the CFU with some reservations:

> The curtailment of film making for Government Departments could be a serious blow for our members, but we hope to be given credit for taking the broader view. It would be extremely dangerous to our economic survival and to our position as a first class Power to deprive the nation of the essential means for expressing and interpreting our political, social and industrial objectives throughout the world.
> (*Kinematograph Weekly*, 14 February 1952)

Overall, however, it was probably fortunate for the government that any significant outcry against closure of the CFU was swiftly muted by worry over the health and subsequent death of King George VI, which effectively relegated concern over government filmmaking in the news agenda.

Although modern sources do exist for the study of the film units, they normally address them as more or less peripheral to the main topic and thus tend to fall within a number of related categories which are subsequently reviewed in more detail below: individual film monographs, film history and especially that of the documentary movement, biographies and autobiographies of the most prominent, and film and propaganda.

Unsurprisingly, the most complete and tangible records of the Empire Marketing Board, General Post Office and Crown film units are the films themselves. During their twenty-two years of existence, about 375 films of varying length, subject matter and quality were produced. Most of these films are archived and available through either the BFI or the Imperial War Museum (IWM). Many have also recently found their way on to YouTube and other free access internet sites, having been uploaded from a variety of sources. Yet, despite this ready availability – and the fact that the original screenings of many of the short films had formed regular parts of individual cinema programmes, and also that there was a flourishing non-theatrical exhibition circuit, both of which guaranteed a substantial contemporary audience – very little has been written about the films from the perspective of either historical or film analysis.

Of course, there are notable exceptions to this and these tend, generally, to fall into two categories; either individual film monographs or, more frequently, as part of film histories which are usually thematically or chronologically titled. In the former category, Kenneth Short's (1997) *RAF Bomber Command's Target for Tonight*, which was a review of Harry Watt's 1941 film, neatly encapsulated some of the key features of subsequent CFU productions examined later in this research:

> *Target for Tonight* must be judged, in its own right and in its own time; applying those criteria, *Target for Tonight* was a fine piece of moviemaking by a very talented filmmaker… What Watt achieved in 1941 figuratively blew away audiences and critics alike with the realism of his camerawork and his unmatched skill in leading non-professional actors to authentic performances, immeasurably enhanced by the skilled cutting of Stewart McAlister. And yet the film was still largely artifice; *Target for Tonight* was not the real thing, including the compression of an eighteen-hour period into forty-eight to fifty minutes. It was still 'Lights, Camera, Action!' in a cut-open Wellington fuselage on a sound-stage at Denham Studios. (Short, 1997, p. 200)

As will be discussed later, much of the contemporary success of such feature films was attributed to their realism and authenticity. However, as Short observed, a great deal of the production was traditional film craft and deception.

Short's review was followed a few years later by Brian Winston's 1999 BFI study of Jennings' *Fires Were Started*, which stands out as an exemplar of an in-depth analysis of a particular CFU film. Along very similar lines Adrian Smith focussed on another Jennings film,

The Heart of Britain (1941), in 2003. His and Winston's approach differ slightly from Short in that the films are primarily vehicles for examining the methods and ideas of the director, Jennings. Smith, for example, considered Jennings' depiction of the working class, asking;

> Did *Heart of Britain* simply confirm the prejudices of Jennings' fiercest critics on the left, not least those admirers of John Grierson grouped around the *Documentary News Letter* who lambasted the supposedly naive, romanticised, sentimentalist view of a 'mass observation lad'?... Jennings' view of a class from which, for all his good intentions, he remained so detached [was probably influenced by] trudging the rubble-strewn streets of Coventry or the East End. (Smith, 2003, p. 135)

In his later wartime CFU films Jennings continued to present 'ordinary' people as idealistic and heroic – as, for example, the miners in *The Silent Village* (1943), the firemen in *Fires Were Started* and Goronwy and Bill, respectively, the miner and train driver, in *A Diary for Timothy* (1945).

This director-focussed approach has been adopted elsewhere in the occasional review of individual productions which have appeared in a variety of collected works. Most notably, in the BFI's *Projection of Britain: A History of the GPO Film Unit* (2011) a section is given over to discussing particular films. So, for example, David Matless reviewed *The Horsey Mail* (1938) and Wendy Webster *The Silent Village*. The latter film, a homage to those Czech citizens of Lidice massacred by the Nazis, was also reviewed by John Hartley and emerged, somewhat bizarrely, in *Beautiful Things in Popular Culture* (McKee, 2007).

However, discussion of the films produced by the EMB, GPO and Crown film units appear most frequently in those texts which can be described as histories of film and these also usually fall also into two distinctive, but inevitably overlapping, categories. In both cases the authors' choices of films tend to be limited to a few of the more famous feature-length productions. In the former category, the films feature significantly in books concerning the documentary movement, whereas the latter would include those about films, both contemporary and later, concerning the Second World War and its aftermath.

The post-war academic reflection on the importance of the British documentary movement commenced in some senses with the work of Elizabeth Sussex who, in 1975, published *The Rise and Fall of the British Documentary*. Sussex made substantial use of the reminiscences of many of the individuals who played an important part in both the British documentary movement and the CFU in particular. For example, she quoted the May 1943 resignation letter of Ian Dalrymple, the CFU executive producer, who clearly identified the uneasy relationship between the unit and the cinema owners: 'the commercial exploitation of our films [was] exposed to the mercy of the whims and waggles of private distribution, with the result that the same old artificial conditions are created to prevent the producer covering his costs' (Sussex, 1975, p. 151). It was a common complaint from Alberto Cavalcanti to John Grierson and beyond that government-employed documentary filmmakers would be far better remunerated in the private sector. Grierson also made an early appearance in Sussex's book, which to some extent may be seen as something of a response to Grierson's own 1946 book, *On Documentary*, which had been reprinted in 1969. As far as the documentary movement was concerned, it is hardly surprising that Grierson should have pride of place, given that he credited himself with inventing the term 'documentary':

> I suppose I coined the word in the sense that I wasn't aware of it being used by anybody else. I mean to talk about documentary film was new, and I know I was surprised when I went to Paris in 1927 and found them talking about *'films documentaires'*... When I used the word 'documentary' of Bob Flaherty's *Moana*, I used it as an adjective. Then I got to using it as a noun, 'the documentary'. (quoted in Sussex, 1975, p. 3)

Grierson was, of course, pivotal in the creation of, firstly, the EMBFU and then the GPOFU and his influence both in the style of filmmaking and the collective approach adopted in production continued after he left in 1937. He was a powerful influence also on many of the CFU directors and, after his return from Canada in 1948, he was appointed the CFU's controller of films. Unfortunately, just as he had a decade earlier, he came up against the somewhat bureaucratic and financially conservative hand of the civil service and in 1950, once again, resigned. Although a great deal has been written subsequently about Grierson and the documentary movement (Ellis, 1984, 2005 (with McLane); Aitken, 1992, 1998), the film units did reflect much of his intellectual and production ethos. There can be no doubt that Grierson's somewhat catholic and eclectic approach to filmmaking struck a particular chord amongst a group of generally middle- and upper-class independent filmmakers during the 1930s. Grierson's film *Drifters* (1929) was generally accepted as the seminal work of the British documentary movement combining, as it does, American influences (Robert Flaherty's 1922 film *Nanook of the North*, for example) with the cutting techniques of Eisenstein and his own social imperative. Although there was a convergence of opportunity and personality, according to the histories of the movement, Grierson's importance to the development of the film units lay not so much in his own productions but rather in the areas of the training and recognition of talent, the identification and exploitation of alternative distribution means and, finally, in the proselytising of the documentary movement to which many of the filmmakers professed adherence.

Much of the eventual success of the documentary movement and, by implication, the EMB, GPO and Crown units, was owed to Grierson's skill as a publicist. He wrote prolifically, founding such journals as *Cinema Quarterly* and *World Film News*, and was a regular contributor to debates in both the national press and trade journals such as *Kinematograph Weekly*. An example was his post-war clarion call in support of the CFU and the value of documentaries, when he wrote:

> We have, in short, to realise the part we [the documentary producers such as the CFU] shall be required to play in giving men the kind of mind and spirit that will bring the world to order. This involves a new measure of understanding and a will to use the medium more directly than we have done in the past. (*Kinematograph Weekly*, 20 December 1945, p. 63)

Despite this it is probably true to say that, like the documentary movement itself, his influence was essentially metropolitan and intellectual rather than widespread and popular. According to Jack Ellis and Betsy McLane,

It [the Documentary Movement] had prestige among the educated classes and fit [sic] in with the thirties' ideas about art in relation to society. A movement with trained and skilled workers, it offered a distinct style as well as purpose and innovations in form and technique that are arguably Britain's most important contribution to the development of the motion picture. (Ellis and McLane, 2005, p. 105)

Grierson's success was to define the nature and role of the documentary, which was, he said, 'the creative treatment of actuality' (Grierson, 1933, p. 8). Newsreels, on the other hand, were essentially visual newspapers which, although capable of being editorialised, tended to be two-dimensional and, unlike much of the documentary output, lacked the narrative framework and exploitation of commercial cinematographic techniques. Certainly, most of Grierson's acolytes were happy to take on the terminology and call themselves 'documentarists'.

Although Grierson can be recognised as the founding father of the British documentary movement, it remains a moot point whether he would have achieved that status or the implied success without the support and advice given by Stephen Tallents,[3] who had been secretary of the Empire Marketing Board between 1926 and 1933. Tallents had not only recruited John Grierson but also, with him, introduced and developed the idea of using documentary films to support the board's objectives. Furthermore, having moved to the GPO to be in charge of public relations, he was able to facilitate the move of the entire EMBFU and Grierson to the GPO when the unit was forced to close.

Subsequent film historians have returned every decade or so to review the British documentary film movement. At the end of the 1980s Paul Swann, for example, produced his history of the same name which included a thoughtful review of the EMB and GPO film units. However, Swann's assertion that 'the Crown Film Unit's predilection for feature length films portraying the heroic British people at war steered it away from films dealing with social issues and, particularly, specific problems caused by the war' (Swann, 1989, p. 164) could be challenged by a review of the variety of both themes and duration of Crown's film portfolio.

A decade later Ian Aitken consolidated the existing state of scholarship regarding the British documentary with his edited collection, *The Documentary Film Movement: An Anthology* (1998). Certainly, his description of the institutional and organisational features of the documentary movement were neatly encapsulated as a

> set of affiliated, often loosely connected organisations, concerned primarily with film production and film distribution, but with also the questions of public education and corporate publicity production... The mode of (film) production was craft, rather than mass production-based and had little connection with the commercial film industry. (Aitken, 1998, p. 9)

Although an excellent review, its range and scope mean that occasionally it does contain a number of generalised contentions which could be reconsidered. For example, Aitken assured the reader that the 'one significant fact connecting [the documentarists] is that they were old enough to have been directly affected by two of the most important radicalising events of the first half of the twentieth century; the Great War and the General Strike' (Aitken, 1998, p. 7). There is nothing especially wrong with this assertion although it does significantly omit to mention the Great Depression or the Spanish Civil War, both of which were equally radicalising events – see Peter Miles and Malcolm Smith (2013), Tom Buchanan (1997), Paul Preston (1978) and David Archibald (2005). This book will certainly seek to rectify or qualify such claims made in respect of the film units.

Furthermore, given that the film units produced their work during a very turbulent period, it is hardly surprising that they should feature both in general film histories as well as those directly concerned with, especially, the Second World War. Books by Frances Thorpe and Nicholas Pronay (1980), Anthony Aldgate and Jeffrey Richards (1986, 1994, 2007) have contributed significantly both to the scholarship and understanding about cinema and film in wartime. However, the CFU's appearance again tends to be limited, as in *Britain Can Take It* (Aldgate and Richards, 1986) the representative films chosen were *Fires Were Started* and *Western Approaches* (1944). As far as more general film histories are concerned the film units are barely a footnote. So Neil Rattigan in Wheeler Winston Dixon's *Re-Viewing British Cinema, 1902–1992* discussed the 1955 film *The Dam Busters* and briefly mentioned that it can be seen as a linear descendant of the CFU's *Target for Tonight* (Rattigan, 1994, p. 149). In a more restricted time frame,

Charles Drazin published in 1998 *The Finest Years: British Cinema of the 1940s*. As the title suggests, this was a comprehensive review of film production and reception during the decade. Again, as might be reasonably expected, a great deal of the text was given over to those commercially produced feature films which were deemed box-office successes, such as *Henry V* (1944) and *Brief Encounter* (1945). However, this is one of the few texts which included a substantial section on films produced by the CFU although, as with other authors, there was a tendency to review from a director-focussed perspective rather than from a thematic or contextual approach. For example, Harry Watt's contribution to filmmaking was summed up as his 'importance to the British Cinema lay far more in his ability to inspire others with the cause of realism in his own films, which are on the whole rather crude' (Drazin, 1998, p. 142). Watt was, of course, the director of the critically acclaimed *Target for Tonight*. His film also featured in an earlier review of wartime cinema in Clive Coultass' 'British Feature Films and the Second World War' (1984) but, as the title suggests, the discussion of the CFU's output was quite limited. Some years later, in 2001, Simon MacKenzie's *British War Films, 1939–1945* was essentially a review of successful commercial films produced during the war, such as *In Which We Serve* (1942). The same omission of the CFU is generally true of the varying texts and articles written subsequently about British films in wartime, such as Robert Murphy (2005). Even those authors who have reviewed the British war films produced in the 1950s (such as Geraghty, 2000 or Ramsden, 1998) only give scant recognition to the work of the CFU as precursor.

As has already been mentioned, the biographies and autobiographies of those employed or interacting with the film units can be fertile sources of information. There are biographies of the key personnel and these seem to have been published on a regular basis. The latest Grierson biography was by Jack Ellis in 2000 and that of Humphrey Jennings by Philip Logan in 2011, and no doubt others will be in preparation. Of all the film units' directors, Jennings does appear to generate a significant academic discourse, as a spat in the *Journal of British Cinema and Television* demonstrates. This commenced with a review of documentary films by Martin Stollery in 2013 that was followed by a riposte from Brian Winston (2014) a couple of issues later and subsequently a rejoinder by Scott

Anthony and Patrick Russell (2014). Winston had been defending the more traditional periodisation of British documentary which essentially views the post-war years, especially after 1951, as one of decline. Stollery, Anthony and Russell take a much more nuanced perspective on the supposed decline. No doubt this debate will continue over the next few years.

Of course, those with a less high profile or more limited contact with the film units tend to have fewer biographies or autobiographies, and often the unit is dismissed in a few sentences or paragraphs. The autobiographies of Basil Wright (1976) and Pat Jackson (1999) show some insight both into the production of films and the workings of the units. However, for some important participants in the later development of the units, such as Sir Kenneth Clark, who was head of the MoI's Films Division in 1939, their film roles warranted only a small flippant aside. Clark regarded his appointment as inexplicable and went on to explain it in his autobiography, *The Other Half*, '[as] commonly attributed to the fact that in those days films were spoken of as "pictures" and I was believed to be an authority on pictures' (Clark, 1977, p. 10). Clark was, of course, director of the National Gallery and surveyor of the king's pictures. Other biographies can be quite obscure and appear to be rarely accessed. Representative of this category would be Cally Trench's (2012) brief but obviously heartfelt online tribute to her father, Terry Trench, who worked for the CFU as both a director and editor. Among a long list of documentary films until his death in 1975, Trench's CFU credits included editing *The True Story of Lili Marlene* (1944) and *This Was Japan* (1945) and directing *The Way from Germany* (1946). According to his daughter, his work was characterised by the realisation that, as most cinema audiences see a film only once, 'no editor should be pleased with a film which, however ingenious, is not clearly understood and does not make an emotional impact first time' (Trench, 2012).

Trench's observations, like those found in many of the relevant biographies and autobiographies, provide substantial information about the individuals concerned but also sometimes about the workings of the units. It is still possible to hear some of the reminiscences of employees as a few have been recorded as part of the Broadcasting, Entertainment, Communications and Theatre

Union (BECTU) History Project, and are available through the BFI's Reuben Library. Occasionally, of course, the self-justification aspect of the recollections successfully camouflaged the reality, but normally this can be filtered to provide snippets of information about the units' filmmaking activities. For example, in her BECTU interview in 1994, Nora Lee revealed that the development of shooting scripts and the careful consideration of camera angles was often determined by the need to be economical with film stock which was in short supply during the war years.

Despite the difficulties of filmmaking, any examination of the units must also consider the nature of film exhibition and audiences in the period, as this underpins the argument that their output had a significant importance for the study of pre-war, wartime and post-war Britain. Unlike the more conventional commercial film studios which essentially provided films for commercial cinema, the units' exhibition outlets were many and varied. There was a thriving non-theatrical exhibition circuit in which films were loaned, normally free of charge, to almost any organisation which had access to a 16 mm film projector and, later, associated sound equipment. Others were literally taken onto the street corners of Britain by a fleet of cinema vans operated by the units' sponsors. So, as will be seen, films were distributed and shown in factory canteens and village halls to audiences that ranged from war workers and the Salvation Army to Boy Scouts. As more men and women were conscripted into the forces in the 1940s the films were shown in Navy, Army and Air Force Institutes (NAAFI) both in the UK and wherever British forces were fighting.

Although the majority of the units' films fell into the short category of between five and twenty minutes in length, their productions also included feature-length titles such as the already mentioned *Target for Tonight* and *Western Approaches*, which were exhibited as main attractions on the commercial cinema circuits. The cinemas themselves ranged from the massive 2,000+ seater 'picture palaces' such as the Odeons which had been built in many city centres during the 1930s, to the mid-range, often independent houses, such as The Regent in Portsmouth which has been studied in depth by Sue Harper (2004, 2006). Finally, there were the very small cinemas, often in rural situations, with seating for a hundred or so people. These types of cinema are just about recognisable in the early part of the twenty-first century, but the newsreel cinemas, which in the 1940s were often to be found in most city centres, often in railway stations such as Baker Street (a major London Underground interchange), have almost entirely disappeared. The newsreel cinema was an American import of the early 1930s and concentrated on regular, repeated, hour-long shows of, unsurprisingly, newsreels, but also increasingly animated cartoons and travelogues. Normally the newsreel theatres were tied to one of the main newsreel producers such as Pathé or Movietone. However, during wartime, MoI shorts, including CFU-produced ones, were also inserted into their daily programmes.

Although the majority of GPOFU films reflected the interests and operations of their sponsor, Crown productions were commissioned by the government and were exhibited regularly in various ways to a national audience. This has almost inevitably led to the films being categorised as propaganda. Watching today, on television or increasingly digitised through the internet, a CFU production from the 1940s, with its cosy stereotypes and worthy storylines, there is sometimes an uncomfortable feeling that this really is propaganda dressed up as documentary. It is by no means as brutal or blatant as *Triumph of the Will* but the films could possibly fit at the opposite end of the same continuum. This impression is hardly surprising as, after all, the CFU was an organ of government directly responsible to the MoI, which itself was responsible for government publicity. Clark, the unlikely head of the MoI Films Division, was an early and passionate advocate for the role film could play, announcing to *Kinematograph Weekly* that:

> no film is good propaganda unless it gives entertainment. A bad film transfers boredom to the cause it advocates. Secondly, it must be realised that the essence of successful propaganda is that people should not be aware of it. If you make people 'think' propaganda their resistance to it is increased. (*Kinematograph Weekly*, 11 January 1940)

This observation was made despite the reluctance of many in government to become actively engaged in something as nefarious as propaganda, and this perspective was quite deeply ingrained. The official *History of the Second World War* does not include a volume on the MoI and even the ancillary volume on *Morale* by

Lieutenant-Colonel J. H. A. Sparrow (1949) referred almost entirely to morale within the armed forces rather than that of the civilian population. It was not until some thirty years after the conflict that Ian McLaine (1979) published *Ministry of Morale*; his study on the MoI in turn seemed to spawn a number of journal articles and books over the next forty or so years which began to use the word 'propaganda' in their titles. The apparent acceptance of the term enabled film historians and others to reflect and examine film production and distribution within a new context. Thus, for example, T. J. Hollins in 1981 examined the use of film in his *English History Review* article, 'The Conservative Party and Film Propaganda Between the Wars', and a few years later Tom Wildy looked at the post-war situation in his *From the MOI to the COI – Publicity and Propaganda in Britain, 1945–51* (1986). Books published on this topic range from Nicholas Pronay and D. Spring's *Propaganda, Politics and Film* in 1982, through William Crofts' 1989 *Coercion or Persuasion? Propaganda in Britain After 1945* and culminating at the end of the millennium with James Chapman's 1998 *The British at War: Cinema, State and Propaganda, 1939–1945* and Nicholas Reeves' 1999 *The Power of Film Propaganda: Myth or Reality?*. Thus, over a period of twenty or so years, what had been avoided previously had become so conventional that recent studies of the films sponsored by the MoI, and its later iteration, the COI, have been generally ascribed to the 'propaganda' category. Reeves (1999), for example, entitled his chapter on the CFU and other productions 'Official Propaganda in Britain During the Second World War', and by 2007 Jo Fox was able to conflate into the same conceptual idea what would have seemed inimical forty years before as *Film Propaganda in Britain and Nazi Germany: World War II Cinema*. However, before accepting these assumptions, it is worthwhile to review exactly what 'propaganda' can and does mean in the context of the films sponsored by the MoI and later the COI.

Trotsky's description of cinema and film as 'the best instrument of propaganda' (cited in Taylor, 1998, p. 16) has been echoed by politicians of every persuasion almost from the beginning of film. Film is able to communicate a visual message to a mass audience in a way that does not require the mediation of literacy. Visual images and simple storylines could, for the first time, be transmitted to large groups of people in a single event. Not only was this medium extremely powerful but the very novelty engaged audiences in an unsophisticated and uncritical manner. Although film and cinema were well over thirty years old by the time that the EMBFU was created, much of this early enthusiasm for the moving picture was still evident in cinema and non-theatrical exhibitions in Britain. The apparent power of the medium, and the potential passivity of the audience, inevitably drew those who wished to utilise it for purposes other than entertainment.

Predictably, perhaps, although there are propaganda studies of many nations, much of this work has concentrated upon reworking themes within the Nazi and Soviet systems.[4] Consequently, it is often difficult to employ the term 'propaganda' without being aware of its pejorative connotations. Most obviously its negative and insidious associations were aptly reinforced as early as 1933 by Joseph Goebbels, who required of propaganda the achievement of the following aim: 'It is not enough to reconcile people more or less to our regime, to move them towards a position of neutrality towards us, we want rather to work on people until they are addicted to us' (cited in Reeves, 1999, p. 88). More recently, with the work of David Welch (in 1993, 2003 and 2017) and others, propaganda has been placed on a scale of advocacy which governments and institutions have adopted for centuries: 'Throughout history the governors have always attempted to influence the way the governed see the world. Propaganda is simply what the other side does, while one's own side concentrates on "information" or "publicity"' (Welch, 1999, p. 24).

The origins of the term propaganda lie with the creation in 1622 by Pope Gregory XV of the 'Congregatio de Propaganda Fide', the Congregation for Propagating the Faith. In response to both the spread of the Reformation and the conquest of the New World, this was a committee of cardinals charged with the responsibility of overseeing the spread of Catholicism and the regulation of ecclesiastical affairs in non-Catholic countries. The Latin root *propagare* conveys a sense of both propagation and spreading. According to Welch:

> the first official propagandist institute was a body charged with improving the dissemination of a group of religious dogmas. The word 'propaganda' came to be applied to any organisation set up to

Introduction 19

spread a doctrine; then it was applied to the doctrine itself which was being spread; and lastly to the methods employed in the dissemination. (Welch, 1999, p. 25)

In many senses the impact and influence of these propaganda messages is symbiotic with the development of the media which carry them. Although there were examples of printed pamphlets and newsletters proselytising political and religious ideas during the English Civil War, it was only with the spread of general literacy on the one hand and steam and electric printing presses on the other that both the vehicle and the audience existed for mass persuasion. The 'public' and public opinion began to be seen as phenomena capable of being manipulated.

Thus, the utilisation of the media, and especially the visual media, whether at the extreme end of advocacy in propaganda or merely mundane advertising at the other, has generated an academic study with its own literature and language. A major debate in this area has revolved around the manner in which 'ideas' and especially 'propaganda' are transmitted to the public or audience. Although there are number of competing theories, the three principal ones are the 'Hypodermic Needle' or 'Magic Bullet' (Lasswell, 1927); secondly, the 'Two Step Flow Theory' (Katz and Lazarsfeld, 1955); and finally, 'The Diffusion of Innovations Theory' (Rogers, 1995). In the first case it was suggested that the mass media, and especially visual media such as film and television, can influence a large group of people directly and uniformly by 'shooting' or 'injecting' them with messages designed to trigger required responses. In many ways this was the assumption that lay behind much of the propaganda efforts in wartime Germany and the Soviet Union. The audience was perceived to be passive and, providing that there were no alternative sources of information, they would end up believing and accepting what was 'injected' into them. The 'Two Step Flow Theory' is slightly more sophisticated in that it postulates that certain individuals within society are opinion formers or opinion leaders and it is these people who need to be 'targeted'. This approach has been adopted frequently by the advertising industry in its attempts to sectionalise and classify markets. Products are therefore often promoted with celebrity endorsement to encourage sales within particular groups in society. There is less evidence that this approach has been taken to 'spin' political ideas and opinions through the productions of the film units, although celebrities, such as the Crazy Gang, Bernard Miles and others, do occasionally appear in reassuring rather than actively indoctrinating roles. The more complex 'Diffusions of Innovation Theory' argues that, although opinion formers are important in the spread of ideas and innovations, there are social and psychological factors which predispose individuals to accepting or rejecting a particular view or commodity. Amongst these factors would be the terminal level of education, for example, or perhaps the perceived need for the change. The theory identifies five 'adopter' categories: (1) innovators; (2) early adopters; (3) early majority; (4) late majority; and (5) laggards. Although it might be conceivable to review Nazi propaganda activity in Germany from the 1920s onwards on the basis of this perspective, it is outside the scope of this study. However, within EMB, GPO and Crown productions it is possible to identify recurring themes which could be interpreted as either reinforcement of ideas and opinions or as addressing slightly different audiences who may be examples of the adopter categories.

It is certainly plausible to suggest that the output of the units were 'propaganda' as they were, after all, government organisations producing films directly for the government. However, as will be seen, there were very few films which reflected a negative propaganda that encouraged the audience to hate the 'enemy'. A few, such as *Men of the Lightship* (1940) or, more obviously, *The Silent Village*, dwelt upon the iniquity of the Nazis. Once that war was over and a new enemy had been identified, Crown did produce *Alien Orders* (1951) and *The Waking Point* (1951) amongst a few anti-Communist films. However, most of the film units' productions from 1930 onwards were less hard propaganda, but rather sought to persuade, encourage and reinforce as well as to provide entertainment and information. Although overall many productions could easily be described as public information films, it is possible, by adopting some of the concepts from business, to refine them further into public relations or direct advertising films. In the former case the underpinning purpose behind the film was to create or reinforce 'brand' awareness. Much of the GPOFU catalogue is exactly that, giving the public sufficient information in a suitably digestible format to make them aware of the multiple services on offer from the Post Office. This differs in one major sense from the advertising film, as its purpose was to provoke an active response from the audience. Perhaps the most obvious example of the advertising film would be for the annual 'post early for Christmas' campaign, which in 1948 was promoted by Cyril Fletcher, a comedian famous for his *Odd Odes*, in the short *Postman's Nightmare*.

Another type of film which might come under the PIF umbrella was the educational film. As early as 1933 Grierson was asserting in the last annual report of the Empire Marketing Board that nearly 68,000 schoolchildren had attended the cinema in the Imperial Institute to watch various films. However, given the importance of the non-theatrical exhibition for the film units' various productions, schools were a major venue for their output from the 1930s onwards. The school 'film show' in a darkened hall was a feature of British education until well into the 1960s. Grierson was certainly an advocate of the 'educational' value of film but perhaps assumed too readily that it was education for an adult audience. Swann (1983, p. 27) calculated that, although Grierson claimed an annual non-theatrical audience of more than 4 million in 1934, the majority must have been children as the loans record showed 54 per cent going to schools and a further 13 per cent to juvenile organisations. There were certainly films which appear more suited to a younger audience, such as *God's Chillun* (1938) about the slave trade, or *Steps of the Ballet* (1948). Others, like *Britain's Countryside* (1934), were more in the travelogue vein and would probably appeal to audiences across the age range. Occasionally there were films which were specifically created for educational purposes although these, like *How the Teleprinter Works* (1940) and *Introduction to Aircraft Recognition* (1947), often had particular audiences in mind, such as GPO engineers and naval ratings.

There is an inherent difficulty in classifying or categorising such a varied and diverse canon as the output of the film units from 1930 to 1952. The edges between categories are frequently blurred and each and every film could probably be assigned to a number of different areas. In most cases they can be allocated to the public information film category but not all – some films, such as *Harwell Assembly* (1952), were actually secret and not declassified until the 1960s. Without an attempt to provide a framework of classification there is little possibility of examining and evaluating the entire film catalogue. This book develops a means by which the interconnection between the films and the historical context in which they were produced can be appreciated.

However, the core of the research underpinning this book's analysis and conclusions are the films themselves; but these are historical artefacts liable to decay and are often highly flammable. Consequently, unless an archive has taken the time and trouble to record them onto a safer and longer-lasting medium, or kept them in a dry environment, there is a high probability that the films will have been lost or damaged irretrievably. Many duplicates of EMBFU, GPOFU, CFU output and other contemporary films have already been lost, often having been destroyed, sometimes deliberately, in an attempt to recover the silver content from the film stock. This means that the availability for viewing of a particular film will depend upon a number of, seemingly random, variables; principally whether it has been lodged within an archive such as the BFI or the IWM and whether it is in a safe condition to be viewed. Understandably, the archives are reluctant to chance a researcher reviewing a fire risk film or to pay for its safe duplication when demand to see it is minimal.

Those relatively few, mainly feature-length, films directed by the more famous unit personnel such as Jennings or Watt have often been made available to other platforms such as television or, more recently, through the internet; in this way they have effectively been given both a wider audience and been saved for future generations to appreciate. This, unfortunately, cannot be said about the majority of the EMB, GPO and Crown productions which have languished, usually unseen, for well over seventy years. Most of these films however exist in the BFI and IWM archives, along with a small number of often specialist films available in a variety of collections – such as, for example, Jennings' *Spring Offensive* (1940) which is in the University of East Anglia's film archive.

An annoying practical complication that confounds research into the film units' catalogue is that it is sometimes surprisingly difficult to confirm a particular film's production provenance. The research for this book quite early on established that the listings held by both the BFI and the IWM are neither comprehensive nor entirely accurate. Even a contemporary catalogue, such as that in the trade journal *The Cine-Technician* (November–December

1952, p. 143), has errors. In these circumstances it was decided to include films in this study which had either the appearance of the appropriate name or logo in the introductory credits or, exceptionally when it is absent, the direct mention of its production in the documentary record. However, even these basic criteria have often raised anomalies – as one unit morphed into another, films already in production were sometimes prefaced by a later name or logo. Some films, for example, such as *Men of the Lightship* (1940), have no production acknowledgements other than the ubiquitous MoI Films credit. At the other extreme, *Christmas Under Fire* (1941) confusingly has both GPOFU and CFU logos. In order to accommodate these inconsistencies, and where a date can reasonably be ascertained, films are allocated to the EMBFU between 1930 and 1933, then the GPOFU from late 1933 until it became directly under MoI control in April 1940, before it formally became the CFU on I January 1941. Unfortunately, in the later 1940s the Crown logo itself was inadequate as evidence of CFU production as the imprimatur had been expropriated by the COI for its own use. Even when a film may be safely verified as having been produced by the one of the three units it was often the case that the credits omit mention of the director or production staff. This, of course, does reduce the opportunities for differentiating or analysing films on the basis of the production personnel.

The absence of any form of production credit was especially true of the brief sixty-to-ninety-second trailers or 'flashes' which were a regular part of cinema programming in the 1940s and continued well into the subsequent decade. In wartime these addressed such issues as preventing waste or encouraging salvage collections or recruitment to various nationally important roles such as telephonists or hospital domestics. In the post-war era public information film 'flash' topics have included road safety or, bizarrely, encouraged people to volunteer for agricultural 'holidays' to bring in the potato harvest. Some of these would have been produced by the CFU but this form of PIF did not normally identify the production company and were, in wartime, prefaced only by the MoI logo. This uncertain authenticity is further compounded as the documentary record about wartime and post-war 'flashes' is neither exhaustive nor complete. In these circumstances these very short sixty-to-ninety-second films have been excluded from this book.

Therefore, the selection of films has been determined essentially by the survival and safe availability of the films themselves. Not only is the filmic record of the units incomplete; so, too, is the associated documentation. As has been indicated above, there is a significant canon of published material that provides an important element of secondary evidence for the study. The main archival source for the film units is the National Archives at Kew and those documents relating to them are to be found principally in the INF1, 6 and 12 classifications. As far as the GPOFU is concerned, the majority of the archival material has been transferred to the Post Office archive in the Postal Museum in London. The locations of the relevant documents are clearly indicated in the text, normally prefaced by the abbreviation TNA (The National Archives). Other documentary evidence of direct relevance to the units exists in a number of university and related libraries. This category includes the Grierson Archive in Stirling, the Conservative Party Archive at the Bodleian Library, Oxford and Mass Observation at Sussex. As far as contemporary journals are concerned, the BFI library is well stocked with trade journals such as *Kinematograph Weekly* and specialist film ones such as the *Documentary News Letter*. Newspaper and relevant magazines were available through the British Library at Wetherby, West Yorkshire. Local newspapers, such as the *Yorkshire Post*, supplied some non-metropolitan evidence for regional critical review and audience response. Other artefacts were found elsewhere, frequently quite randomly – cinema posters, comments by local history societies or parish magazines; often these are reported recollections which, of course, have to be considered cautiously given the problems associated with historical ethnographical research.

Sadly, as the last of the units closed down over seventy years ago, all of the active participants have now passed away. The original idea behind the book was generated many years ago following a discussion with the sister of cameraman Jonah Jones and his immediate family. Later conversations were also had with Nora Lee before she passed away in 2009 and also with Humphrey Jennings' daughter, Mary-Lou. These are all, of course, anecdotal but they provide an important impression of what it was like to be part of the collective style of operation which pervaded the units. More personal reflections were also consulted in the BFI's Reuben

Library where the BECTU History Project resources reside. These are interviews with leading member of the British film industry, including many early documentarists. Their personal reflections give background colour, providing assertions and assumptions which can be challenged or confirmed by other source material.

The book acknowledges in particular the work of James Chapman, Mark Glancy and Sue Harper, admirably summarised in their book *The New Film History* (2007). As far as the EMB, GPO and Crown film units are concerned, their analysis situates most of the early published works on the units clearly in either the auteur or textual analysis branches of film history, and certainly these approaches still feature in this study. However, they have gone on to argue that the analytical framework of what they refer to as 'New Film History' is far more complex and is concerned as much with the importance of the context in which the film was both created and exhibited as with its direction and content. As they explain:

> films are shaped and determined by a combination of historical processes (including, but not limited to, economic constraints, industrial practices, studio production strategies and relationships with external bodies such as official agencies, funding councils and censors) and individual agency (representing the creative and cultural competence of their art directors, composers, costume designers, directors, editors, producers, stars, writers, etc.). (Chapman, Glancy and Harper, 2007, p. 6)

Chapman has further argued that New Film History has extended the traditional debate about whether films provided an accurate historical representation to one which considers more thoughtfully the political and social context that underpins them. This, in turn, impacts upon the 'extent to which popular cinema contributes to the discourse of nationhood and national identity' (Chapman, Glancy and Harper, 2007, p. 65). This point is especially important to an investigation of the production of public information films by the government film units, as not only did they latterly produce feature-length films[5] which are frequently referred to in histories both popular and academic, but also in television shows and documentaries. An early example of this was the BBC documentary *Operation Jericho* (first broadcast on BBC2 on 29 October

2011) which used footage from the CFU's *Target for Tonight*. If it can be reasonably assumed that the small number of feature films contributed towards the debate on nationhood and national identity by constructing and reconstructing significant moments in the nation's history, then surely those myriad shorts exhibited from 1930 to 1952 and beyond provided an unconscious underpinning to the contemporary appreciation of that national identity. Therefore, if feature films such as *Target for Tonight* provided key and stark prompts in bolstering the ideas surrounding British nationhood, the many shorts were more subliminal, a wallpaper of moods and situations which reinforced and strengthened the overall sense of national identity, particularly during wartime.

This perspective can be examined more thoroughly using the perspectives recently developed by reception studies. Harper's work on audience reception and response which, according to *The New Film History* places the 'film text at the nexus of a complex and dynamic set of relationships between producers and consumers' (Chapman, Glancy and Harper, 2007, p. 7) has been very important in determining an appropriate methodological approach. Harper has extended and anglicised the approaches adopted earlier by Janet Staiger (1992) and later by Barbara Klinger (1994) and has emphasised the importance of audience response and reaction in evaluating the context and, perhaps, success of a particular film. The nature of the individual audience member's response was, of course, complicated by a variety of social, cultural and immediate factors, such as the reason for attending the cinema or reaction to posters and reviews among many other things. Some contemporary reactions to the EMB, GPO and Crown films are available in newspaper, journal and other miscellaneous sources; however, there are others which are essentially recollections made decades later and published in a variety of periodicals. These latter sources combined with interviews with the rapidly diminishing demographic of those who remember going to the cinema in the 1940s present problems from a strictly ethnographical perspective. Such recollections, although offering interesting perspectives, are essentially coloured by subsequent life experiences and have often lost much of their contemporary perspective and clarity.

This book seeks to examine the full catalogue of the films produced between 1930 and 1952 by the EMB, GPO and Crown film units. It will evaluate their importance in the contexts in which they were produced and also the legacy which, amongst other things, provided exemplars for the future development and production of public information films.

Notes

1 Dartington Hall, near Totnes, Devon, is the headquarters of a charitable trust specialised in, amongst other things, investigating and supporting the arts.
2 Many Conservative politicians were hostile to the whole idea of government information services – for example, Duff Cooper (the wartime Chancellor of the Duchy of Lancaster and subsequently ambassador to France) was quoted as saying: 'I believe the truth of the matter to be that there is no place in the British scheme of Government for a Ministry of Information' (McLaine, 1979, p. 280).
3 Sir Stephen Tallents (1884–1958) was a career civil servant who pioneered the role of public relations within government.
4 See, for example, Mariel Grant (1994), *Propaganda and the Role of the State in Interwar Britain*; Philip Taylor (1999), *British Propaganda in the Twentieth Century: Selling Democracy*; George Roeder (1993), *The Censored War: American Visual Experience During World War II*; or Judith Proud (1995), Children and Propaganda: Il etait une fois…: Fiction and Fairy Tale in Vichy France.
5 The BFI has defined 'feature-length films' as those over forty minutes.

1

A shaky start – the British government and film, 1900–30

It took the British government some time to appreciate the political potential of film. Towards the end of the nineteenth century the general perception of film was that it was a minority interest and probably likely to remain so given the cumbersome nature of the technology required both for filming and exhibition purposes. No doubt, too, the early films often inserted as short interludes in variety and music hall shows condemned it to being regarded as entertainment for the masses and not at all acceptable for the establishment figures represented in both Conservative and Liberal parties.

The Boer War and the early use of film

As has often sadly proved to be the case, war and conflict not only provided ample fare for on-screen entertainment but also hastened the development of film technology and alongside that audience expansion. The Boer War (1899–1902) saw the production of the first films which purported to represent realistic scenes of not only a current conflict on the screen but also one in which an increasing number of Britons were actively engaged. This was achievable as, by the turn of the century, film technology had reached the stage where a short film, normally of one to two minutes, could be shot and presented for exhibition. As Stephen Bottomore (2007) has described, these shorts were often included amongst a variety of media – lantern slides and photographs and so on – as part of patriotic shows in local venues.[1] These shows ranged from the traditional variety bills of the music halls to lectures given by a local worthy.

The short films produced at the very beginning of the twentieth century seem to have been essentially private and local arrangements rather than government-sponsored public information films. Some films of combat preparations and manoeuvres were shot by intrepid cameramen working for commercial companies who were embedded with the troops in South Africa.[2] Sadly, however, according to Luke McKernan, 'no film from this period is known to survive' (McKernan, 2002, p. 2). In order to provide for domestic audiences, then, 'other companies filmed only troops departing or returning to Britain or resorted to "fake" recreations of battlefield scenes' (McKernan, 2002, p. 2).

Most of the films released during the Boer War were therefore not those of actual combat but rather fictional recreations, a practice which was to continue in some of the more famous GPOFU and Crown films later in the century. However, around 1900 the films frequently had a narrow or parochial feel as they addressed the needs of local audiences keen to see relatives marching away or returning from the war. The Mitchell and Kenyon (M&K) archive, for example, includes some twenty films of this kind, featuring ten volunteer regiments. According to Stephen Bottomore (2007, p. 6), 'of the 120 towns and cities surveyed for the M&K filmography in the period between 1900 and 1902, every exhibition associated with this company listed a Boer War themed title'. The local focus was evident in such titles as *The Bradford Artillery in Camp at Morecambe* (1902) which, unsurprisingly, was exhibited in the Bradford area. The titles of the films themselves tended to be brief descriptions of content – after all, the duration rarely exceeded two minutes – rather than titles in the modern sense. Other examples of this include *The Coldstream Guards Embarking on the Troopship 'Gascon'* (October 1899) and *Gordon Highlanders in Ladysmith* (1900). Vanessa Toulmin (Toulmin, Popple and Russell, 2005) has made a detailed study of the short films of the Boer War and identified a number of genres including troops on exercises and at manoeuvres, tableaux of army life, soldiers departing and returning and the 'celebrities' – famous leaders and commanders. The Boer War was the first conflict in which the British citizen at home would see moving images of both British and enemy commanders, enabling them more easily to identify with, or become hostile to, respective friend and foe. *The Arrival and Reception of Lord Roberts at Cape*

Town (1900) and *Cronje's Surrender to Lord Roberts* (1900) were one-minute examples of this type of brief film.

The positive audience response to these short newsreel-type films as reported by Bottomore (2007, p. 4) appeared to have encouraged some entrepreneurs to produce films purporting to show military action in South Africa. Examples of these from the Mitchell and Kenyon archive include the *Dispatch Bearer* and *Shelling the Red Cross* (Figure 1.1); both produced in 1900, these were intended, as the latter film title certainly suggested, to reinforce a public perception of the iniquity of the Boers. In this particular short film, a Red Cross nurse was shown tending the wounded in a hospital tent, supposedly in South Africa. A Boer shell exploded in the tent and the film concluded with the wounded being rescued from the tent, with the Red Cross nurse amongst their number. Although these early Boer War films had some of the features of those produced later by the GPOFU and CFU between 1940 and 1945, they were neither funded nor authorised by anyone in the government. Cinema in Britain at the beginning of the twentieth century was essentially, in both production and exhibition terms, a private enterprise. Although the Boer War lasted for some two and a half years, and demonstrated that there was an appetite amongst the populace for

Figure 1.1 In *Shelling the Red Cross* (1900), an early propaganda film, the Boers target a hospital tent with inevitable results

material which purported to be factual representations of the conflict, there was little contemporary evidence of the direct interest from the government as to the potential value of film.

The experience of the First World War

It was not until 1914, with another altogether more terrifying and closer conflict, that the possibilities of film were considered and harnessed to the British war effort. Karel Dibbets and Bert Hogenkamp (1995) and Nicholas Reeves (1986, 1999) have written extensively about the government's approach towards the relatively new medium and its uses in the propaganda battle against the Central Powers. This conversion to the political value of film had been quite slow in its development and, according to Nicholas Hiley (1995, p. 161), was probably a reflection of the class-based attitudes of those in government – this may also explain the lack of much official interest during the South African conflict. Hiley explained that, before and during the First World War, cinema-going was essentially a working-class activity with little intrinsic attractions to the middle and upper classes. Moreover,

> for working class patrons, the cinema was not so much a place for watching films as a comfortable venue in which they were greeted warmly by the proprietor and enjoyed a novel experience of being in public space which they could dominate and control. Many simply bought tickets in order to meet their friends, to sit in their favourite seats, and to enjoy the sensation of being an audience, whilst others hoped to find in the darkness and privacy that which they could not enjoy at home. (Hiley, 1995, p. 161)

The slightly subversive atmosphere and role played by the new cinemas, of which there were 5,400 in 1915 (Hiley, 1995, p. 162), caused some anxiety in government circles. These cinemas were accommodating a mass audience so that by January 1917 weekly attendances had reached some 21 million (Hiley, 1995, p. 162). Inevitably this figure included multiple attendances by some individuals, but it remains a spectacular concentration of the population in particular places. These venues were increasingly seen by government alternatively as opportunities for publicity or propaganda, places to be controlled and, inevitably, as major sources of revenue for the Exchequer.

It was realised quite early in the war that the cinema offered significant advantages in disseminating the government's message. This was because, as Mr T. L. Gilmour of the Department of Information, in his evidence to the Cabinet Committee on Overlapping in the Production and Distribution of Propaganda in the autumn of 1917, reflected:

> There is a further advantage which the Cinema has over the newspaper as an agent for influencing public opinion. The Tory, the Liberal, the Labour man, the Socialist, buys for the most part one newspaper – naturally that which is most in sympathy with his preconceived views – and is daily confirmed in his devotion to the political creed he has adopted. At the cinema theatre the Tory, Liberal, Labour man and Socialist must sit side by side and see the same thing presented in the same way, and insensibly their views are affected by what they see. (TNA: CAB 27/17)

In order to exploit this perceived advantage, the very first British official film of the First World War, the forerunner of all later productions, was the Wellington House production *Britain Prepared* (produced by Charles Urban), which premiered on 29 December 1915 at the Empire Music Hall in London. Wellington House was the home and *nom de guerre* of the War Propaganda Bureau, a semi-secret organisation set up by Prime Minister Herbert Asquith in 1914 with the initial responsibility of 'influencing public opinion abroad' (Reeves, 1999, p. 20). However, Wellington House's venture into filmmaking was also released for domestic audiences, mainly at the insistence of the cinema proprietors who were anxious for something appropriate to exhibit. The result was a somewhat slow and repetitious film of 'exceptional length' (MacKenzie, 2001, p. 7). At over three hours, *Britain Prepared* was a series of essentially separate sections that ranged from 'Training the New Army' – cheery non-slackers undergo PT, drill and bayonet practice, mounting and sabre drill for cavalry (reel 1) – to the manufacture of munitions and the royal visit to Vickers (reel 8) (IWM: cat. 500). The film did, however, incorporate some of the values which were to remain constant in British propaganda and documentary films for the next thirty or so years. In line with what Grierson later advocated as the 'creative treatment of actuality', as much as possible of the footage shot should be as authentic as possible. Perhaps as a result of not only its authenticity but also its novelty, *Britain Prepared* seems to have been well received by domestic audiences, having been shown in over 100 cinemas in the major cities in Britain by the summer of 1916. According to Reeves (1993, p. 480), the film 'attracted enthusiastic acclaim from all sides'. It was applauded overseas, as well, as the British ambassador to Bucharest noted in a memorandum to the Foreign Office, arguing that such films supporting the war effort should be 'real British war films, as distinct from faked war dramas' (Reeves, 1999, p. 23).

Unfortunately, technological difficulties, not least the cumbersome camera equipment and the assiduity of military intelligence, restricted the opportunities for taking action shots on the Western Front or elsewhere in the early part of the war. Thus, *Britain Prepared* is essentially a catalogue of shots of military and naval training and munitions manufacture. Subsequent productions over the next few months tended to be similar, if not in duration then at least in content, much to the increasing displeasure of both audiences and cinema proprietors. The trade journal *Cinema* had, as early as January 1916, commented that official films were no less than 'a fraud on the long-suffering British cinema-going public' (cited in Reeves, 1999, p. 25). However, all this was to change on 21 August 1916 with the release of *Battle of the Somme*. This seventy-five-minute film included footage shot by Geoffrey Malins and J. B. McDowell of the preparations, the artillery bombardment and the initial assault of the battle which commenced on 1 July.[3] According to Reeves (1997, p. 7) 'for an official propaganda film, its extended sequences of the physical devastation of war, the battlefield landscape, the prisoners of war, the wounded and, above all else, the footage of the dead, construct a remarkable and remarkably powerful representation of the war on the Western Front.' It was certainly a box-office success, as it has been estimated by Hiley (1995) that *Battle of the Somme* was seen by over 20 million people in the six weeks after release – although perhaps this owed more to familial interest in the actions of Kitchener's volunteer army than to the film's intrinsic artistic merits.

Over the next few months similar battlefield 'spectaculars' – most notably *The Battle of the Ancre and the Advance of the Tanks* (January 1917) and *The German Retreat and the Battle of Arras* (June 1917) – were released to a country hungry to see the evidence of the progress of the war about which they could read regularly in their newspapers. A feature which seems to have resonance later in the mid-1940s is that audiences appear to have become quickly satiated by the diet of lengthy battlefield action-based newsreel films. As Reeves has argued:

> It is the financial data that perhaps reveals the extent of the propagandists' failure most clearly. In the first three months of their exhibition, *Battle of the Somme* and *Battle of the Ancre* grossed £65,000; in the eighteen months from January 1917 to June 1918, the total income achieved by all official films amounted to the princely sum of just £70,023. That figure looks small enough in itself, but given that it includes the £35,000 earned by *The Battle of the Ancre*, the failure of the later official films becomes all too clear. (Reeves, 1986, p. 29)

Another characteristic of these First World War propaganda films, which was reflected during the Second World War, was the frequent inclusion of members of the royal family. In the CFU's *Listen to Britain* (1942), for example, the Queen is shown listening to a Dame Myra Hess concert. The monarchy as a focus of patriotism made its first appearance during the First World War in *The King Visits his Armies in the Great Advance*, which went on release in October 1916. Its portrayal of the monarch in a less formal environment reviewing the troops in France seems to have been well received by audiences. According to Reeves (1993, p. 472), the spectacular success of the film was exemplified by it achieving an almost unheard of eighty-six simultaneous screenings on the London cinema circuit. *The King Visits his Armies in the Great Advance* also appears in some way to have endorsed and legitimised the 'volunteer' army whose relatives made up most of the cinema audiences in Britain. Towards the end of the war, the shadowy hand of Wellington House behind propaganda film production was replaced by a more official, if no less secretive, Department of Information in February 1917, which a year later metamorphosed into the MoI. However, as Prime Minister David Lloyd George placed the MoI under the leadership of Canadian press baron Lord Beaverbrook, there was little chance of it retaining its somewhat reclusive profile. Beaverbrook's opinion, according to A. J. P. Taylor (1972, p. 145), that propaganda was 'the popular arm of diplomacy', did nothing to endear him to other members of the War Cabinet and the establishment, who tended to regard it as something of a black art and demeaning to a British gentleman. The often-vituperative battles within government over the use of propaganda in 1918 have been admirably described by Taylor (1972, pp. 137–52). It was during this latter period that the government, through the auspices of the National War Aims Committee, decided to produce a full-length propaganda feature film to address issues such as domestic war-weariness and growing industrial unrest. *National Film* (1918) was a misbegotten adventure from the very beginning. A lengthy production schedule, and associated problems including a fire which destroyed much of the film stock, meant that by the time the film was finished, so was the war, and it was never released.

At the same time as the government was producing these somewhat worthy films extolling the prowess of the nation under arms with stirring images of tanks moving into battle, it was not averse to using the medium in an often much more mundane way. It had been very much a reluctant conversion to the value of the cinema in promoting a message; in his evidence to the Cabinet Committee on the Overlapping of Production and Distribution of Propaganda in 1917, T. L. Gilmour of the Department of Information, reminded the committee members that:

> when war broke out the Cinema was universally regarded as an instrument for the amusement of the masses: the educated classes thought of the 'pictures' as responsible for turning romantic shopboys into juvenile highwaymen, as a sort of moving edition of the 'penny dreadful'. (TNA: CAB 27/17, Oct/Nov 1917)

Ironically, amongst those converted in Britain to the value of the cinema was the press baron Lord Northcliffe, who observed in September 1917:

> As a newspaper man I hate to confess it, but the motion picture is doing more for the Allied cause than any other means of thought transmission. Not everyone reads the newspaper, and those that do

forget what they have read, but no one can forget what he has actually seen. (TNA: CAB 27/17, Oct/Nov 1917)

The practical application of this approach was only slowly appreciated by individual government departments. The realisation was especially important as one of the consequences of the stresses and strains of what had become a total war encompassing all aspects of economy and society had resulted in an increasingly dirigiste approach to public policy. By 1918, however, in what was very much a model for what occurred two decades later, a discrete government department, the MoI, was given the responsibility for commissioning short, silent films for general exhibition to the British public, exhorting them to, amongst other things, save bones which, apparently, could be made into fertiliser, glue and even explosives (*Old Mother Hubbard*, 1918).

These film tags – so called as they were one- or two-minute features 'tagged' on to the end of the main feature in the cinema – were essentially some of the earliest public information films produced and exhibited throughout the UK and, later, the Empire. However, in May 1917, in order to give the films a degree of conformity and also to maximise their audience potential, the government, through the War Office, reached an agreement with the Topical Film Company to produce these short films and to 'tag' them on the end of the bi-weekly cinema newsreel, also produced by Topical. This arrangement, however, only lasted a brief time, as in October of that year Topical was bought out by the government and it became, like the EMBFU, GPOFU and CFU later, effectively the government's own film production unit. Reminiscent also of the CFU during the Second World War, it was eventually situated in the MoI, as one of Lord Beaverbrook's first actions as minister in May 1918 (TNA: INF 4/2, 'Publicity during the Great War', 26 October 1943).

Many of these short film tags have disappeared, but enough survive to enable a brief comparison with those PIFs later produced by the EMBFU and its successive government film units. Before the involvement of the MoI, each individual government department had used film, or not, as often determined by the attitude of the minister or senior civil servants to the medium. Occasionally, as in the time of the Boer War, individual commercial companies produced their

Figure 1.2 An animated propaganda film showing the German High Seas Fleet shelling the UK's east coast towns in December 1914

own patriotic offerings. In 1915 the Cartoon Company produced a five-minute short, entitled *John Bull's Animated Sketchbook, No. 4*, in which the iniquity of the Germans was shown in an animation of the shelling of the east coast towns in December 1914 (Figure 1.2).

Later in the war, much of the Cartoon Company's output showed humorous caricatures of the Germans. In 1917 the *Sketchbook No. 15*, drawn on screen by 'our famous artist', was a somewhat simplistic propaganda piece. Three comic-book stereotypical German troops with bent and battered *pickelhaubes* (spiked helmets) sheepishly moved across the screen from right to left, then returned clutching three gas meters; behind them the artist revealed that Berlin announced 'last night we gained three metres'. The humour may have dated somewhat, but the final sketch is interesting as it included a cartoon Charlie Chaplin destroying a zeppelin. Chaplin, along with George Robey, another famous contemporary music hall and screen performer, often appeared in either cartoon form or live action in these early tags. This use of popular entertainers in such propaganda films was, of course, repeated in the Second World War with, for example, the inclusion of the Crazy Gang's Flanagan and Allen singing 'Underneath the Arches' in Jennings' *Listen to Britain* (1942).

Inevitably, a comparison between the wartime short films produced by the MoI in 1918 and the much larger portfolio of the EMB, GPO and Crown film units between 1930 and 1952 is made more difficult by both the different demands and pressures and the dramatic improvements in film technology; but it is still possible to discern some similarities, especially in content, and link them with the later productions. These may be examined more easily under the headings that follow.

Morale or general reinforcement

Although the First World War had been progressing for well over three years before the MoI's Cinematograph Department took over the commissioning and production of films, it was still not certain that the Allies would prevail. The long years of stalemate on the Western Front, and the terrible toll in casualties, meant that the government wished to remind the domestic audience of the reasons for the conflict. An example of this approach was *John Bull's Animated Sketchbook* series (1915–18), which has already been mentioned. As far as the later productions were concerned, one of the first films in this category, 1941's *Christmas Under Fire*, reinforced both why Britain was fighting Germany and the sheer awfulness of the Nazis in bombing civilians. Perhaps more interesting in this category was *The Woman's Portion* (1918), a moralistic tale of the wife of an enlisted soldier who would prefer him to have been killed on the battlefield rather than suffer the shame of his desertion from duty. There is little in the GPOFU/CFU catalogue which can be said to directly compare with *The Woman's Portion*, although the small cameo storyline was an approach that was frequently adopted. An example of this is Crown's 1941 film *The Pilot Is Safe*, which, as the title suggests, was a reconstruction of the rescue of a pilot shot down in the English Channel.

Savings and the post-war world

A key government message in the latter stages of the First World War was to encourage the population to save more to help to fund the war effort. As such, war bonds and war savings certificates were issued, and some PIFs were produced which encouraged their purchase. A number of these not only emphasised that the money would be used to 'rid the world of Huns' (*Simple Simon*, 1918), but also that after a five-year investment period there would be a significant return [£1 for 15s 7d (78p) saved] which would enable individuals to purchase houses and their contents (*Jack and Jill*, 1918). Although there was nothing in the First World War film catalogue directly encouraging the civilian population to save, later there were several films produced by the GPOFU, like *The Saving of Bill Blewitt* (1936), which enthusiastically endorsed it. However, after the Second World War, with the increasingly dire economic situation, Crown did produce films, such as *Pop Goes the Weasel* (1948), which sought to explain the crisis and encouraged hard work and thrift. Perhaps a more surprising contrast between those early tags and the later films was in the suggested post-war treatment of the Germans. In *The Leopard's Spots* (1918), the film links rape and violence in Belgium with the post-war Germans attempting to sell goods to the UK – the obvious but crude message being that Germany must suffer for its part in the war and this could be achieved by embargoing their future exports. By 1944, however, the message contained in the Crown productions is much more sophisticated. In *The True Story of Lili Marlene*, and more obviously in *A Diary for Timothy*, Crown director Jennings was far more conciliatory, asking rhetorically of Tim, for example, about the future of Mozart's great music.[4] It was clear that the legacy of the treatment of Germany at Versailles in 1919, as predicted by *The Leopard's Spots*, was not to be repeated after the Second World War.

Handy hints and national advice

There was a more obvious comparison between the 1918 productions and those films produced during, and immediately after, the Second World War in the area of domestic advice to the civilian population, mostly, although not entirely, about reducing the amount of waste. *Father and Lather* (1918) was a salutary tale advising men not to leave the cake of soap in water while shaving as this caused it to deteriorate quickly. Similarly, *The Secret* (1918) and *Give*

'Em Beans (1918) were short films about preparing meals: the first about the substitution of grated potato for suet and the latter self-explanatory. Although during the 1940s these short handy domestic hints tended to be produced by film companies other than the GPO or Crown units, advisory films for the farming industry, for example, bear comparison. Thus, the 1950 CFU production *Insect Pests in Food* directly echoes the earlier *Cure for Potato Blight* (1918) in its emphasis on spreading the message to farmers about expanding domestic food production by controlling pests and blights.

By the end of the First World War the public information-type film had certainly become a significant part of the government's communication strategy. According to Reeves (1993, p. 465), 'at least 240 films were released during the years in which (Britain's official filmmakers) were at work and, in addition, between May 1917 and the end of the war a further 152 issues of the bi-weekly official newsreel were produced'. Even though the MoI's 1918 film production catalogue was unsophisticated and limited, the fact that the ministry was responsible for and used film in a variety of contexts provided an administrative and operational template for what was to happen when Britain and Germany once more went to war in 1939.

It is also probably fair to say that another major factor underpinning the government's approach to film and, especially, audiences during wartime was one of control. In both world wars this attitude was primarily prompted by a desire to ensure that nothing was screened which would either compromise national security or induce demoralisation both in the UK and abroad. In evidence given in 1943 to the Enquiry on Publicity during the Great War, Mr Brooke-Wilkinson reported that:

> Early in 1915, Mr Bedford and I were invited to attend a conference at the War Office, when we were informed that the total prohibition of the export of films from this country was under serious consideration. Apparently, there were many reasons for this course of action, one being the possibility of improper communication and messages being sent abroad, another was due to the receipt of information that the films were being exhibited abroad which was detrimental to the State and were causing reports to the effect that our new armies were inefficient and worthless. (TNA: INF 4/2, 'Publicity during the Great War', 26 October 1943)

Domestically, the administrative and legislative foundations for control had been laid as early as 1909 with the Cinematograph Act, which prohibited the exhibition of film except in licensed premises. In addition to this, three years later the British Board of Film Censors (BBFC) was established, with the role of giving initial guidance as to the 'suitability' of films released commercially in the UK. Although the BBFC was supposedly an autonomous body, the government retained a powerful influence, as the Home Office was responsible for the appointment of the president. Thus, while the BBFC issued 'certificates', exhibition licences were granted primarily by local authorities in England or Wales and the conditions imposed by them tended to be very parochial.

However, the censorship of newsreels and putative documentaries tended to be at the production rather than at the exhibition ends of the process. In moves that vividly anticipated the confusion and restrictions of the first weeks of the Second World War, the army and navy excluded all journalists from the front until May 1915. This was undoubtedly an unnecessary action, as Field Marshal Douglas Haig later observed: 'the correspondents have played up splendidly' (quoted in Bourne, 1989, p. 208). In other words, they were putting a far more optimistic spin on their stories than perhaps the field marshal could have reasonably expected. As far as film cameramen were concerned, forays to the front were always conducted in the company of intelligence officers who 'vetted' the location and shots. It is highly probable that this unwanted companionship may have saved the lives of several cameramen, as the professional soldiers were more likely to identify safer areas within a battle zone for an operator to set up his bulky and highly visible equipment.

By November 1918 the British government had recognised that, at a time of national emergency, the cinema had advantages both as a vehicle of propaganda and a ready source of revenue through the introduction in May 1916 of a tax on cinema admissions.[5] However, whether that realisation would extend beyond the end of the war was a moot point.

Notes

1. There is a comprehensive discussion of music halls during the Boer War in Attridge (1993), Chapter 1.
2. According to Luke McKernan, 'eight British commercial cameramen are known to have filmed in South Africa during the Boer War; William Kennedy-Laurie Dickson for the British Mutoscope and Biograph Company, Walter Calverley Beevor and Sydney Melsom (there are doubts over his identity) for Robert Paul, John Benett-Stanford, Edgar Hyman and Joe Rosenthal for the Warwick Trading Company, all filmed in the period up to the fall of Pretoria in June 1900. Sydney Goldman, Rosenthal's replacement, and C. Rider Noble remained to film the later stages of the war' (McKernan, 2002, p. 2).
3. Geoffrey Malins (1886–1940) was probably the more famous of the two wartime photographers. He published his memoirs in 1920 as *How I Filmed the War*. These are remarkable for Malin's redrafting of his role in the war; he never once mentions his colleague, McDowell.
4. Mozart's Piano Concerto No. 17 in G.
5. An Entertainment Tax was introduced in May 1916 which imposed, according to the exhibitors, a fairly swingeing ½d on cinema tickets up to 2d and, for the more expensive 6d seats, a 1d tax. As the numbers are very small it is difficult to give a modern, post-decimalisation comparison. However, in percentage terms, the tax on the first ticket was 25 per cent and on the second, more expensive one, 12.5 per cent.

2

The Empire Marketing Board Film Unit: Tallents, Grierson, documentaries and the revival of government interest, 1930–33

Although the experience of the First World War had changed the political, social and economic environment significantly as far as film was concerned, most in government saw little need for further involvement in the production or commissioning of films. Films, or at least their exhibition in the commercial sector, were primarily regarded as a source of revenue for the Exchequer. However, this position began to change quite dramatically from the mid-1920s onwards.

There were several reasons for the increasing awareness that films in both theatrical and non-theatrical settings were likely to have some communication value given the potential audience numbers. This was not least because of the rapid expansion of cinemas throughout the UK, but also due to the multiplying opportunities for non-theatrical exhibition. Much of this was driven by the changing technology, firstly with the more easily available 16 mm projectors for non-theatrical showings and later the arrival of synchronised sound. In the political arena the Conservative Party seemed anxious to exploit the opportunities which film provided for political propaganda. An early Tory proponent was Joseph Ball,[1] who was the chief publicity officer in the 1927–29 period and subsequently head of research until 1939. In many senses this was a reaction to the implications of the new mass electorate, following the 1918 and 1928 Representation of the People Acts. Ball foresaw that the days of the outdoor political orator and the town hall meeting where generally the 'converted' were gathered, although not yet dead, were limited. Means had to be found of addressing the new electorate near or where they congregated.

Direct exhibition within the commercial cinema was precluded by both cost and the fact that the owners were reluctant to exhibit films of an overtly partisan nature; however, the cinema-going habit could be exploited by the introduction of non-theatrical display such as cinema vans. Somewhat ironically given the hostility of some Conservative members to the government film unit in 1951, twenty years earlier criticism often came from the political Left. In a critique of the newsreels, the *New Leader* (a left-wing journal) announced that they, 'By the mere fact of their regularity, must play a large part in the forming of popular ideas and in the moulding of public opinion... Its object is not to present news but to breed a race of society gossipers, sports-maniacs, lick-spittles and jingoes' (*New Leader*, 31 May 1929, p. 2). Even as late as 1940 Labour leader Clement Attlee thought that the MoI was part of the Conservative Party's propaganda machinery (Reith, 1949, p. 368) The appreciation of the potential value of film as a means of disseminating a message coincided with the development of what was beginning to be called public relations, even though, in the 1920s, the means of presenting government party policy or commercial messages still tended to rely heavily upon the more traditional media rather than film. The establishment of the Empire Marketing Board in 1926 was a prime example of this approach.

The Conservative government's manifesto at the general election of December 1923 had espoused the cause of imperial preference. In essence, this meant erecting tariff barriers to protect trade, especially from the Dominions. The unfortunate consequence of this was the likely increase in food prices, a feature which was exploited successfully by the Conservative Party's political opponents. Although a year later Conservative premier Stanley Baldwin was returned to office with a healthy majority after the brief Ramsay MacDonald Labour government, the argument in favour of imperial preference had not been won. Baldwin therefore wanted to wean the public off their, somewhat traditional, support for free trade and convince them that there was a self-interested case for imperial preference. In order to achieve this, at the end of November 1924, the government advised the Dominions of its intention to appoint an Imperial Economic Committee with the aim of encouraging UK consumers to purchase products from imperial sources which, in turn, would, it was hoped, benefit both consumers and producers. Thus, the permanent organisation proselytising these policies became a political reality in 1926 with the establishment of the Empire Marketing Board (EMB).

Although the EMB was quite short-lived, becoming a casualty in 1933 of the economic fallout of the Great Depression, much of its success was down to the dynamism and far-sightedness of the EMB secretary, Stephen Tallents. As Atkins (2003) has pointed out, Tallents later reflected that he had received little by way of a detailed briefing from Leo Amery, the secretary of state for the colonies and minister with overall responsibility for the EMB, and was therefore able to build a remarkably creative and energetic organisation, 'set at a tangent to the usual stereotype of dull Whitehall bureaucracy. It was small, never larger than 120 employees, because "the agreed policy is to work through other agencies wherever possible and undertake as little direct work as conditions permit"' (Atkins, 2003). The 'little direct work' eventually became the EMB Film Unit. The actual agreement to the establishment of the EMBFU was in a minor note in the minutes of the EMB committee in April 1930. This gave authorisation for an expenditure of £2,350 to fund a film unit and the rental for two rooms initially in Wardour Street, London (TNA: CO 760/37).

The role that Tallents played in the development of firstly the EMBFU and later the GPOFU cannot be underestimated. His sponsorship of John Grierson and enthusiasm for the role of film as a persuasive medium in both public relations and marketing was evident in the development of both film units. Although he was reputed to be a taciturn figure, by the mid-1920s he was already known as a regular columnist in the *Manchester Guardian* as well as the author of two books of poetry. Tallents not only saw film as an important medium for accessing and perhaps manipulating public opinion in favour of imperial preference, but he also convinced the government to appoint Grierson as the assistant films officer in 1927. Much has of course been written about Grierson and the documentary movement – Aitken (1992), Barnouw (1993), Winston (1995) and indeed Grierson himself in 1946. From these it is possible to identify those aspects which formed the intellectual and production ethos that underpinned much of the output of the EMB and its successor film units. There can be no doubt that Grierson's somewhat catholic and eclectic approach to filmmaking struck a particular chord amongst a group of generally middle- and upper-class independent filmmakers during the late 1920s and early 1930s. He was also fortunate in that his pioneering film *Drifters* would probably not have been made, or at least not have achieved such wide distribution, had it not coincided with the government's slowly evolving change of attitude towards protectionism and its corollary imperial preference.

As Grierson's *Drifters* is often acknowledged as the founding film of the British documentary movement, in some senses it sets the tone and standard for future productions. There are aspects of *Drifters* which are reflected in the films produced by the government film units. There is, for example, the depiction of the tension between the old traditional ways and the new modern, usually industrialised methods – the latter, of course, also being championed by both the GPO in *Line to the Tschierva Hut* (1937)[2] and, as late as 1949, in Crown's Oscar-winning *Daybreak at Udi*.[3] Although *Drifters* predated the EMBFU, it utilised real people rather than actors and showed the workings and trials of a particular industry, in this case the Scottish and North Sea herring fleets. However, the choice of topic probably owed less to Grierson's intrinsic interest in fishing but rather to Tallents' appreciation of the power of persuasion, if not flattery. The first secretary of the Treasury, Arthur Samuel,[4] had written a book called *The Herring: Its Effect on the History of Britain* (London, 1918) and Tallents took the opportunity of persuading him to grant funds to make a film on the Scottish herring industry. He apparently further encouraged Samuel to be supportive of the role of film in general by suggesting that he should become a 'consultant adviser' on *Drifters*. Therefore, by successfully translating Samuel's book into a film format, Tallents and Grierson were able to show it as a valuable means of disseminating information in support of a political or personal objective. However, even though Tallents had secured important political support for the role of film, it was always the least regarded of the media employed by the EMB. As late as 1933, the annual report places film and cinema in last position in terms of advertising, well after posters, leaflets, lectures – and even horticultural display.

Despite the regard in which *Drifters* has been held, another film was the first to be commissioned directly by the EMB. Walter Creighton, an acquaintance of Rudyard Kipling, produced *One*

Family, which was released in 1930 under the auspices of British Instructional Films. Creighton's appointment was perhaps indicative of the perceived novelty of film and the lack of suitably experienced filmmakers. His background was that of a pageant master who, at one time, had been responsible for staging the annual military tattoo in Aldershot. The assumption, presumably, was that he had the experience of producing a visually spectacular event for the public. However, he did realise that he needed some training in the new medium and so left the UK to spend the next eighteen months in Hollywood learning the craft of filmmaking. Whereas Grierson's *Drifters'* reputation has only been enhanced over the years and is regularly referred to and shown in various university courses and at film aficionados' meetings, its near contemporary has almost disappeared entirely. Yet there are probably as many, if not more, features in *One Family* than in *Drifters* that were later reflected in GPO and Crown films. On the negative side, the film is certainly overlong at just under fifty minutes, even after the silent version's intertitles had been removed and an annoying soundtrack dubbed. The clipped received pronunciation seemed very much at odds with the visual representation of a working-class family. Of course, Creighton's film was, in one sense, quite avant-garde in that, prior to 1929, film was a silent medium where the message, political or not, was essentially interrupted by the inclusion of the intertitles – the short explanatory captions. Once sound was available in both recording and exhibition, the opportunities to confirm the message aurally were increasingly important.

As far as *One Family* was concerned, Creighton utilised a common plot device with the film dominated by a dream sequence. A young schoolboy, having seen the ingredients list of the king's Christmas pudding in his father's morning newspaper, falls asleep in school. He dreams about visiting Buckingham Palace where, after meeting the king off camera, he began a search for the ingredients of the pudding. Accompanied by a chubby palace retainer, no doubt to provide some comedic elements, he eventually encountered in one of the palace's rooms the embodiments of the Dominions. These ladies, apparently recent debutantes and scions of aristocratic families, were attired in flowing white dresses set off with headdresses which included representations of the major exports of the countries. Thus, Miss South Africa's head was garlanded with grapes and oranges. Similar items adorned the heads or dresses of the other Dominions, namely Australia, Canada, India, the Irish Free State and New Zealand. Within the dream sequence the boy was encouraged to visit the countries and see the production of various foodstuffs. Inevitably, most countries were represented by shots of large orchards, vineyards, grain fields and, in New Zealand's case, the cattle required to produce butter. It is slightly confusing that Miss India seemed to have nothing to offer the king's pudding and, despite Canada's prairie grain fields, when searching for bread for the pudding the boy goes to Scotland and Ireland to be offered loaves by a suitably tartan-clad female baker and the same from unshod scruffy children in Ireland. The dream ending, the boy was shown back at home where his mother was making the Christmas pudding and, according to tradition, he was given an opportunity to stir it. Had the film ended there it would have perhaps been understandable; however, there then follows a fairly long sequence featuring a stereotypical British policeman, chubby and jovial but with a sense of authority. The policeman was shown gathering representatives of the children's counting rhyme: 'Tinker, tailor, soldier, sailor, rich man, poor man, beggar man, thief.' Having assembled the entire eight-man cohort, he escorted them to a local pub and requested a tankard of beer for each. The drinks are provided, and the last scene is of them all drinking the king's health at Christmas. Even if it is assumed that the practice of public relations and marketing were in their infancy, especially in the context of the use of film, *One Family* is, according to a BFI reviewer, 'baffling'. The narrative is at best disjointed, and the latter section appears to be totally unrelated to the rest of the film. Even after the addition of the sound dubbing, the evidence of audience reaction was not very positive. Creighton's film, which cost £15,740, a not insignificant part of the EMB's total film budget for three years, premiered at the Palace Theatre, London on 7 July 1930, but was withdrawn from commercial exhibition a week later, having failed to attract an adequate audience. *The Observer's* film critic summed up the general press reaction the following Sunday: 'It is because I believe implicitly in the fine possibilities of British propaganda that the EMB film *Our Family* oppresses me with such a feeling of waste and disappointment… Here is the stuff of adventure and romance with enough raw material to serve half a dozen films with beauty. It is timid and respectful, tentative and yet traditional. It is put together without any urgency and passion for its content' (*The Observer*, 13 July 1930, p. 12).

This failure was ironically recognised by Grierson, who commented a year later, in the EMB 1931 annual report, that the long dream sequence was 'not quite the dream which the film public was accustomed to turn over in their minds. The lesson we learned was that cinema can only at peril depart from the dreams and aspirations of common people'. However, despite the inadequacy of the production, the lack of commercial success and the hostility of the contemporary audience, the film does demonstrate features which later became the mainstay of productions of the government film units. *One Family* was essentially a drama documentary in which the public relations message was intertwined with a story narrative. Similarly, *One Family* was a sponsored film produced with a particular cause in mind – in this case the EMB and imperial preference. There was a nod in the direction of that sponsorship with the few brief frames showing the recipe of the pudding and the importance of the Empire, especially the Dominions, in producing its ingredients. The soundtrack also reminded the audience, through the limited statements of the society ladies, that their assigned country had natural and agricultural resources necessary for the UK. Although hardly a successful film by any measure it did point the way to the development of government-sponsored films designed for, nominally, public information but more likely public relations purposes.

The actual establishment of an in-house film production unit in April 1930 came quite late in the history of the EMB. Although the gestation period was quite lengthy, Tallents, the secretary of the EMB, had long been an advocate of film as a means of communicating a national ideology. In his booklet *The Projection of England* (Faber, 1932), he praised the success of post-revolutionary Russian cinema, not only Eisenstein's *Battleship Potemkin* but also Vsevolod Pudovkin's *Storm Over Asia*, Viktor Turin's *Turksib* and Oleksandr Dovzhenko's *Earth*. His comments on *Earth* are enlightening in that they reflect the approach taken frequently by the EMBFU and its successors and are well in line with Grierson's opinions. '*Earth*', he wrote, despite 'its enforced and tendentious story, is fundamentally a hymn of the soil and of the people who live by the soil. Its beautiful procession of villagers to the young man's funeral, its simple and lovely dying fall of rain descending upon apples, are nearer to true poetry than any other film within my knowledge' (Tallents, 1932, p. 223). The booklet encouraged British filmmakers to emulate their Russian counterparts and produce such films: 'the countryside and the country life, which have inspired so noble a body of English poetry and painting, we have themes not less beautiful than that of *Earth*, and we are under no necessity, as was Dovjenko, to disguise them under the appearance of political propaganda' (Tallents, 1932. p. 224). The final comment in this sentence might be regarded as somewhat disingenuous given that Tallents was responsible for attempting to alter public opinion in favour of imperial preference.

The Projection of England was also important as not only did Tallents recognise the need for film production but also for the development of exhibition outlets. He was convinced that the tide was turning. 'There are signs already of a public demand for a new type of entertainment, in the development both of special theatres devoted to news items and of non-theatrical performances in schools and elsewhere. I suspect that there is a great potential audience, in England and overseas, which could in time be led to add their patronage to the picture houses, if they could count upon finding, at least in some of them, other matter than the sex and crime material of which two-thirds of our present programmes are composed' (Tallents, 1932, p. 224).

Despite Tallents' endorsement of the role of film, the reality was it only provided a very small element in the strategy pursued by the EMB. The more traditional media which had been used quite successfully in the First World War were again vigorously revived in the late 1920s. These included leaflets, of which nearly 10 million were distributed according to the 1932–33 annual report of the EMB. Posters, too, remained important, with over 27,000 schools receiving them, according to the same report. Inevitably, the effectiveness of these media is difficult to assess given that public relations was in its infancy and the techniques for judging advertising campaigns were as yet underdeveloped. Even the success of posters, which are perhaps the most tangible and retrospectively famous of the EMB's publicity campaign methods, was based upon hearsay rather than concrete evidence. Certainly, as far as film was concerned, a note of caution is necessary, as its impact or influence in altering the public's perception of the post-war role of the Empire was probably politically diminished somewhat as a large number of the non-theatrical venues were schools and the audience children.

Although both *Drifters* and *One Family* were produced prior to the foundation of the EMBFU, most of its early film work was actually editing reels shot by various companies and individuals both in the UK and the Empire. Grierson had suggested, according to Hoare (2010), that the unit produced over 100 films for the EMB between 1930 and 1933 (Hoare, 2010, p. 207). This is perhaps somewhat disingenuous as most of these edits were created mainly for non-theatrical exhibition or, occasionally, as flashes for the commercial sector. However, almost more important than film production at that time was the establishment of a means of distribution of the films. In the first instance these were loaned, usually for free, from the Empire Film Library based at the Imperial Institute in London. This initially provided the means both of film storage but also distribution to, mostly, non-theatrical settings. In its various iterations the centralised lending facility remained a valuable resource for this form of exhibition until the closure of its direct successor, the COI, in 2011.

The movement away from being merely a post-production facility to filmmaking came in 1930 when the EMB film committee sanctioned the small grant of £2,350 for these purposes, as well as the rental of a small office space initially in Wardour Street, London, but soon nearby in 37–39 Oxford Street. Amongst one of the final sets of minutes for the EMB in May 1933, the situation was neatly described. It explained that the offices,

> include[d] besides the Board's Chief Film Officer, Mr John Grierson, a small staff of producers, cameramen and editors, which varies in size in accordance to current requirements and current resources. The Unit's work has been directed primarily at the making of documentary films illustrating the production and marketing of Empire commodities. The films so produced are in some cases designed for showing in public cinemas on a commercial basis. In other cases they are reserved for non-theatrical showing. The Board's main purpose has been to produce, within the limits of their own commission, films of high design and quality, and to secure wide distribution for them. They have not been primarily concerned to secure commercial profits. (TNA: CO 760/37)

This short paragraph, situated very near the end of the minute, identified some of the key issues which continued to feature in the histories of all the government film units. On the positive side they were encouraged to make documentary films of 'high quality' for both commercial and non-theatrical exhibition. There was also an implication, evident in the phrase 'directed primarily', that alternative sponsors and sources of income could be tolerated. However, on the negative side, the numbers of personnel of the film units often fluctuated in line with oscillating costs, which frequently brought them into conflict with the civil service bureaucracy of which they were nominally members. There was also little support from the commercial film industry who became antagonised by the units as competitor organisations which did not need to conform to the normal economies of production. The very organisational flexibility, which owed much to Grierson's determination to make the EMBFU semi-independent of government and attractive to a number of like-minded filmmakers, also made it anathema to the Treasury and many in the commercial sector alike.

However, the early prospects for the success of the EMBFU in April 1930 might have looked reasonable, as not only was it now a recognised production facility but it had already received its first commissions from the EMB – films on *Children of the Empire* and the *Port of London*. Unfortunately, there were also issues both of a technical nature and, perhaps more importantly, the wider national and international economic climate which were to cause both production problems and, eventually, the demise of the unit itself. The major technical change was, of course, the introduction of synchronised sound in the late 1920s and the rapid adaptation of the commercial cinema to accommodate what soon became an essential feature of film viewing. The initial lack of sound recording facilities available to the EMBFU meant that most of its productions were essentially silent where the visual message was reinforced by intertitles. However, given that the cost of sound systems was often prohibitive to schools and church halls and similar venues, it did mean that early on EMBFU productions had a ready market in non-theatrical settings.

When examining the films produced by the EMBFU during its brief three-year existence some caution is necessary, as establishing the provenance of these early films is often problematic. Not only are some of the films no longer extant but, in other cases, the change in titles from commission to production combined with an absence of on-screen credits make analysis and discussion problematic. Furthermore, there is, of course, the necessary observation that film is a dilatory medium, often taking months from idea to exhibition. So much of what was commissioned during the life of the EMBFU did not actually achieve exhibition in either non-theatrical or commercial venues until the unit itself had been disbanded. In the main, the films produced by the EMBFU were short documentaries, often only a few minutes long, but which, for the first time, enabled people to witness events unfolding that had been previously largely confined to print. Despite these caveats, it is possible to suggest that what the EMBFU produced fell into certain categories which, in the main, reflected the sponsor's requirements. It is also perhaps unsurprising that the unit's approach was reflected later by the GPO and Crown units, as inevitably some of the personnel moved, usually harmoniously, from one to the other. So, for example, Basil Wright and Stuart Legg were amongst the early EMB filmmakers who continued to work, not always uninterruptedly, with the government film units. One of the major successes of the EMBFU, which continued with the GPO and Crown units, was that it had quickly developed a reputation as an in-house film production unit that other government departments and agencies appeared increasingly happy to contact. The EMB's final annual report noted that, amongst other sponsors, films were produced for the Ministry of Agriculture, the Admiralty and the Air Ministry. It is not possible at this distance in time to discover whether these commissions were as a result of the unit directly seeking outside sponsorship or the government departments themselves seeking to exploit the opportunities presented by an in-house production facility. It was highly likely that the two approaches existed side by side.

As far as the actual films are concerned, the relatively short life of the EMBFU, combined with the time required to get a film ready for exhibition, even if the duration was rarely more than twenty minutes, meant that the number of films which can be securely attributed to the unit was only around thirty. Although they were produced by the EMBFU, as has been stated their actual distribution and exhibition often occurred well after the unit had been disbanded, so the exact date of completion can only be estimated.

Unlike its successors, the GPO and Crown units, the small number of films fall into relatively few categories with only rare outliers. As will be seen, what was perhaps both significant and apparent quite early in the history of the EMBFU was that, although nominally created to publicise the advantages of the Empire, especially for the British citizen, the wider-ranging creative licence approved by Grierson and tolerated by Tallents was quickly exploited. It is possible to identify a small number of categories into which most of the production catalogue falls.

Publicity for the Empire Marketing Board

Given where the EMB unit was situated organisationally and in terms of its basic funding, it was hardly surprising that about one-third of the unit's productions were created as public relations pieces with the intention of changing or reinforcing public perceptions in favour of the Empire and, more specifically, the importance of imperial trade. Having said that, the production catalogue of these films is quite small, at about six. With titles including Paul Rotha's *Australian Wines* (1931) and *Windmill in Barbados* (1933) – which was actually about sugar production – it seems highly likely that a major reason for this was the sheer distance involved in acquiring the appropriate film footage at a time when passenger air travel was in its infancy. A couple of films in this category exemplify the public relations combined with travelogue approach taken by the EMBFU.

People and Products of India, which was produced in 1931, demonstrated some of the difficulties in explaining complex concepts in a visually attractive way without the addition of a sound commentary. Consequently, this film has a plethora of intertitles interspersed with supportive images. It commenced with a map of British India, which then stretched from what is now Pakistan in the west to Burma (Myanmar) in the east and included Ceylon (Sri Lanka) off the south coast. It had, according to the intertitle, a population of over 300 million people and was a land of mosques and temples. Life in India was dominated by traditional agriculture, itself relying, according to the film, on the annual purchase of seeds often financed by loans from moneylenders. Not only was the production of wheat seen as quite backward but that also appeared to be the case for several other agricultural products. The areas for growing silk, rice, sugar and jute were illustrated with their own map and brief visual illustration of the production methods, which still relied heavily on manual labour supported occasionally by oxen. Despite this, there were increasing examples of technological improvements and the development of new farming methods, such as the mechanisation of sugar production post harvesting. The penultimate section of the film perhaps bizarrely included a section on the 'greatest danger to man and beast – the man-eating tiger'. The evidence of the mass slaughter of these animals gave the film a certain edginess and probably coincided well with the prevailing attitude toward wild carnivores which existed in the inter-war years. However, the key message in the film is left to the last few frames. The products of India are shown being loaded onto merchant ships bound for the UK. The final intertitle announced that 'Big Ships keep Britain and India in touch'.

A later version of the same theme and approach can be found in Wright's eleven-minute silent, *Cargo from Jamaica*. Here there is a direct and obvious comparison between the traditional methods of growing, harvesting and transporting bananas to the technological approach to unloading and storing them after the vessel arrives in London. The contrast is most noticeable with the numbers of workers hauling banana bunches by hand from carts, into small barges and then, also manually, filling the holds of the waiting vessel. On arrival in the UK the mechanical unloading is supervised by one man. Not only is the value of Empire emphasised as a ready source of food, but also the differences, perhaps superiority, of technologies are made visually evident. Other films in this category addressed the importance of the Empire as a source of raw materials, rather than just food. So *Lumber* (1931) and *Axes and Elephants* (1931) concentrated upon the timber industries in Canada, New Zealand and Burma.

The best of Britain

By far the largest group of films produced by the EMBFU focused on what was occurring in Britain in the early 1930s. This is perhaps unsurprising as, with the possible exception of Canada, the film industries in the other Dominions and the Empire at large were at best nascent and in most cases non-existent. The time, effort and cost of sending a film crew to distant lands was indulged in a few cases but, inevitably, it was easier and quicker to film closer to home. It is possible to describe this output as travelogues, but that somewhat trivialises the underlying message. The early directors, often emulating the style and approach pioneered by Grierson in *Drifters*, not only emphasised the visual attraction of traditional crafts and landscapes but usually juxtaposed them against the new industrial developments in the particular sector being examined. Although both sets of images are often visually arresting, the audience would, in an age of modernity, almost certainly appreciate the obvious tensions between them.

The stresses between old and new were evident in the one EMBFU film made by the American Robert Flaherty. His earlier films – *Nanook of the North* (1922) and *Moana* (1926) – had been important in Grierson's developing understanding of what he was to call the documentary. When the opportunity presented itself, Grierson invited Flaherty to create a film for the EMBFU, eventually released in 1932 under the title *Industrial Britain*. Unfortunately, Flaherty's somewhat idiosyncratic approach to filming and extravagant use of film stock meant that the final product was actually the result of Edgar Anstey's editing following Flaherty's dismissal. Having said that, the film itself bears several hallmarks of later GPO and Crown productions. It also must have had contemporary cinematic value, as it was amongst the six EMBFU films to be selected by Gaumont-British Pictures for the addition of a soundtrack and exhibition in the company's cinemas. Much of the camerawork reflected the somewhat romantic approach taken by Flaherty in his earlier films. There were the windmills and looms of previous centuries, enhanced by shots of traditional craftsmen including potters, glassmakers and engravers. However, the old order was changing and steam and smoke became its symbols. The modern world needed coal to provide its power and this was still, in the main, hewn by hand. The film asserts that there were still over 1 million miners employed in the UK. Similarly, the scenes of steelmaking were powerfully dramatic but essential for the modern world. Despite power and mechanisation, the film concluded that, behind it all, there remained a need for human involvement. Skilled workers, for example, were required to produce lenses for aerodrome lights. Even the massive steel construction of a modern hotel at Marble Arch in London required the 'man at the lever'. The basic message behind *Industrial Britain* was that, although the heavy industries of coal and steel underpinned transport and manufacturing, the role of the skilled workman was still essential. Future government film unit productions often used the juxtaposition of old-world scenes and modern technologies to create an impression of progress. The footage shot by Flaherty appears in a few subsequent shorts, such as *The English Potter* (1933) and *The Glassmakers of England* (1933). Furthermore, *Industrial Britain* emphasised authenticity by using individuals playing their normal roles rather than actors, which itself became a key aspect of many future government film unit productions.

Another one of the 'Imperial Six' productions bought by Gaumont-British to be recut and have sound added was *Shadow on the Mountain* (1932), originally *An Experiment on the Welsh Hills*. This, too, has the juxtaposed message of traditional farm activity with modern scientific research. It commenced with quick cuts of Welsh mountain scenery and threatening weather. In an early scene of British transhumance, farmers and their dogs are shown heading to the hillsides to round up the sheep to take down to the valleys for the winter. This traditional, presumably centuries-old, activity was then contrasted with a section on grassland research. Included are shots of scientists in white coats (again, a theme frequently utilised by later unit films) manipulating pollens via bees to improve the grain harvest. The result of this is also automation, as hand sowing and horse-drawn ploughing gave way to mechanisation in the form of the motorised caterpillar tractor.

Although *Shadow on the Mountain* was one of the Imperial Six, it does appear to lack some coherence, especially in respect of the section on the seed research station. However, there is no doubt that the message was one of the march of progress through even traditional industries. Despite this, there also appears to be a smaller number of films which are less message orientated but more lyrical and reflective. Contemporaneously with the production of *Shadow on the Mountain* was Basil Wright's *O'er Hill and Dale* (1932), also bought by Gaumont-British. This generally upbeat film was also released under the title *Shepherd's Spring in the Cheviot*

Hills and deals essentially with similar issues from a northern rather than Welsh perspective. In this case, the focus is far more upon the individual, Martin the Shepherd, and his life during lambing. Martin's tasks during April and May are observed, from the bizarre concoction of gin and linseed oil given to the sheep to, apparently, ward off dysentery to the brutal skinning of a dead lamb and then placing it over an orphan to encourage the mother to adopt it. As a winter storm threatens, the shepherd rescues another orphan lamb and takes it home for his wife to keep warm in the kitchen. The final shots of gambolling lambs demonstrated a successful lambing season. Again, *O'er Hill and Dale* confirms the approach taken in many of the EMB and subsequent film units in that the narrative revolves around 'normal' people undertaking their regular activities (Figure 2.1).

Over the three years existence of the EMBFU, there were several films which conformed to the practice of showing the activities of 'normal' people working in traditional ways, such as *Upstream* (1932), about salmon fishing in Scotland. *Our Herring Harvest*

Figure 2.1 *O'er Hill and Dale* (1932) showed the tough existence of hill farmers

(1932) was slightly unusual coming so soon after *Drifters*, but this film was about the North Sea herring fleet working primarily out of Suffolk and concerned the operation from catch to dispatch on trains to London. From an agricultural perspective the unit released *The Shepherd* (1933), which utilised footage shot for earlier films. The sharing or multi-use of footage became a feature of the government film units' modus operandi, probably both as a result of the cooperative style of operation within the units and the fact that, until they had access to larger studios, the majority of film was shot outdoors and post-production occurred within a relatively small set of rooms.

Amongst the cutting staff of the EMBFU was Grierson's sister Marion, who was originally employed to edit footage coming from Canada and was also a member of the film unit of the Travel and Industrial Development Association (TIDA). Probably because of family connections, both units initially operated out of the same building. Marion began producing her own films, released initially under both EMB and TIDA names. *So This Is London* (1933) was fairly typical of her films, being essentially a travelogue and an observation of a day in the life of the nation's capital. The focus on London was emphasised from the beginning with the caption 'All Roads Lead to London'. This film also conforms to the juxtaposing approach taken by other filmmakers of the unit. There were many scenes of traditional historic London, including the Houses of Parliament, Westminster Abbey, the Tower of London and so on. However, this was contrasted with modern landscapes of Battersea Power Station, the sixty miles of docks and London's financial centre. The contrast between old and new was not just architectural but also shown in terms of the people. There were the flamboyant Cockney pearly kings and queens alongside the military and judicial pageantry, but the majority of Londoners were now office or shop workers who used the excellent transportation links and whose leisure time was in the great London parks, traditionally reserved for the better off. In a further nod to modernity, London was shown as the city which never sleeps as, according to the soundtrack, 'when night falls the city of pleasure takes over from the city of commerce' and the film concluded with scenes of a jazz nightclub.

Another female filmmaker who began her career with the EMBFU was Evelyn Spice (later Cherry). She had originally worked with Grierson in Canada and had come over to the UK where she was initially his secretary. Her history demonstrates both the collaborative working practices of the unit as well as the fact that novices were both tolerated and encouraged. Her first EMBFU film was *Spring on the Farm* (1933), which was notable in using a child for the voiceover. The film itself was a somewhat bucolic and pastoral review of the animals and their young that can be found on a farm in springtime. Although Grierson's colleagues have often been described as his 'documentary boys' this should not be at the expense of the 'girls'.

Direct advertising

The line between creating a favourable impression, which is the principal aim of most public relations exercises, and direct advertising of a particular good or service is inevitably very blurred. However, one of the consequences of increasing mass literacy towards the end of the nineteenth century had been the rise of the mass circulation newspapers, especially the national popular dailies, such as the *Daily Mail* in 1896 and the *Daily Mirror* in 1903. A symbiotic relationship quickly established itself between the newspapers and the nascent advertising industry. To the newspapers, advertisements were a welcome source of income which kept the cover price down; to the advertisers, it was an easy opportunity to get their message into many homes. The prospect of film as an advertising medium had been trialled during the First World War, but this was mainly in the context of government 'short' messages such as *Jack and Jill*.

The blurred line between public relations and advertising films is certainly evident in some of EMBFU projects sponsored by the Ministry of Agriculture and Fisheries in support of its 'National Mark' campaign. In 1928 the Agricultural Produce (Grading and Marketing) Act was designed to encourage standardisation in agricultural produce, such as eggs, beef and apples. The National Mark would be a guarantee of quality in home-produced food and the EMBFU made at least a couple of shorts to advertise the new system. An early example of this was *Plums That Please* (1931) which, as the title implies, was a comprehensive explanation of the growing, harvesting, distribution and retailing of plums. Having highlighted the National Mark scheme at the beginning, the film commenced with shots of plum orchards in blossom in the Vale of Evesham. These initial scenes emphasised some of the traditional skills, with men climbing ladders to prune the trees. The introduction of new technologies appeared after the plums had been picked and the film follows the journey of the Purple Pershore variety. Once harvested, they were weighed and graded which had, by the late 1920s, become a highly automated process. The graded plums were then packed and loaded on to trains bound for London where they were seen being auctioned at Covent Garden Market. The message, of course, was that not only were the plums of a consistently high standard but their journey from tree to consumer was short. To complete that trip the film concluded with a section 'for the housewife' explaining and demonstrating how the fruit could be canned or bottled for later use. *Plums That Please* (Figure 2.2) was quickly followed by a more wide-ranging exploration of the value of the National Mark in the somewhat self-congratulatory *Record*

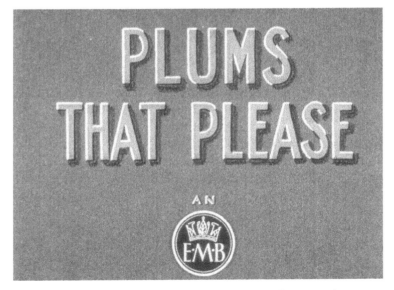

Figure 2.2 *Plums That Please* (1931): one of the EMB Film Unit's simple advertisements

of *Achievement* (1931), which reviewed its success in several food production areas.

It was not just government departments that appeared to value the expertise of the EMBFU. The unit was also making inroads into providing films for the private sector. Wright's *Liner Cruising South* (1933) is a descriptive account of the Orient Line's SS Orford Caribbean cruise. The journey, which was essentially a tour of British possessions, would have been sympathetically viewed by the EMB, being in line with the policy of imperial preference; but it was also valuable advertising for the shipping line. Similarly, in 1932 Arthur Elton produced a film on the production of gramophones and radios for HMV called *Voice of the World*.

Miscellaneous

Although most of the EMB's films were created for widespread and unrestricted exhibition, a few were designed for a highly selective audience. This 'specialist' type of film remained a small part of the catalogue of the EMBFU and its successors for the following two decades. Although premiered before a press audience in 1932 with surprisingly supportive reviews, Arthur Elton's *Erecting Aeroplane Engines* was highly technical. There were long visual descriptions of different types of aeroplane engines, both water- and air-cooled. Shots of engineers tightening bolts were accompanied by the salutary intertitle 'bearings must fit, but not too tightly!' The penultimate scenes in the film were essentially a list of British aero engines: the Rolls-Royce Kestrel, the Bristol Pegasus and so on. It is only in the very last scenes that shots of flying aircraft demonstrated the purpose of the engines. *Erecting Aeroplane Engines* could easily fall into an 'instructional' category as it is difficult to see the intended audience other than those with a significant technical bent or interest in aviation. The categorising of the films produced by the EMBFU is, as has been mentioned, a problematic exercise. This is doubly so if there is little documentary evidence extant and the films not readily available. Such is the case with such interesting titles as *Furry Folk* (1931) and *A New Road Transport Train* (1932).

Closure of EMB and the future of the film unit

The collapse of the American stock market at the end of 1929, and its subsequent impact on worldwide trade and financial markets, meant that, in 1931, the new national government in Britain was seeking major economies. There had been little enthusiasm in the Treasury for the EMB and, unsurprisingly, it became an easy target for cost-cutting. The board was finally wound up in September 1933. Needless to say, a collateral casualty of the closure was the EMBFU. In the meantime, Tallents had secured an appointment at the GPO as its public relations officer and convinced his new employers that a film unit would be a valuable aid to developing a national public relations programme. Although the transfer of the film unit directly to the GPO was relatively seamless – and jobs were saved and filming continued – it is possible to make a couple of general but interim observations about the EMBFU. On the positive side, the unit proved to be important in the development of the craft of filmmaking, especially documentary filmmaking in the UK. The announcement of the unit's closure prompted *The Scotsman* to write in 1933:

> The EMB Film Unit is peculiar amongst film-producing organisations in that it has not merely a commercial purpose. Thus free from the need to play for popularity and of the demand for immediate and tangible results, it can take a long-range view, to explore, and build for the future. This is precisely what the film Unit has been doing during the past two or three years and it is just this volume of training for a purpose that is threatened with extinction. When the unit was inaugurated, it was given the task of 'bringing the Empire alive'. Those who founded the organisation were instructed to use the cinema, *or to learn to use it*, to bring the day-to-day activities of the Empire at work into the common imagination. (*The Scotsman*, 3 June 1933)

It has often been remarked by Grierson's biographers that, rather than a filmmaker, he was essentially a propagandist for documentary film and especially for its public information role. In order to achieve this, he seemed to have the ability to spot filmmaking talent and indeed many, such as Humphrey Jennings and Stuart Legg, owe much of their later success to him. The environment in which they worked, initially the two small rooms in Oxford Street, was inevitably conducive to a collaborative style of working which was to continue even when larger studio premises were found in Blackheath and later Beaconsfield. However, it would be remiss to assume that Grierson's talent-spotting activities were restricted to potential directors. At a time before film schools and university courses on filmmaking, much would be achieved by enthusiastic amateurs, as the case of cameraman Frank 'Jonah' Jones demonstrated. Jones had been a not very proficient car mechanic apprentice. Having an interest in films and photography, he wrote to Grierson enquiring about the possibility of a job. Grierson must have thought the young man had potential, as he was subsequently employed as a trainee cameraman. As no formal training existed, it essentially meant copying what others did, but with the ready opportunity of experimenting with the equipment available. Jones was soon to become one of the three main cameramen of the GPO and later Crown film units, along with Fred Gamage and H. E. 'Chick' Fowle. His list of credits, for somebody who was essentially self-taught, are remarkable, from *Night Mail* to *Target for Tonight* and many more. He pioneered camera techniques which are still in use today. An example of this was the creation of a wooden rig built above the conning tower of a submarine. Prior to the CFU film *Close Quarters* (1943), a shot of a submarine diving was always taken from another vessel operating alongside the submarine. With Jones' camera rigged above the top of the conning tower, it was possible for the submarine to commence its dive and the water was seen to be rushing over the bows and coaming (Figure 2.3). Almost all subsequent films which include a submarine diving sequence show it this way. The shot is perhaps even more remarkable as Jones was unable to swim. Had Tallents not been able to convince the GPO to take over the EMBFU in its entirety, it is quite possible that the creative mix would have quickly dissipated.

In a very short time, the unit had developed a reputation as the government's in-house film production facility. Links both official and unofficial had been created to such an extent that, in the EMB's final annual report in 1933, Grierson was able to announce that the unit had made close links with a number of departments across the range of government activity:

Empire Marketing Board Film Unit, 1930–33 65

Figure 2.3 *Close Quarters* (1943) with Jack Lee (director) and Jonah Jones behind the camera. Note the wooden rig on the submarine's conning tower (© IWM D 13211)

For the Ministry of Agriculture the Unit had produced four films on tomatoes, apples, plums and beef. For the Post Office Stuart Legg was working on a film on how to use a telephone dial and the Air Ministry was awaiting a film on aeroplane engine development.

Even though the unit was producing films of reasonable quality, the biggest problem it faced was not the actual creation of films but rather the limited opportunities for exhibition. The decision by Gaumont-British to dub soundtracks on what became known as the Imperial Six was an exception as far as the commercial sector was concerned. In fact, from very early on, the 'trade' had maintained a degree of scepticism regarding public exhibition of government public information films. As early as March 1928, *Kinematograph Weekly* had noted:

> A number of exhibitors in Newcastle and Gateshead have fallen in with a scheme of the Empire Marketing Board, for running special matinees for children. The programme of the matinees will consist of EMB films and will be designed to stimulate Empire buying. The exhibitors are indemnified against loss, and in Newcastle the

Education authority has accepted the responsibility for allocating the children of various schools to the several participating kinemas, so as to avoid overcrowding.

The obvious assumption was that the EMB films were primarily educational and by implication unsuitable for an adult fee-paying audience. This scepticism would persist to a greater or lesser extent throughout the lives of the government film units and the demand for indemnification was subsequently often made. Having said that, the naturally commercial instincts of the cinema owners were already somewhat compromised by the legislative framework under which they operated. Immediately after the end of the First World War the coalition government returned to a laissez-faire approach to filmmaking and exhibition. Unfortunately, they had failed to recognise that one of the unexpected consequences of the war had been the increasing popularity of films produced in the United States. The American use of 'exotic' locations and aggressive marketing began to create concern about the possible demise of the domestic industry and, perhaps more worrying, the British way of life. In one of the first protectionist measures, which predated the economic collapse of 1929, the government introduced the 1927 Cinematograph Films Act, the purpose of which was to protect the British film industry by introducing a quota system. The act provided that, in the first year, renters had to offer at least 7.5 per cent of British-made films in their catalogues and the exhibitors were required to screen at least 5 per cent of these films within their programmes. These quotas were to be raised in stages up to 20 per cent by 1936. There is some debate about the importance of the Cinematographic Act and its influence on the British industry. Paul Swann (1989, p. 10) has stated that 'many British films were "quota quickies"; films made as cheaply as the law would allow, to be displayed so that renters and exhibitors could fulfil their legal obligations to show British films. These films were often shown when cinemas were empty; when they were full they would be given programmes consisting of American feature films'. Not only were these 'quota quickies' often dire in terms of production values but they did not include films 'which depicted mainly news and current events, natural scenery, industrial and manufacturing processes and scientific films' (Dickinson and Street, 1985, p. 12), which were actually excluded from the terms of the Cinematographic Act. Consequently, the commercial exhibitors frequently ignored what was not compulsory and so the early documentary filmmakers, many of whom later worked for the EMBFU, GPOFU and Crown units, were at an additional disadvantage, as their products seemed to fall outside the limited 'safety nets' of the quotas – even though, as can be seen above, much of their output championed both traditional British values as well as modern technical developments.

Although it is impossible to compare audience numbers between trade and non-theatrical exhibition given the problems associated with commercial exhibition, it appears highly likely that the larger audience for EMB films was in a variety of non-theatrical settings. This outlet should not be undervalued, as even a contemporary observer writing in *The Scotsman* after the announcement of the EMBFU closure concluded:

> the Film Unit's work has had an important influence. In the non-theatrical field – schools, film societies and cultural organisations of all kinds – it holds the largest circulation in the country. At present it is responsible for 600 programmes a month.
>
> Last year (1932) the audience of school children was over a million and it is growing steadily. (*The Scotsman*, 3 June 1933)

To this can, of course, be added the numbers visiting the cinema in the Imperial Institute which, according to the final EMB report in 1933, was estimated at 161,000.

Although the transfer of the EMBFU to the Post Office in its entirety was of paramount importance to the development of the government public information film, the continuation of the lending library as a means of distribution and exhibition meant that the unit's – and its successors' – outputs would always be made available to a wide audience.

Notes

1 Sir (George) Joseph Ball (1885–1961) was an intelligence officer, party administrator and businessman. At the outbreak of the First World War, he joined MI5 and remained in the service until 1927. He was persuaded by J. C. C. Davidson (later Viscount Davidson), chairman

of the Conservative Party, to join the party organisation as director of publicity. Davidson said of him: 'he is undoubtedly tough and has looked after his own interests... On the other hand he is steeped in the Service tradition, and has had as much experience as anyone I know of the seamy side of life'. From 1940 to 1942, Ball reverted to his earlier profession as an intelligence officer and served as deputy chairman of the Security Executive. He was, however, a quintessential éminence grise, and his influence on affairs cannot be measured by the brevity of the printed references to him (Robert Blake, writing in *Dictionary of National Biography, 1961–1971*. Oxford: OUP, p. 68).
2 A film about the arrival of the telephone in a remote Swiss valley.
3 *Daybreak at Udi* compares traditional medicines with the arrival of new modern approaches to healing.
4 Arthur Samuel (1872–1942) was a Conservative politician and secretary for overseas trade (1924–27) involved with the setting up of the EMB. Latterly, he was first secretary of the Treasury (1927–29) and later became Lord Mancroft.

3

The General Post Office Film Unit in peacetime, 1933–37

Not only was the direct transfer to the Post Office very welcome in terms of job security for the EMBFU personnel, it immediately placed them in an operating situation with far greater scope for filming. This was enhanced significantly when soon afterwards the unit vacated its small rooms in central London for a proper studio set up in Blackheath. The principal advantage of this was that it gave the unit greater opportunities in filming on set and, later still, with the introduction of an improved sound recording system. Although, as Grierson has pointed out, the EMBFU was important in developing the craft of filmmaking amongst a small group of like-minded individuals, it is difficult to envisage the possible success of its films in changing the public's attitude toward imperial preference. Having watched *One Family*, for example, would the regular drinker of Spanish sherry forsake a favourite tipple for a South African alternative, or swap Californian dried fruit for its imperial competitor? In most cases the purchase decision would almost inevitably be determined by price which, of course, became especially important during a time of economic austerity.

Unlike the EMB, which was a temporary and small aspect of government activity, the Post Office was a major department which, perhaps more importantly, was one with which most UK citizens had daily contact. The postmaster general, a position which dated back in various iterations to the time of Henry VIII, was, by 1933, a senior Cabinet appointment. Kingsley Wood[1] presided over a large and very diverse empire. Not only was he responsible for the mail that was daily delivered across the nation, but almost every village and town in the country had its own post office, a natural community meeting point as well as the vendor of stamps and other services – and, increasingly important in the inter-war years, a safe haven for savings in an era when most individuals did not have bank account. The Post Office was certainly a labour-intensive organisation, being the nation's largest employer of well over a quarter of a million people in that period. However, perhaps more importantly from a film perspective, it was also at the forefront of a technological revolution in communication. As early as 1904 the Wireless Telegraphy Act had given the Post Office control, through licensing, of all radio communication in the UK. It was also responsible for the developments in wired technology and the 1930s saw a rapid expansion in domestic telephone usage as well as such innovations as the telephone dial. All of this meant, according to Swann, that 'the Post Office spent more on publicity, advertising and public relations than any other Government body during the 1930s… the London Passenger Transport Board was the only comparable [although regional] entity in Britain at the time' (Swann, 1989, p. 53).

It was hardly surprising, then, that the Post Office provided the scope, the ready support and a potential audience for a film unit in terms of both customers as well as in-house employees.

Grierson was fortunate to have Tallents as his mentor and supporter, as one of the conditions of his appointment negotiated with Wood was that he requested that the film unit and its associated film library should be transferred directly to the Post Office. Doubly fortunate, too, as this coincided with Wood's intention to put the organisation on a more commercial footing. Tallents' role was to be the Post Office's first public relations officer, with the responsibility of convincing both general public and employees that the Post Office was, according to a memorandum he wrote for the Select Committee on Estimates:

> an undertaking which renders services of social and economic value and provides employment on a self-supporting basis, to remove friction in work by 'bringing alive' and explaining to the public the activities which the Post Office conducts in its name… It was also to develop among Post Office staff a better understanding of the Department's diverse and scattered activities. (TNA: PO M12039/1934)

These 'diverse and scattered activities' would provide ample opportunities for the creative skills of the now General Post Office Film Unit, as well as significant prospects for exhibition.

Wood's desire to publicise the activities of the Post Office, as well as the need to instruct the public in the use of the new technologies, accorded fully with the attitudes of both Tallents and Grierson. According to Swann, 'the G.P.O. Film Unit was seen by [them] as a model for official information machinery, utilising all the mass media to educate the public about the rapidly growing range of government activities' (Swann, 1983, p. 21). It is possible that this aspiration to reach out to the public was an appreciation that the political landscape had changed. Since 1928, universal suffrage of all adults over the age of twenty-one meant that public relations became more important for government and its agencies. Without such public explanations, there was likely to be a danger of political upheaval through the ballot box. Thus, much of the GPOFU's output can be seen as the harnessing of the creative element to the demands of its sponsor. It was an opportunity of which even a somewhat sceptical commercial sector represented by *Kinematograph Weekly* could initially approve:

> Government departments are at last awake to the value of films, both for educational work inside the departments and for the description of their working to the general public. The complexities of departmental work and its contacts with the public at a thousand points make the film activities increasingly necessary. (*Kinematograph Weekly*, 28 September 1933)

Although much of the subsequent reputation of the GPOFU has rested upon a very few films, such as *Night Mail* and a limited selection of the work of directors like Jennings' *Spare Time* (1939), most of its production catalogue featured films that reflected the activities and needs of its sponsor. The novelty of these and subsequent films by the GPOFU and CFU was the personalisation of the topic, using snatches of dialogue and frequently individuals performing the roles they did in real life – although the authenticity which this appeared to suggest was normally part of a tightly scripted and structured production to meet the sponsoring department's demands. As might be expected, most films produced by the GPOFU, especially in the years before 1938, were directly or indirectly related to the activities of the Post Office. Of the just over one hundred films which can be credited to the GPOFU from 1933 to 1940 nearly 70 per cent would easily fit into this category. This percentage would be higher still if the films of 1939 and early 1940 were discounted as, by then, the sponsor had become the MoI. Consequently, although much of the output would sit in the 'documentary' genre, and there are plenty of examples of experiments in that area, the GPOFU was essentially a public relations film production company. As will be seen, much of the GPOFU catalogue ranged from public information films in support of the wide range of activities of the Post Office to direct advertising such as, for example, Norman McLaren's 1937 film *Book Bargain*, which extolled the value of the telephone directory. Although the principal production focus of the unit was upon Britain and issues facing the British citizen, it was clear that international developments in the late 1930s began to change the tone and approach of these films. This chapter seeks to examine those films produced up until early 1938 when, after the Anschluss, the incorporation of Austria into the German Reich, it became difficult to ignore the growing threat in Europe.

EMB 'legacy' films

Perhaps inevitably, given the sudden demise of the EMBFU and its transfer to the Post Office, a small number of EMB films were already in production and were released under the GPO logo. Amongst these was Basil Wright's *Song of Ceylon* (1934), the funding for which came from the Ceylon Tea Propaganda Board. *Song of Ceylon* was an important film in the catalogue as it had wide success, winning its category in the Brussels International Film Festival the following year. The film itself was somewhat unusual, especially given the nature of its sponsorship, as tea only features in a few frames. It could easily be described as a travelogue, but was presented in four discrete labelled sections. Firstly, the audience was introduced to the Buddha and shots of pilgrims climbing Adam's Peak (Sri Pada), the mountain where the Buddha was supposed to have left his footprint. This footage was supported by scenes of natural flora and fauna of Ceylon (Sri Lanka). Moving on to the next section, headed 'The Virgin Island', the film became a straightforward documentary description of life for most Sinhalese people. In quick succession there were shots of water being pumped by foot, local women collecting both water and firewood and men fishing with hand-held nets. In one sense, this film reflected a consistent theme which regularly permeated EMB and the later units' productions. The visual message, often reinforced by the commentary, emphasised an appreciation of the dignity of labour, be it industrial or, as the case here, in an agricultural and peasant community. Much was made of the skills of individuals and the self-help aspect of community life, so the harvesting of rice was a cooperative project, with the narrator explaining that in Ceylon working for hire brought shame on the family. However, the community aspect of work was regularly relieved by celebrations with much dancing and singing. This paean to the bucolic existence was suddenly shattered in the third section of the film, 'Voices of Commerce', which introduced the viewer to 'modern' Ceylon. A railway locomotive was shown thrusting its way through the hills, contrasted with shots of elephants pushing trees. The audience must have quickly realised that Ceylon's real importance was as a supplier of raw materials. In quick succession, the exploitation of timber, copra and tea using modern methods and technology was introduced and modern transport conveyed these materials down to the docks where they were loaded onto British-registered ships, in this case the SS Orford. Yet, as suddenly as the film introduced modern Ceylon, the final section, 'Apparel of God', was a descriptive piece on the values and qualities of Buddhism illustrated by workers making offering to the Buddha and, once again, dancing. Overall, *Song of Ceylon* was an unusual film with strictly delineated and contrasting segments. However, the international jury in Brussels must have been appropriately impressed.

The GPOFU often utilised footage already shot either to produce a shorter film, often for educational purposes, or to be included in another production entirely. This happened in the case of *Song of Ceylon*, as a shorter version was released under the title *Negombo Coast* (1934) and footage included in the later *Gardens of the Orient* (1936). This latter film, also funded by the Ceylon tea industry, was more obviously an advertisement. It commenced in travelogue style with somewhat contemporary stereotypical shots of a British expatriate climbing a mountain, but suitably attired with collar and tie. However, it quickly moved to its focus which, according to the soundtrack was, 'Tea, the most popular beverage in the world'. There followed a brief resumé of both the history of tea growing in India and Ceylon and an explanation of how the product was grown, harvested, packed and transported to the UK. The emphasis was very much on claiming that the success of the industry was a result of the British entrepreneurship and technology which enabled some 450 million tons of tea to be produced annually. The film does, however, emphasise that this development was not at the expense of the indigenous population, which now had access, at least on the plantations, to education and modern health care.

At this distance in time, and without modern analytical tools, it is impossible to know whether the three films had any significant impact on tea consumption in Britain in the 1930s; they were, however, amongst the last of the imperial preference type produced by the GPOFU. In this category there were only a couple of other legacy films which had started production prior to the transfer of the unit to the GPO. These were *British Guiana* (1934) and *King Log* (1934). The former, probably produced by Wright on his 1933 trip around the Caribbean, described the landscape and agriculture of the then British colony in Central America and concluded with the, perhaps inevitable, shots of locally grown rice and sugar being loaded onto vessels bound for the UK. The latter was a compilation of various pieces of film initially edited by Wright and released as *Lumber* in 1931, but re-edited by Evelyn Spice to become *King Log* and one of the Gaumont-British Imperial Six.

General public relations films for the Post Office

It was hardly surprising given Kingsley Wood's desire to publicise the range of the Post Office's activities that most (33 per cent) of the films produced by the GPOFU reflected the wishes of their employer. This, too, coincided with the intentions of Tallents, the newly employed public relations director, and was initially accepted by Grierson. From the filmmakers' perspective, they were assured of reasonably secure employment and facilities, and the management style was reasonably 'hands off', enabling them to experiment and develop ideas and techniques which were then regarded as novel.

Wood understood the potential value of film in explaining the range of activities for which the Post Office was responsible and a significant number of the releases between 1934 and 1938 were essentially exercises in public relations. Indeed, in 1935 the postmaster general commissioned a film of himself welcoming new recruits into the Post Office and extolling its virtues. It is probably worth noting at this point that the audience for these productions was fairly restricted, often directed at the Post Office's many employees. Even when the films received wider distribution and exhibition, it was not on general release to the commercial cinema circuit. Many were produced in 16 mm format and shown in non-theatrical settings, sometimes by the GPO itself through local showings or cinema vans.

The range of topics addressed by the film unit in the mid-1930s was quite catholic. Many of these films tended to be straightforward explanations of the new technologies which were being introduced during the inter-war years. One of the films which spanned the transfer of the unit from EMB to GPO was the 1933 production by Grierson and Legg entitled *The Coming of the Dial*, which was also one of the first to utilise a Marconi-Visatone sound system. This short film explained how scientific advances had made the candlestick telephone system redundant and that it was being replaced by direct dialling. A very science-based film, it demonstrated how the electrical impulses generated by dialling were translated into eventually ringing the number of the desired telephone. It is a little unclear as to the intended audience for such a film, but it had the novelty of a new and practical future technology.

Many of the films produced by the GPOFU over the next four years or so were essentially short documentaries explaining the new developments in telecommunication rather than directly advertising the Post Office's various undertakings. In this category were short films with often self-explanatory titles such as *Cable Ship* (1933), *Telephone* (1934) and *CTO – The Central Telephone Exchange* (1935). Others such as *Under the City* (1934) and *The Copper Web* (1937) explained the developments in telecommunications and the need for cabling either through trenches or telephone poles while *Droitwich* (1935) introduced the audience to the building of massive radio masts to facilitate international communication. A more comprehensive account of the Post Office's responsibilities in underpinning a significant part of British economy and society was Evelyn Spice's sixteen-minute *Calendar of the Year* (1936). The film commenced with winter scenes and the audience was assured that GPO engineers would repair telephone wires in all weathers. Similarly, its wireless monitoring stations would be always at the ready, monitoring the airwaves for sea distress calls. Spring, of course, brought other perhaps less dramatic issues. The telephone or telegraph was important to the farmer to ensure, in the example given, that his spring flower crop could be transported punctually to market. Spring was also the time for laying new cables, erecting radio masts and, in a nod towards novel developments, the audience was introduced to the coaxial cable essential for the development of television. Summer enabled the director to reflect upon national and local events such as trooping the colour, Cowes sailing regatta and the Derby. However, it was emphasised that the success of the radio outside broadcasts depended upon the preliminary work of the Post Office engineers who had installed all the sound cables. Summer, of course, meant holidays and the audience were reminded that over 10 million people set off for the seaside every year where they then proceeded to send more than 180,000 postcards to their friends and relatives by Royal Mail. As summer moved into autumn, the focus turned to the countryside as the farmers harvested their products and sent them to market. In other sectors of the economy, heavy industry was working at full power and shipping was unloading and loading in the Port of London and elsewhere. All parts of the British economy relied on good and secure communications to be successful and profitable. The end of the year provided the opportunity for traditional Christmas scenes of turkeys, shopping and Salvation Army bands. However, the Post Office message was again reinforced by the recruitment of extra staff to manage the more than 10 million parcels that were sent during the festive season. *Calendar of the Year* was an uncomplicated but visually impressive exercise in public relations for the Post Office and, as such, was symbolic of a significant part of the role of GPOFU productions (Figure 3.1).

There were other productions which could easily be placed in this category but where the message was far less obvious. This was the case in *Locomotives*, one of Jennings' first films for the GPOFU that was released in 1934. This film, primarily intended for a school audience, commenced with visual discussion of the

Figure 3.1 Evelyn Spice's *Calendar of the Year* (1936) was an annual review of the many tasks carried out by the General Post Office

development of the steam engine, via colliery usage to railway locomotives. Much of the footage was shot using models from the Science Museum is South Kensington, London. Jennings pointed out that the Royal Mail began using the railways only a few short years after Stephenson's Rocket had made its initial journey in 1829. Since then, the railways had become increasingly important in the transportation of mail. The film concluded with shots of mail being collected in London, sent to Paddington Station and then sorted in the travelling post office on the Cornish Riviera Express. Again with a nod towards the importance of technology, some of the mail was shown being delivered and others collected by a trackside apparatus while the train itself was still travelling.

While not quite in the realms of subliminal advertising, the GPOFU did experiment with other formats in its mission to publicise the role of the Post Office. Len Lye was an accomplished animator who produced a few films for the unit. In 1937, for example, perhaps at the prompting of Grierson whose name also appears in the credits, Lye produced *Trade Tattoo*, an experimental animation urging the public to post early in the day. This film was also unusual as it was completed in Technicolor, although it followed a somewhat stereotypical GPOFU approach. The emphasis was on the rhythm of work in Britain, ranging from the spectacular blast furnace images on one hand to the dangerous work of fishermen on the other. The message, of course, was that these industries could only be successful by using the power of correspondence. Trade was, it was visually argued, maintained by the regular rhythm of the daily postal collection and delivery.

By the mid-1930s, however, the declining international situation was not only beginning to impinge upon the British public through newspaper articles and radio discussions but it began to feature almost unconsciously in GPOFU productions. In a sense the film unit was reflecting the fact that European and world affairs were increasingly encroaching on the consciousness of the British public. This view could be seen in such films as *Message from Geneva* (1936). Ostensibly the film was about the technology required for telephone communications between London and Switzerland. BBC News had wanted to take a live feed from the League of Nations in Geneva but, for that to happen, the GPO needed to check that the telephone line was ready. Subsequently, after a few brief shots of Geneva, the audience was reminded that the League of Nations was established after the First World War as a 'clearing house for disagreements throughout the world' which would 'eliminate economic as well as political anarchy'. The Post Office supported this contention practically as, it asserted, 'wireless is important in ensuring the rule of law between nations'. It concluded with a declaration that 'radio was the best means of international communication'. Although the contemporary audience might have hoped the claims in *Message from Geneva* were accurate, the international crises in China, Abyssinia and, soon, Spain had clearly demonstrated the inadequacies of the League of Nations.

Public relations films for the postal service

As the origin of the Post Office was primarily to collect and deliver the Royal Mail, it is hardly surprising that several films – about

12 per cent of the output – were produced by the GPOFU to remind the public of the importance of the postal service. Perhaps the most important of these, certainly when viewed retrospectively, must be *Night Mail* (1936). Of all the films produced by the GPOFU, Watt and Wright's visual description of how mail posted in London travels through the night to arrive by morning in Scotland is very famous. Of course, the impact of the film was enhanced by the poet W. H. Auden, whose rhythmic lines towards the end of the film match the sound of the train as it goes over the rail track joints. Technically, *Night Mail* demonstrated the lengths to which the cameramen Chick Fowle and Jonah Jones would go. Cameras were rigged up on wooden structures both on top of the locomotive's tender and on the buffer bar. Both were extremely dangerous and isolated positions but, for the cameramen, they achieved sequences which were both novel and spectacular. The popular view of the locomotive rushing north during the night underpinned by the constant metre of Auden's poem occasionally obscures the fact that these scenes feature towards the end of the film – and that the film itself is about the delivery of mail. At the beginning, the audience was introduced to the collection and sorting of mail in London where, apparently, 'forty post office workers sort over half a million letters'. The relevant mail bags were then transported to Euston Station and loaded on to the 'parcel special', which was due to leave at 8.30 pm. The film followed the express northwards, delivering and collecting mail by the automatic trackside apparatus and stopping 'for thirteen minutes at Crewe' to unload and load mail from Ireland via Holyhead. Unlike the exterior scenes in *Night Mail*, the interior of the travelling post office was recreated as a set in the Blackheath studios and the mail sorters were told to sway in the same way as they would have done normally with the train in motion. Although the GPOFU and Crown's reputation rests to some extent on the authenticity of their films, much was down to cinematic artifice. Regardless, *Night Mail* was visually spectacular even though underpinned not so much by Grierson and Legg's commentary as by the rhythm of the poem towards the end. *Night Mail* is sometimes seen as one of the most famous creations of the documentary movement, although at the time its cost at £3,456 was deemed excessive and the Treasury demanded an investigation. Yet, despite its subsequent fame, *Night Mail*'s purpose was essentially as a public relations

exercise to remind the audience of the effectiveness of the postal system (Figure 3.2).

Other, less popular films were subsequently produced by the GPOFU with the same objective as *Night Mail*. A year earlier, to celebrate George V's silver jubilee, the unit released *The King's Stamp*. The film unit had been experimenting with the use of actors in a very few films over the previous couple of years and this film, which was essentially an historical review of the development of both the stamp and the postal system, used actors to play Queen Victoria and Rowland Hill (the 'inventor' of the postage stamp). Its director, William Coldstream, also shot some of the scenes in colour while others remained in monochrome. While concentrating upon the history and latterly the production of stamps, the film also assured the audience that the postal system was not only important for business but had been instrumental in increasing literacy from the mid-nineteenth century onwards. It also pointed out that Brazil was the next country to introduce the postage stamp and that the system soon became the international method of funding postal services. It also, of course, encouraged a new popular hobby, that of philately. Unfortunately, the impact of the film was significantly

Figure 3.2 In *Night Mail* (1936), the travelling post office was a studio set

reduced as George V only survived the jubilee celebrations by just over eight months, dying in January 1936. The film was later re-edited and released again after the king's funeral as *How Stamps Are Made*.

Another film in this category which used actors to communicate the theme was Richard Massingham's *Daily Round* (1937). As the title suggests, this short film related the daily activities of a country postman. It commenced with the postman sorting the mail and then followed him walking his round. There were obvious reminders to the audience about such postal services as telegrams, air mail and parcels, although in the latter case the parcel was not delivered because it was labelled COD (cash on delivery). The film also had a comedic element, with the postman falling off a bank for example, and it also adopted a dream sequence device which injected more humour. The postman, in his dream, was dressed in a naval admiral's uniform as he watched Morris dancing from the top of a hill which he was encouraged to join. Afterwards, his customers, lined up in military parade fashion, were reviewed reading their mail. On waking refreshed the postman continued his round. Other films which were essentially public relations exercises for the postal services included Jennings' *Post Haste* (1936), an historical review of the development of the Royal Mail. The same year *6.30 Collection* and *Air Post* described, as their names suggest, the sorting of mail and its overseas transport using the new opportunities provided by improvements in aviation. The GPOFU continued to produce a few films annually which were essentially reminders to the public of the range and value of the postal service. In 1937, for example, as well as *Daily Round*, the self-evidently titled *Letters to Liners* was released.

The importance of saving through the Post Office

During the First World War the government had appreciated the value of using film to encourage the UK population to buy war bonds, as in the 1918 short *Simple Simon*. The concept of national savings was not new, as the Post Office Savings Bank was founded by the Palmerston government in 1861 with the aim of providing a simple investment opportunity for, principally, the industrial working class and also a ready source of funds for the government. The impact of the Great Depression and the ensuing austerity measures appear to have encouraged both government and the general population that savings were mutually beneficial. As national savings were operated through individual post offices throughout the country, the GPOFU was urged to produce films which emphasised the value of small-scale savings.

One of the GPOFU's first films was Arthur Elton's *John Atkins Saves Up* (1934), which was typical of the approach adopted by the unit for encouraging savings. It was a short romantic comedy in which John (played by Leslie Higgins) was a cautious individual whose daily commute was from Brent into the City of London. En route he was attracted to a poster of a girl (Eileen Lee) advertising holidays in Summersea. The unspoken message, prompted by a dream sequence of the girl amongst the sand dunes, was, of course, how could he afford such a holiday? The perhaps inevitable solution was that he made weekly savings deposits in his local post office. The important point of the film was that even small deposits were safe and handled with care and security. Elton showed how John's paying-in slip was sorted, transferred to the ledger and then processed centrally with the interest added. Eventually John has saved sufficient and collected £3 over the post office counter, apparently sufficient to pay for his holiday! John subsequently travelled by train to Dawlish and there met up with the girl in the poster who, surprisingly, has a copy of his post office paying-in slip. The short story approach to encouraging savings was often adopted by other films in this category. A rather more sombre example was shown in 1936 by Alberto Cavalcanti and Harry Watt in *The Saving of Bill Blewitt*. Whereas professional actors were used in *John Atkins Saves Up*, for this film Watt adapted a story around the villagers of Mousehole in Cornwall (Figure 3.3). Bill Blewitt was in fact the village postmaster. Once more the focus was upon saving for a particular purpose, in this case replacing a wrecked fishing vessel. Bill had to seek employment elsewhere in the quarries of Cornwall but, from his wages, he managed to buy a five-shilling national savings stamp every week. After two years he had saved sufficient to enable him, after some negotiation, to buy another vessel, the Faithful. The film concluded with Bill heading off to sea, a fisherman once again.

Figure 3.3 Post Office staff count daily savings slips in *John Atkins Saves Up* (1934)

Other GPOFU films which promoted the Post Office Savings Bank included Legg's descriptive *Savings Bank* (1934) and in the same year the similarly self-explanatory *Banking for Millions*. However, even the mundane topic of savings could be addressed in an experimental fashion, as was the case of the *Rainbow Dance* (1936), another semi-animated film by Len Lye in which the value of saving was manifested as a crock of gold at the end of a rainbow.

Direct advertising

Most of the GPOFU's productions made specifically for the Post Office between 1933 and 1937 addressed their topics from a general public relations perspective and could probably be reasonably described as public information films. Inevitably, the time needed from pitching the idea to actually releasing the film, mainly to a non-theatrical audience, was usually many months. Consequently, there was a strong possibility that events might overtake the message of the film, as certainly occurred later in 1939–40. Despite this possible handicap, there were a few films which were date or activity specific and can easily be described as advertisements. One of the first of these was Cavalcanti's *The Glorious Sixth of June* (1934). This production, which was almost entirely filmed in a studio, demonstrated again that the unit was experimenting with different genres to get its message across. In this case the approach was the use of slapstick humour, which might seem a bit bizarre when it is realised that the date in question marked the lowering of telephone charges. Everything was somewhat over the top. The reduction of the charges was described as 'an epic of human endeavour' and the on-screen action included a stereotypical spy attempting to prevent documents getting to Parliament where the minister would announce the reductions. After the use of many on-screen devices culled from the silent movies, including fights, bombs, flying through windows and a cameo performance by Humphrey Jennings as a post office messenger boy, the papers got to Parliament and the reduction in telephone charges was announced. Although there are many instances where the GPOFU and Crown utilised humour, it rarely ever again reached the level of slapstick found in *The Glorious Sixth of June*. Other films which could be recognised as advertisements were not so date specific and tended to fall into the category either of those which advertised a new service or product or those which were reminders.

The 1930s saw a rapid expansion in the number of domestic telephones and this development was no doubt enhanced by the introduction of the dial model. By the end of the decade there were over three and a half million households with access to a telephone. This in itself created the demand for such associated products as the telephone directory. In 1937 the GPOFU produced *Book Bargain* about the value of the directory, although the film concentrated upon the London directory which, it was revealed, was updated four times a year. Obviously for much wider circulation was the earlier Cavalcanti short *Pett and Pott – A Fairy Story of the Suburbs* (1934), which encouraged the more affluent middle classes to purchase a telephone. The film was a relatively moralistic and semi-comedic comparison between two couples who were living in similar suburban detached houses, themselves a feature of the house-building expansion in the mid to late 1930s. Mr and

Mrs Pett lived in 'Peacehaven' and were shown bathing a baby and encouraging their four other children to say their prayers at bedtime. Meanwhile, next door at 'Kismet', Mrs Pott was reclining on the sofa in a black cocktail dress, smoking and reading a somewhat salacious novel – all of which occurred during the day. Being advised of local burglaries, the Petts opted for a telephone, whereas Mrs Pott preferred to hire a maid. Further comparisons were made between the two couples: the Petts were very family orientated but Mr Potts, in particular, was seen enjoying the pleasures of the London night life. Needless to say, the maid arranged for the house to be burgled but the Pett children heard the commotion, and the police were summoned by telephone. They arrived in full Keystone Cops style, and the burglar and maid were arrested. In the final scene of the film the judge admonished the Potts and recommended that they purchase a telephone, thus driving home the advertisement message of the film.

The moralistic cum comedic approach was also adopted when reminding the Post Office's customers of some of the implications of the services. *N or NW* (1937) was a short film about the collapse of a young couple's relationship resulting from the failure to write the correct postcode on a love letter, NW1 being written instead of N1. Of course, the Post Office managed to correct the code and the lovers were reunited. The soundtrack of this film included the 1935 Fats Waller hit 'I'm gonna sit right down and write myself a letter'. The GPOFU and its successor, Crown, had an unfortunate reputation for a fairly liberal interpretation of the music rights laws and it is quite possible that this film contravened them.

Other Post Office services

Three films produced in this period were narrative descriptions of particular industries where the role of the Post Office was integral to their overall success. These were Spice's *Weather Forecast* (1934), Legg's *BBC – Voice of Britain* (1935) and Coldstream and Legg's *Roadways* (1937). In the first, the Post Office, through the Central Telegraph Office (CTO), had the responsibility of coordinating communication between meteorological observation posts and the wider community. Meanwhile, Legg had pitched the idea for a film to the BBC during the last few months of the EMB. The role played by the Post Office in *BBC – Voice of Britain* was limited to the building and maintaining of the large radio masts at Droitwich. The rest of this near hour-long film was a comprehensive review of the role of the BBC, as the audience was offered a tour of all the broadcaster's facilities, including studios where they were introduced to some celebrities of the day such as G. K. Chesterton, the author, and Henry Hall, a famous band leader. There then followed a comprehensive review of the BBC's programming – from outside broadcasts exemplified by the annual Oxford v. Cambridge boat race, children's and educational programmes, music personified by Adrian Boult, to SOS messages and the time signal. Also regarded as important was the coverage of news and current affairs; the BBC, the narrator explained, 'would always report of the great events of the day' be that overseas or domestic, which visually was confirmed by footage of the launching of the Queen Mary in September 1934. The BBC's entertainment brief was also not forgotten, as amongst the last scenes of the film were ones of London's night life with Henry Hall's orchestra and Dinah, a famous 1930s jazz singer.

The final film in this small category was a little unusual as it was one of the first road safety films produced by the unit and was a foretaste of those released after the Second World War. The background to *Roadways*, emphasised in the film, was the toll of road casualties which, it was stated, had reached over 6,000 per year. Leaving aside some initial patronising comments about lady drivers, the film charted the development of road transport, especially that of the combustion engine and the lorry. Roads now carried the industrial world and more traffic created greater dangers. Consequently, the government had to step in and introduce licences and legislation to reduce the excess driving times which, apparently, were the cause of many accidents. Alongside this, new road signs, speed restrictions and even the L-plate were introduced. The film concluded with its perhaps customary plug for the Post Office, assuring the audience that the GPO took its safety responsibility seriously and ensured that its vehicles were in good condition and the drivers fully trained.

The best of Britain

A few of the films produced by the GPOFU in the mid-1930s appear not to have been made in support of the unit's sponsor but were rather more general observations of life in Britain. In that sense they continued the pattern established by the EMBFU of films primarily evoking the spirit of Britain, often expressed in sequences extolling the dignity of labour. One of the first films in this category was Grierson's *Granton Trawler* (1934) which, in one sense, was unique, as it was very much a personal project; from writing to camerawork to post-production. As the name suggested, this was a short film of the daily life of a Scottish trawler out of Granton on the Firth of Forth. Grierson's approach appears to have been heavily influenced by Russian filmmakers with the focus on worker as hero, undertaking hard and dangerous labour. The film used sound very effectively to emphasise that theme. It has no narrator and the roar of the sea was minimised in contrast to the wailing of the wind and the cries of the gulls. The trawlermen, including the skipper, talked relatively quietly throughout, although the broad Scottish accents often make understanding problematic.

Similar in approach, but examining a very different industry, was Cavalcanti's *Coal Face* (1935). This film was a reminder of the importance of coal mining to the British economy and the message was hammered home with many statistics, an approach which featured in later PIFs. So, according to the film, of the annual coal production in the UK, 40 million tons were for household use, 10 million tons for electricity, 12 million tons for the railways, 15 million tons for shipping, 85 million tons for industry and over 50 million tons for export. Not only do these figures explain the key importance of coal for Britain, but the film emphasises the obvious point that, as an extractive industry, it relies upon the labour of over three-quarters of a million miners. These men worked in a very dangerous industry, where four miners on average were killed every day and one in five were injured every year. Despite this, the miners had developed their own communities which revolved around the pit and this was exemplified by sequences of Welsh miners' choirs.

Another theme which was evident in these mid-1930s' productions could be classified as travelogues, best illustrated by the work of Grierson's sister Marion. She produced three films in 1934, the titles of which are self-explanatory: *St James's Park*, *Edinburgh* and *Britain's Countryside*. The six-minute silent *Edinburgh* was typical of this genre. The audience was introduced to the many attractions of Scotland's capital city, described as the 'modern Athens', including Princes Street, St Giles's Cathedral, Holyrood and the castle with its time gun. Although perhaps not remarked upon at the time, despite being about Edinburgh this piece remained London-centric, commencing with the rail journey from the nation's capital. The shots of the train, although visually interesting, show it passing over the Forth Bridge, which being north of Edinburgh would never have occurred.

Miscellaneous

Any attempt at categorising films will inevitably reveal anomalies, films which are unique or, in some cases, presage what developed during the CFU years. Although, by the mid-1930s, the international situation was deteriorating, with crises in China, Abyssinia and, most recently, in Spain, a significant proportion of the British public favoured relying upon the League of Nations rather than in rapid rearmament. The Peace Ballot of 1934–35 resulted in a massive majority endorsing the league. This attitude was reflected in the 1937 film *We Live in Two Worlds*. Previous references to the developing international crises had been quite oblique, as in *Line to the Tschierva Hut*, *Men of the Alps* and *Four Barriers*, also all released in 1937 and all describing the development of telecommunications in Switzerland. The latter film, for example, contains the observation that the Swiss are hardworking people who 'know little of international crises'. However, *We Live in Two Worlds* also focused on Switzerland and was much more direct in tackling international events. It was narrated by J. B. Priestley, the successful author and broadcaster, who became even more famous during the Second World War for his radio talks. Priestley's introduction compared the growing global communications with an increasing fear of Germany which had sparked an arms race. The anxiety being felt in Britain was not, apparently, shared by the Swiss, who were shown enjoying themselves drinking and attending church in a 'charming and medieval manner'. Priestley moved on to argue that the world had a choice between nationalism and internationalism. The latter, of course, with its improvements in telephone and wireless technology, offered a more civilised future for the world. There were, he went on to argue, 'no frontiers in the air'. Although Priestley was discussing the value of radio in international communications, unfortunately the lack of barriers in the air had been amply demonstrated by the bombing of Guernica in Spain in April 1937. Priestley's optimism, which may have been shared by a large proportion of his audience, was regrettably found to be misplaced over the succeeding months.

Not only was 1937 the year in which mid-decade optimism began to fade, as was reflected in the later GPOFU films, but it was also marked by John Grierson's resignation and subsequent appointment as the first commissioner of the National Film Board of Canada. Although no doubt his influence remained amongst his 'documentary boys (and girls)', he was not directly involved again until being appointed as controller of the CFU in 1948. It is probably true that he had become increasingly frustrated by the bureaucratic demands of both Post Office and civil service. His position as head of the film unit had become progressively more difficult after Tallents had resigned to join the BBC in 1935.

A consequence of Grierson's departure was that some of the more maverick work practices previously tolerated were brought into line with contemporary civil service operations. The unit was no longer run by a films officer but rather by a production supervisor who, in this instance, was Jack Holmes, recruited from Gaumont-British Instructional Films with the intention of introducing more commercial influences to the film unit. It eventually fell to Holmes to navigate the transition of the sector-based GPOFU into the national filmmaker, the CFU.

Note

1 Sir (Howard) Kingsley Wood (1881–1943) was a Conservative politician with a reputation as a significant innovator in all the official positions he held. He was, for example, one of the early advocates for a Ministry of Health and also pioneered the introduction of modern business methods into the departments for which he was responsible.

4

Rumours of war and the creation of the Crown Film Unit, 1938–40

There was an obvious dichotomy in the types of films produced by the GPOFU in the last two years of peace. On the one hand, it continued to release films which directly reflected the services offered by the Post Office. As will be seen, the deteriorating international situation often could not be avoided, even when covering some of the more mundane topics. On the other hand, although the government had sought to enforce a more bureaucratic operating framework for the unit, it was increasingly clear that the national and international situation required an effective 'in-house' film production unit for both emergency preparation and propaganda reasons. As early as October 1935 a sub-committee of the Committee of Imperial Defence had been established to determine guidelines for the dissemination of official news and propaganda in the event of war. It reported the following year that a Ministry of Information would be established to 'present the national case to the public at home and abroad in time of war' (quoted in Chapman, 1998, p. 16). Ironically, it is certainly possible that film itself had reinforced fears about the possible course of a future war. Alexander Korda's *Things to Come* (1936) appears to have played a very influential role in predicting in fiction what actually happened in Spain and elsewhere. The role of smoothing the transition from a peacetime to a wartime footing had been originally given to Sir Stephen Tallents. Unfortunately, Tallents' lack of success in convincing Whitehall to utilise the potential of film, combined with his somewhat prickly personality, led to his leaving his position soon after the signing of the Munich Agreement in September 1938. Amid the panic and confusion increasingly engendered by the worsening international situation, the government finally acknowledged the potential value of film propaganda and, despite some reluctance from its parent organisation, the GPOFU was designated the official film production unit in the event of war. Therefore, in September 1939, at the outbreak of war, the unit and its costs, if not initially management control, were transferred from the GPO directly to the MoI as part of the putative Films Division (TNA: INF1/460).

The GPOFU's film production catalogue of 1938 and 1939 progressively reflected both the increasing crisis in Europe and the needs of its sponsor. It still produced films which can be categorised as in the previous chapter, but latterly there were those which not only presaged war but all too soon began to show it on screen.

General public relations films for the Post Office

The last of the general public relations category of film was released after the war began in 1940 and was entitled *How the Teleprinter Works*, presenting a short colour explanation of the operation of the machine. This film appears to be the second in a series of technical accounts of telecommunication which began in 1937 with *How the Dial Works*. Also in this area, Humphrey Jennings completed a short descriptive film on the transatlantic telephone entitled *Speaking from America* (1938). As an indication of the declining international situation, the film included a short sequence of President Roosevelt speaking about world peace. Somewhat less technical, but still referring to the possibility of war, was Cavalcanti's *Midsummer Day's Work* (1939). This film was a description of a day in the laying of an underground telephone cable from Amersham to Aylesbury, which was apparently necessary for the defence of Britain. The film explained the very labour-intensive process where gangs of about twenty men dug trenches in preparation for cable-laying. This hard but necessary work was contrasted with bucolic and peaceful images of the poet John Milton's cottage,[1] children, blacksmiths, thatchers and farm workers at the village pub. The implied message was, of course, quite stark. Although the country was presently at peace and basking in the midsummer sun, preparations for war were going ahead at pace.

Public relations films for the Postal Service

As the anticipation of war increased dramatically during 1938 and 1939, it was realised that postal deliveries would be an essential element in retaining public confidence. *News for the Navy* (1938) was a ten-minute short story documentary which followed a package sent by Evelyn to her fiancé, Bert Higgins, a seaman aboard HMS Incredible, a fictitious warship. The parcel was tracked from the large sorting office at Mount Pleasant in London until it was delivered to Bert aboard ship. Some humour was injected when Bert was required, even on station in Bermuda, to pay a one-halfpenny surcharge. The main message, though, which was enhanced by a naval music soundtrack, was to remind people that letters and parcels would be delivered irrespective of where in the potential conflict zones. There were, of course, other short films released at this time which reminded the audience of the more traditional role of the Post Office in delivering the Royal Mail. Jennings' *Penny Journey* (1938) was a story of a postcard being sent from Manchester to Graffham in West Sussex. Once again, it followed the journey from posting, sorting and transport all the way to hand delivery by the village postman. Despite the mundane and eventually pastoral scenes, the audience could not have failed to observe the ARP (Air Raid Precautions) signs, which were becoming a feature of British street furniture. Also emphasising that, whatever the difficulties and dangers involved, the Post Office would ensure that the mail was delivered, was an early Pat Jackson film, *The Horsey Mail* (1938). Horsey in this case was a village in Norfolk which, owing to a breach in the sea wall, had become cut off by the ensuing floods. However, the intrepid local postman was able to deliver the mail by rowing boat, scenes which were injected with a little humour by the accompanying soundtrack of 'I do like to live beside the seaside!' Visual humour was also a feature of the animation *Love on the Wing* (1939), which was a reminder of the opportunities offered to contact friends and relatives overseas using the Post Office's Air Mail service. Although completed, it was one of the GPOFU's films which was never released as, apparently, the postmaster general thought that the images were too phallic.

The importance of saving through the Post Office

The proximity of war did not reduce the government's drive to encourage people to save – and when war began savings propaganda became even more ubiquitous. *The Tocher* and *Mony a Pickle*, both released in 1938, demonstrated a particularly Scottish orientation to the subject. The former was a short five-minute balletic animation by Lotte Reiniger in which the hero secured his bride-to-be with a tocher (dowry) in the form of a Post Office Savings book. With an even more pronounced Scottish slant was *Mony a Pickle*, a ten-minute film containing five comedic vignettes all on the theme of saving in Scotland, from a young couple dreaming about installing modern conveniences in their new house to an elderly miner extolling the safety of his £200 savings.

Direct advertising

Similarly, the number of direct advertisements produced by the GPOFU during the last two years of peace was also very small. *At the Third Stroke* (1939) was a short, humorous piece advising the public how to use the Post Office's telephone speaking clock service, which had been introduced three years earlier. Also with a numeric title was *Nine for Six* (1939), which this time concerned telegrams and recounted a story of a local football team contacting their opponents by telegram to request them to bring a ball to their forthcoming match. *Nine for Six* was an advertising slogan, as a nine-word telegram could be purchased for six pence.

Other Post Office services

What's on Today? (1938) is one of the few films produced by the GPOFU in which the exact date can be identified. It starts with a man listening to the wireless on 24 August 1938 who becomes ecstatic when English cricket batsman, Len Hutton, scored a record 364 runs against Australia in the Fifth Test match at Lord's. The narrator then announced that an appreciation of sport was something which all social classes had in common. Without the Post

Office laying cables, 'of occasionally seventy miles in length', outside broadcasts on the BBC would not be possible. So the Post Office's activities enabled the British public to listen to such sporting events as the Isle of Man TT Races, the Cup Final and the Derby. The other Post Office service represented on film was much more specific. Jennings' *North Sea* (1938) was a story documentary of a real event, an approach which was to be used more frequently later by the CFU. It recreated the story of an Aberdeen trawler, the John Gillman, which had got into difficulties during a storm. Its radio distress calls were picked up by a GPO shore monitoring station and relayed to other ships in the area, which stood by the stricken vessel. Perhaps inevitably, repairs were made aboard the John Gillman and it returned safely to harbour. The film concluded with the assertion that Post Office wireless stations 'guard our ships'. Also reflecting some of the techniques used in later productions, most of the scenes inside the trawler were shot in the GPOFU's studios at Blackheath.

The best of Britain

The realisation that there was a danger of a general war breaking out in Europe again after just two decades perhaps promoted a more national or patriotic aspect to some of the GPOFU's output during 1938 and 1939. During this period the GPOFU appeared to be favoured by the government, as not only did it have preferential access to departmental contracts, but its facilities were improved at the taxpayers' expense. In early 1939, for example, the Treasury authorised the purchase of a state-of-the-art sound system, an RCA Photophone. It is, of course, possible to argue that this was a prudent measure given the general international climate of the time, but to other documentarists in the commercial sector this was just an example of government partisanship in favour of the GPOFU.

There was probably some truth in this, as other documentary film companies sought commissions and sponsorship from organisations both in the private sector and amongst semi-public bodies. The resulting productions tended to be either in the form of public relations films or documentary 'type' films. In the former case, sponsors tended to be as diverse as Imperial Airways, the gas companies and, perhaps most famously, Shell Petroleum. In the latter category, the National Council for Social Service and the Land Settlement Association sponsored films which were more likely to be shown in non-theatrical settings. An obvious example of this type was Edgar Anstey's 1936 Pathé Production *Housing Problems* which, although praised by the Ministry of Health and critically acclaimed, was actually financed by concerned philanthropists at Rowntree's, Sanderson Wallpapers and the International Bath Association.

However, amongst an unspectacular group of films released by the GPOFU during these two years was the last of John Grierson's major contributions, which came out after his departure. *On the Fishing Banks of Skye* (1938) was another observational film of traditional Scottish fishing methods. Other industries and places were revisited by such shorts as *The Farm* (1938), *The City* (1939) and Cavalcanti's *The Chiltern Country* (1939). There were two films which presage some of the approaches taken later by the CFU. *God's Chillun* (1938) was a highly moralistic anti-slavery film which was probably created for non-theatrical exhibition in schools and similar venues. With words by W. H. Auden and music by Benjamin Britten, both its theme and its presentation would today be regarded as at best patronising, and possibly even offensive. It did not shy away from the responsibility of British slave traders in removing people from the West Coast of Africa and subjecting them to a dreadful Atlantic crossing of up to three months, when perhaps half would die on the journey. Those who survived to work on the sugar plantations of the West Indies or cotton fields of the southern states of what became the USA were, according to the film, 'the absolute property of their owners'. There were several uprisings against the slave owners and the film related positively the story of Toussaint Louverture,[2] who led the Haitian revolt in 1791 against predominantly French slavers. The film then proceeded to describe the eventual response of the British government which, in 1807, banned the transportation of enslaved people. It went on to argue that the situation was far better in the late 1930s where most of the descendants of the original enslaved people now had reasonably secure employment working on the sugar, banana or cocoa plantations. Although, interestingly from a modern perspective, the film concluded that while these plantations were owned mostly by Europeans and the wages were small, there was access to education. On the positive side, the film's conclusion was that much remained to be done.

More famous retrospectively than *God's Chillun* was Jennings' fourteen-minute short, *Spare Time* (1939). This was a descriptive comparison of how workers in the steel, cotton and coal industries spent their spare time. Each industry had its own daily cycle of work which was punctuated by particular leisure activities. The film commenced with steel which, it was revealed, was a twenty-four-hour operation. As the blast furnaces could not be shut down, the workers operated a three-shift system, meaning that their spare time could be morning, afternoon or evening. Their interests such as whippets, pigeons, bicycles, football, the pools and betting were cut against a traditional northern brass band. The same approach was taken to examine the other two industries. Perhaps most famously, the hobbies of the cotton workers – gardening, wrestling and dance halls – were contrasted with the performance and somewhat manic dancing of the local works kazoo band, a musical instrument which has lost its popularity in recent years (Figure 4.1). Unsurprisingly, miners were represented by a Welsh male voice choir, against which were shown scenes from the pub with miners playing billiards and cribbage. Younger miners, apparently, had access to sporting facilities such as boxing, but no alcohol, in the local YMCA. The film presented the days and hobbies of the workers in three of the great industries of the UK in the months before their lives were disrupted by the outbreak of war.

Figure 4.1 The kazoo band in Humphrey Jennings' *Spare Time* (1939)

Preparation for war

It was already established that the moment war broke out the GPOFU would be transferred to the MoI. However, the film unit had already begun to include scenes or commentary that acknowledged the imminence of conflict. *SS Ionian* (1939), for example, another of Jennings' short films, was ostensibly about a merchant ship travelling through the Mediterranean. Leaving Gibraltar, it travelled eastwards to Malta, arriving in the Grand Harbour, Valletta, on 3 July 1939. The battleship HMS Barham was shown in dry dock and the merchant vessel observed the old tradition of the sea in dipping its ensign in a salute to those ships of the Royal Navy. As SS Ionian headed eastward, it encountered other vessels of the Mediterranean fleet: HMS Malaya in Alexandria, HMS Garland and Greyhound in Haifa and HMS Warspite off Cyprus. Wherever the Ionian was delivering or collecting cargo, it was under the obvious protection of the Royal Navy which, according to the film, was 'the greatest in the world'. Sadly, propaganda would encounter reality over the next few years. SS Ionian was sunk by a German submarine, U-20, at the end of November, barely five months after filming. Similarly, HMS Greyhound was sunk on 22 May 1941 and HMS Barham later in the year on 25 November. Although all the crew of the Ionian survived, the combined death toll for the other two vessels was nearly one thousand.

The imminence of war convinced the government, through the Home Office, to commission the first GPOFU public information film. In this case it was neither public relations nor advertising, but rather direct advice for the general public as a whole. *If War Should Come* (1939) was the film response to the deteriorating situation in Europe and especially the invasion of Czechoslovakia on 15 March 1939. This occupation demonstrated that Hitler was no longer just interested in acquiring territory which was ethnically German and prompted Neville Chamberlain, the British prime minister, to guarantee the security of Poland. These events made war in Europe if not inevitable then highly probable; so the government not only ramped up its armament programmes but also began to prepare the general population for what might happen. It was in this context that *If War Should Come* was conceived

Figure 4.2 In preparation for the imminent conflict, the threat of gas attack loomed large, as shown in *If War Should Come* (1939)

for general release and public information (Figure 4.2). In early September 1939 the film was retitled *Do it Now* to reflect the German invasion of Poland and the British response.

The film is a combination of reassurance and instruction. Its message was that Britain was well prepared and that eventually 'democracy will triumph'. However, to achieve that end the citizen must take certain steps. On the one hand, these included modifying behaviour such as not paying attention to rumours nor panic buying. On the other hand, there were specific instructions in respect of preparing for air raids. So, in anticipation of incendiary bombs, lofts had to be cleared and buckets of water available on every floor of a house. As the greatest contemporary fear was that the Germans would use poison gas, everyone, babies and children included, had to keep their gas masks with them. Furthermore, in an announcement which foreshadowed the early days of the war, residents were advised that they must not interfere with the government's plans for evacuation.

The GPOFU in the first year of the Second World War, 1939–40

Although the GPOFU was technically able to deliver films – as *If War Should Come* had shown – the experience of the first few months of the conflict reflected what was being called the Phoney War in that there was no strong direction from its new parent department, the MoI. According to James Chapman (1998, p. 18) much of this turmoil was the result of the inadequate political direction caused, initially, by 'the appointment of a Minister who sat in the House of Lords [who] was unable to answer criticisms made of his Department in the Commons. Lord Macmillan, a Tory peer and distinguished judge, was completely ineffectual'. Unfortunately, the early propaganda decisions by the MoI were unmitigated disasters. One of the more famous was the poster which announced, 'Your Courage, Your Cheerfulness, Your Resolution, Will Bring Us Victory'. As Angus Calder somewhat pithily observed 'most working class people thought that "resolution" meant something you made at New Year. But, beyond that, people asked, who was the mysterious "us" to whom "your" efforts would bring triumph? Fat men in the city of London, humourless bureaucrats in Whitehall, the bosses, the generals...' (Calder, 1969, p. 71). This semantic confusion caused the posters to be rapidly withdrawn. Mass Observation noted, as early as October 1939, that 'the source of all Government publicity, the MoI, is almost universally discredited in the eyes of the masses... The position of under-information and lack of steady instructional flow in which the masses place confidence is therefore exceedingly serious' (quoted in Chapman, 1998, p. 19).

Similarly, the part played by the Films Division, the section of the MoI which was responsible for the GPOFU, was hardly inspiring. Joseph Ball, the senior Conservative Party Central Office official who had pioneered cinema vans, became its first head in August 1939. However, the organisational and operational priorities for film propaganda had not been determined effectively and Ball spent much of his time attempting to devise such policies. Unlike Tallents, Ball does not seem to have been particularly sympathetic to the GPOFU, preferring instead that propaganda films should be produced by the commercial sector because these would be seen to be independent and less subject to government direction. As he wrote in the Films Division General Plan of Operation in September 1939, 'we shall be reaching readymade worldwide audiences with films produced by the trade for commercial purposes... and which will therefore, not be suspected of being propaganda films at all' (TNA: INF 1/94 MOI). Korda's *The Lion Has Wings* (1939)[3] which, although made in twelve days without 'official' sanction, epitomises this approach. Cutting together both actual flying footage with studio-based actors, Korda also pre-empted some of the styles of the later CFU productions. However, its cosy dialogue, rigid class distinctions and naive combat scenes made it somewhat incongruous when the Blitzkrieg started in April 1940. By the end of 1939, though, it appeared to most observers that very little had been achieved by the official Films Division and, at the turn of the year, Ball was replaced by an individual perhaps more intellectually and aesthetically in tune with film as an art form. The appointment of Sir Kenneth Clark, director of the National Gallery and surveyor of the king's pictures, as head of the Films Division was also symbolic of the amateurish manner in which propaganda, and films in particular, were viewed by the government. It certainly shocked *Kinematograph Weekly*, the exhibitors' weekly trade paper, which commented:

> It is a cause of wonderment to this tall, quietly spoken, cultured man of art, that he should suddenly be uprooted from the colourful warmth of the National Gallery and translated to the cold cloisters and austere dignity of the Senate House of London University to direct Britain's film effort. (*Kinematograph Weekly*, 11 January 1940)

Despite his self-proclaimed lack of expertise, Clark did see that there was a need to define and formalise what roles film could play in the propaganda campaign both against Nazi Germany and domestically by raising morale. At the end of January 1940, he presented a paper to the Co-ordinating Committee of the MoI in which he identified three basic roles for film: 'What Britain is fighting for', 'How Britain fights' and, finally, 'The need for sacrifice if the war is to be won' (TNA: INF 1/867). Clark went on to suggest the most appropriate type of film genre for each of these three roles. Certainly, he was a passionate advocate for the role film could play; echoing Grierson, he announced to *Kinematograph Weekly* that:

no film is good propaganda unless it gives entertainment. A bad film transfers boredom to the cause it advocates. Secondly, it must be realised that the essence of successful propaganda is that people should not be aware of it. If you make people 'think' propaganda their resistance to it is increased. (*Kinematograph Weekly*, 11 January 1940)

In this he was endorsing the attitude towards film of many in the governing class, which had changed very little since the previous war in respect of the mechanics of propaganda being viewed as essentially 'un-British'.

During the first few months of the war the MoI commissioned, in the main, short 'informationals' such as the 1940 Ealing production of *Now You're Talking* (directed by John Paddy Carstairs), which was received by *Kinematograph Weekly* (28 March 1940) with the understated, 'Let us hope that the Ministry's [MoI] aim of producing 30 short films a year will be on subjects other than gossip!' Such criticism of the Films Division in the early spring of 1940 reflected the general perception of the inadequacies of the MoI itself. Some of this criticism was also levelled at the GPOFU although, in the main, the problems seemed to have been primarily those of organisation and control.

In the absence of much direction from the MoI, the unit produced a few films during the Phoney War from September 1939 until April 1940; these were often commissioned by other government departments, such as the Ministry of Health. *Health in War* (1940), for example, began with a nostalgic look at the last days of peace when there was cricket on the green, hiking in the country and days at the seaside. The film went on to argue that alongside the war with Germany there was another conflict, a much older one, against sickness and suffering. Mothers had a stake in the country to ensure that the new generation was happier and healthier than its predecessors. To achieve this the government, confronted by the war, was ensuring not only that evacuation of the young and sick was carried out but also, for the first time, there was to be a coordinated Emergency Hospital scheme, which became the forerunner of the National Health Service. Patients could take advantage of the fresh air of the countryside as well as the advantages of modern medicine. In particular, all expectant mothers would be entitled to maternity care of a standard equivalent to the best that

Harley Street could offer. This film was unusual, not in the sense that citizens had a right to expect a better life after their sacrifices in war, as that became a common theme in later Crown films, but rather that such future promises were put on hold following the German Blitzkrieg in the west when concerns became more immediate.

Another type of film which became more common later was also produced during the Phoney War. These story documentaries shone a light upon the less glamorous military units that made important contributions to the war effort. The first of these was Harry Watt's *Squadron 992* (1940). The squadron in question was an RAF balloon unit with the responsibility of providing a deterrent to enemy bombers. The film detailed the training of the RAF men and included an interesting assertion, as they were shown sewing a balloon envelope, that they would be ideal husband material with that skill set. The film then recreated an unsuccessful Luftwaffe raid on the Forth Bridge where the flight of the German bomber (actually a British Blenheim) pursued by a Spitfire is cut against two Scottish poachers releasing a greyhound to chase a hare. In both cases, the pursued was caught and the German airman were shown being rescued. The raid prompted the deployment of Squadron 992 to the Forth Bridge where, within twelve hours, a balloon barrage was erected. As with earlier films, the actors were members of the squadron playing their normal roles. Perhaps to enhance the authenticity of the film there were several V-signs and 'bloodys', which was quite unusual for the period. *Squadron 992* was also memorable for cameraman Jones, as he was arrested near the Forth Bridge when scouting for appropriate camera sites and angles, an activity which the local police suspected was more akin to spying (Figure 4.3).

The actual war also featured in a small number of GPOFU films made at this time. Jennings directed the twenty-five-minute *The First Days* (1939), a reflective piece which reviewed the events of September and October 1939 and was easily in line with Clark's 'What Britain is fighting for'. It recalled the last day of peace, 3 September 1939, when religious Londoners were attending church services while others took the opportunity of the good weather to cycle into the countryside. These peaceful pursuits were shattered by Chamberlain's announcement that Britain was at war. This, of course, meant all the panoply of conflict air raid shelters, barrage balloons and sandbags – according to the film, 'millions of them'.

Figure 4.3 The deployment of anti-aircraft balloons in *Squadron 992* (1940)

Jennings suggested that the threat of war had begun to break down social class differences, a theme to which the CFU would frequently return. Despite the overall sense of friendliness, it was clear that the mood was hardening. Although city life appeared to go on as normal, the film showed all the preparations for an expected air attack. The ill, the elderly and children were evacuated, and London landmarks such as the National Gallery and British Museum were emptied and closed. Men were volunteering for the armed forces and women were being trained as ambulance drivers. 'It was', according to the film, 'a time for saying goodbye'. Adieu also to pets, which were either euthanised or taken to the country. The half a million foreign nationals, who made up an important part of London's community, were shown waiting patiently to register as 'aliens'. Shifting to London at night, the fear that the Thames would act as a navigation aid to the bombers was clearly stated, but the film assured the audience that men were watching and waiting and the city was protected by searchlights and anti-aircraft artillery. As night slipped back into day, the BBC addressed both the nation and the world with its famous recognition announcement, 'London calling'. In the City the grass was still growing and new life was welcomed in the form of the previous night's babies. The film concluded with a sequence of the king and queen backed by stirring martial music. *The First Days* demonstrated that, despite all the potential dangers and hardships, the British would face whatever came with determination and resolution. This was a theme which was repeated by the CFU on several occasions during the period up to about 1943. It did rely on several stereotypes to endorse its theme. Thus, for example, cheerful Cockneys are shown singing one of the early popular tunes of the time, 'We're going to hang out our washing on the Siegfried Line!'

The implicit optimism of Jennings' film was also evident in two shorts which celebrated the military alliance with France. *French Communiqué* and *La Cause Commune* were both produced in early 1940, but their scheduled theatrical release was soon overtaken by events. The former described the life of a French *poilu* (soldier) guarding the Maginot Line and the bridges across to Germany. Again, a somewhat stereotypical approach was taken, as the French soldier was seen as essentially a peasant at heart who enjoyed his food and wine, demonstrated by scenes of Christmas celebrations within the Maginot tunnel complex. The film concluded with probably one of the most unfortunately short-sighted statements in any of the GPOFU's productions. This was the observation that, as the earth began to warm, the soldiers' minds were turning to ploughing and planting and the French artillery was sending a message: 'Go back Germans, Jerry, Fritz!' Of course, when the spring came, so did the German Blitzkrieg.

By the latter part of the war, the MoI had arranged that the soundtracks of several Crown productions were translated into various languages for overseas exhibition. *La Cause Commune* was one of the first of these. It was a short film which emphasised the cooperation between Britain and France both on the battlefield and in the production of armaments. Once again, somewhat unfortunately the progress of the war in April 1940 prevented its proposed exhibition.

Although having been made available to the MoI in September 1940, the unit was also producing films with a GPO logo and was accepting commissions from other government departments such as the Ministry of Health. This caused some concern in the Treasury regarding how costs were allocated. As a result, it was decided that the unit would be transferred totally to the MoI on 1 April 1940 and would become the government's own film production facility. As the *Documentary News Letter* later reported, this meant that 'the Ministry will become the supply section of any department or semi-official organisation which wishes to make a film' (Volume 9, August 1940, pp. 4–5).

However, despite the resignation of Sir Kenneth Clark and his replacement by Jack Beddington,[4] who at least had some experience of film, the Treasury in particular was having continuing doubts about the value of a government-controlled production unit. In July 1940, the Select Committee on National Expenditure was concerned about both the cost and relevance of the twenty-eight films which had been completed by the Films Division since the war had commenced. As such, it recommended the establishment of an enquiry, chaired by Harold Boxall, a Gaumont-British executive from Denham Studios, to make recommendations for the future of government-sponsored filmmaking (TNA: INF 1/81). Fortunately for the Films Division and eventually the CFU, the public perception of the role of film had already begun a dramatic shift, mainly because of the Dunkirk evacuation and the potential threat of invasion.

From GPOFU to CFU

The whole wartime environment changed quite dramatically in the early summer of 1940 with the collapse of the Allied Western Front and the subsequent retreat and evacuation of the British Expeditionary Force (BEF). Britain was now isolated on the western edge of Europe, facing a victorious Nazi war machine. At home, Chamberlain resigned on 10 May 1940 to be replaced by a coalition government led by Winston Churchill. In the chaos that ensued with the threat of a German invasion looming, it was perhaps predictable that the general public sought out news and information. As early as 16 May 1940, the *Kinematograph Weekly* headline was 'Newsreels are now top of the Programme'. In these dramatic days it was also unsurprising that the Select Committee's Boxall Enquiry was very sympathetic to the Films Division, as here was an obvious and immediate vehicle by which government could propagandise the British cause – although some of Boxall's criticisms were pretty damning and, from a production perspective, almost incredible. For example, the Films Division had, once again, contravened musical performing rights. 'It is important to obtain clearance from any performer giving the producer all rights in respect of his or her performance,' wrote Boxall (TNA: INF 1/81). 'This is necessary under the Musical Performers Protection Act of 1925. Not a single clearance has been obtained in respect of any of the films produced up to date.' Similarly, the GPOFU's production facilities at Blackheath were themselves also apparently woefully inadequate:

> I was appalled at the conditions under which the Unit work. There is one small stage and three cutting rooms all of which are too small for their purpose. These rooms are badly equipped and with obsolete equipment. There is no storage space, and timber and other goods are stacked in corridors, on the staircase and elsewhere. There is one room on the ground floor for the carpenter's shop which also serves as the main Electricity Switch Room – a combination almost unheard of. This room is typical of the entire place. (TNA: INF 1/81)

Not only were legal obligations ignored and production conditions appalling, but there were other major operational inadequacies. In the pre-production phase, normal access to a film library was impossible, as 'no records are maintained at the moment, with the result that a search of all tins is made before obtaining the desired stock shot' (TNA: INF 1/81). However, perhaps the most telling factor in this catalogue of problems in what was obviously a very amateurish operation was the cost it imposed upon production. Boxall calculated that the cost per foot of film for the GPOFU was a staggering £2 9s 4d, compared with the commercial sector's 18s 2d (TNA: INF 1/81). Put very simply, and given the restrictions on availability of film stock, from the very start the GPOFU and its successor the CFU incurred costs that were over two and half times more than the average of their commercial competitors. In fact, it was this cost differential that remained throughout the history of the CFU and was eventually a major factor in its ultimate demise. Despite this catalogue of problems and potential difficulties, Boxall felt constrained to recommend that 'the Film Unit should continue as an independent unit, not in competition with the film industry but as ancillary to the industry'. However, he did add a caveat that 'the continuance of the film unit [is] subject to it operating in a first class studio' (TNA: INF 1/81).

Even though they had not had access to 'first class' facilities, as has been seen, GPOFU staff had not been entirely idle during the first year of the Second World War. They had become engaged on a variety of projects during this period. Cameraman Jones, for example, went to Dover during the very early days of the Battle of Britain and set up his camera on Shakespeare Cliff. A keen amateur ornithologist, he had pioneered a pan-and-tilt method of following birds in flight – no mean feat given the size and weight of the camera. This particular skill was put to another use in filming a Luftwaffe attack on a small convoy in the Straits of Dover and the subsequent arrival of the RAF. The gentle glide of a burning twin-engine German aircraft (possibly a Messerschmitt Bf 110) into the Channel has now become a stock shot for any film or television programme on the air war (interview with Irene Jones, widow of Frank (Jonah) Jones, 3 August 2005). This footage became part of *The Front Line* (1940), a short film about how Dover was coping with being the closest British town to Nazi-occupied Europe.

It might have been the lack of real objectives or the possible outcome of what was likely to have been a critical report which encouraged Cavalcanti, the senior producer, to seek employment elsewhere. In August 1940, he joined Michael Balcon at Ealing Studios, where he took charge of the new 'shorts' department. Consequently, a replacement had to be found at very short notice for a job which probably would not have existed for very long had Boxall been more critical. Having met with Harry Watt and Jack Holmes, the two senior directors at the GPOFU, Ian Dalrymple was enticed away from the features sector of the commercial industry. It was, by any measure, a remarkable event, more so given that at £900 per annum Dalrymple took a significant salary cut and was employed initially on a weekly basis, so unsure were the MoI of retaining the film unit. One of Dalrymple's first acts was to write to Mr Gaines, deputy director general of the MoI, suggesting that, in the light of the Boxall Report, a reorganised and re-energised film unit should 'be styled the Crown Unit and that the Crown emblem be retained from the present [GPOFU] mark' (TNA: INF 1/81).

It was eventually agreed that the new name should be the Crown Film Unit and, although not formally coming into effect until 1 January 1941, the new operation began using the logo and name from November of the previous year (TNA: INF 1/81).

Notes

1 At Chalfont St Giles in Buckinghamshire.
2 François-Dominique Toussaint Louverture (1743–1803) was a revolutionary who led the first successful revolt against the slave owners in Haiti, which resulted in the eventual recognition of Haiti as an independent state in 1825. Toussaint Louverture became a key protagonist and hero in the movement for Black emancipation.
3 See Short (1997) for a fuller discussion of the film.
4 As director of publicity for the Shell Group during the late 1930s, Jack Beddington was responsible for the production of the famous Shell 'informationals'.

5

The Crown Film Unit's wartime productions, 1940–45

The demands of total war propelled the CFU to produce films which reflected the progress of the war, the anxieties of the British government and, to a greater extent, the concerns of the cinemagoing public. Unlike its predecessors, the EMB and GPO film units, Crown now had ready access to theatrical exhibition. Although its films addressed a variety of themes and topics, it had become essentially the mouthpiece of government and its productions stateendorsed public information films. During this period, CFU films reflected, and to some degree generated, the attitudes and images of Britain in the 1940s which have coalesced into that folklore which underpins many Britons' perceptions of their national identity. The pictures and storylines shown helped to create or at least reinforce a national narrative of the experience of the wartime years, subsequently played back in many of the British feature war films of the 1950s such as *The Wooden Horse* (1950), directed by ex-CFU man Jack Lee, and *Appointment in London* (1952), directed by another ex CFU man, Philip Leacock. Although, as McLaine (1979, p. 12) has noted, wireless, posters and newspapers would play a part, it was the cinema, with its massive audience, that provided an invaluable channel of communications.

The cinema, in return, in the form of the CEA, early appreciated the public's desire for information in a period of anxiety and was prepared to enter into an agreement with the MoI. This was negotiated by Jack Beddington of the Films Division; the exhibitors' journal, *Kinematograph Weekly*, reported on 5 September 1940 that '5 minutes of each programme in every kinema [was] freely given to the screening of the propaganda films'. However, this does not seem to have been as altruistic as it might originally have appeared. The CEA was also anxious to prevent the further development of non-theatrical exhibition. Consequently, it vociferously, if unsuccessfully, opposed both the introduction of more mobile cinema vans and also the development of military camp cinemas.

This deal had given the government, through the MoI, weekly access to the nation's cinema screens during the national emergency. Although some of these MoI short films were produced by the CFU, others came from a variety of independent companies such as Strand or Realist. The sudden increase in short film production which the war had engendered created a need to classify or categorise these films for both the theatrical and non-theatrical markets. At a functional level, categorising the 'type' of film enabled both potential exhibitor and audience to assess its value and appeal.

The commercial sector tended, in the main, to receive its information about individual films from trade papers such as *Kinematograph Weekly*, which every week provided descriptions and technical details of the latest releases.[1] However, for the organisers of one of the myriad venues, such as local NAAFI or film clubs, where there was non-theatrical exhibition of films, it was important to have some idea of the nature and running time of each film before making a request for its loan from either the Central Film Library or one of the MoI's regional film libraries. Given the rapid increase in the number of films produced in the early months of the war, and especially the demand from the non-theatrical sector, the MoI began to produce a regular catalogue. In order to facilitate ordering, the catalogue was divided into sections. For example, in late 1941 the Central Film Library catalogue categorised its available films under the following headings; 'The Fighting Forces, Civil Defence, The British Empire, Labour and Armaments, Food Front, Health and Education, Salvage, Savings and Thrift' (TNA: HO 186/1456).

The key wartime themes

During a major international crisis such as the Second World War, the ebb and flow of the themes evident in the CFU's films tended to mirror the progress of the conflict itself. Of the sixty or so CFU films produced and exhibited between 1940 and 1945, it is possible to identify several recurring themes which reappear in a variety of forms over the period. It was also hardly surprising, given the fact that most of the CFU personnel were ex-GPOFU, that the practices and production values developed during the pre-war years were reflected in later films. For example, *Squadron 992*, the story about a barrage balloon unit which explained the importance of one of the less glamorous but important roles in air defence, was later repeated in *Ferry Pilot* (1942). Similarly, in 1940 the GPOFU produced *Factory Front* (directed by Ralph Elton and Cavalcanti), which emphasised the significance of wartime munitions production in a theme to which the CFU returned over the next few years in films such as *Workers' Weekend* (1943). The principal difference between those films produced in late 1939 and early 1940 was that, compared with the CFU films made later, they lacked any sense of urgency or real threat.

Needless to say, the topics addressed by CFU films during wartime often interwove other strands, but most exhibited the principal characteristics of one or other of the themes outlined below. As in previous chapters, a classification model can illustrate particular themes as well as subtle changes in response to the progress of the war.

1. *Anti-German/hitting back*: Less than a quarter of a century after the Armistice in 1918, Britain was involved in another major conflict with Germany. So it was hardly surprising that an early and major theme of government policy was to reinforce hostility towards the Germans. Initially this tended to be fairly crude and mirrored to some extent the anti-Hun propaganda of the First World War. The approach taken in early CFU films such as *Men of the Lightship* really carried the theme on from films like *The Leopard's Spots*, with its debauched and vicious soldiery now updated to include the heartless Luftwaffe. However, as the war progressed and the evidence of actual Nazi brutality was revealed, the films were able to indulge in a frequent, but perhaps very understandable, demand for revenge. Consequently, these films were primarily concerned with exploiting and developing anti-German feeling and supporting all efforts at hitting back at the enemy.
2. *Reassurance/appeal to patriotism*: A principal purpose of any government propaganda during a modern war is to reassure the civilian population that its sacrifices are not in vain and that

these are being shared across the community. Reeves (1999) argues that this approach was the very 'essence of the MoI's propaganda strategy' and that, 'the people of Britain deserved to be treated as intelligent and sophisticated democratic citizens' (p. 169). Collective deprivations and dangers were important in that they developed and solidified the self-image of a British nation in which all classes were united in their stoic resistance to the enemy. This interpretation of the 'myth' of the Blitz has been challenged by the works of Calder (1992) and later Smith (2000) who have argued, for example, that essentially the many social class divisions which existed before the war continued throughout and that, far from being a unifying feature, the bombing and blackout provided ideal circumstances for robbery and violence, as East End gangster 'Mad' Frankie Fraser, frequently testified (including in the 2005 television documentary, *Bad Boys of the Blitz: Revealed*). However, the contemporary British film industry, and especially productions which were directly sponsored by the government, tended to reinforce the basic ideas and assumptions underpinning the perspective of a nation united against the foe. This type of film was also often distributed overseas not only within the Empire/Commonwealth and the USA but also to non-aligned countries as a way of demonstrating British resistance.

3. *Participation in the war effort*: The Second World War was a total war which required the active participation and commitment to the war effort of all citizens, whatever their occupation, to enable it to be pursued effectively. Often, by cinematic standards, these jobs and roles were less than glamorous and some films were devised to emphasise the importance of the 'support' services, both civilian and military, in assisting those actively engaged in combat.

4. *Looking forward to peace*: The British government realised quite early in the war, especially after the destruction caused by the Blitz raids, that the populace might be heartened by considering what would happen to their lives if, and it became quite quickly when, final victory was achieved. There was an obvious and immediate focus on rebuilding to replace bomb-damaged buildings. However, reconstruction here was not only meant in material terms but also social, economic and educational improvements.

5. *No obvious category*: Within any film classification there inevitably exist several productions that defy categorising.

Even during a period of major national emergency, the CFU found at least one opportunity to indulge individual or departmental whims.

The films situated in the above categories were produced and exhibited against the background of the dramatic events of the Second World War. The volume of literature narrating and explaining the progress of the war from both a domestic and international perspective is, to say the least, enormous and provides the background to the films examined below.

Anti-German/hitting back films

One of the first films which demonstrated all the principal characteristics of this category was *Men of the Lightship*. At first sight this might seem an unusual choice as it was the last film produced by Alberto Cavalcanti prior to his departure from the GPOFU and the MoI's complete takeover of the film unit. However, the official listing of CFU productions held by the BFI records the film as being one of the first CFU productions. Production actually commenced in February but was not completed until the end of July 1940. The final prints were distributed in the late summer of 1940 prefaced, perhaps surprisingly, by the CFU logo and title. The film itself purports to be a reconstruction of a real event and as such there were echoes of some of the anti-German propaganda stories which were circulated during the First World War, such as the scenes of pillaging and murder in Belgium as depicted in the 1918 film *The Leopard's Spots*. It contrasted quite dramatically with the slightly earlier GPOFU reconstruction film *Squadron 992*, which was quite light-hearted with the air combat description reminiscent of a sports commentary. On the other hand, the plot of *Men of the Lightship* revolved around an attack upon a Trinity House lightship which, according to the commentary, for 'over three hundred years has never been regarded as a target'. Even Louis XIV had forbidden attacking such vessels as he was 'making war on the English not on humanity' (TNA: INF 6/353). The film introduced a stereotypical set of English maritime characters aboard Lightship 61 at East Dudgeon off the Norfolk coast, including the comedy figure of Lofty, who was introduced to the audience throwing slops into the wind with inevitable results. This untroubled life was suddenly shattered when an attack by German bombers (looking suspiciously like British Bristol Blenheims) forced the crew, including the elderly, wounded skipper, to abandon ship. To emphasise the perfidy of the 'Hun', the crew were then machinegunned in their lifeboat; the final shot of them was of their bodies washed up on shore, presumably the following day. The message of fortitude in the face of infamy was reinforced as, apparently just two days later, another lightship was towed out to the East Dudgeon site and the audience reminded that the 'Nazis must be stopped, we can and we will stop them!' (TNA: INF 6/353).

The propaganda value of this and later films would be enhanced by sympathetic distribution in the United States where Hollywood-based Britons were encouraged to support and advocate for the Allied cause. In the case of *Men of the Lightship*, a contemporary CFU internal note described how:

> Alfred Hitchcock was approached by MoI to cut and recommentate [sic] the film in order to enhance its chances of theatrical distribution on the American market. Hitchcock agreed and received a mute lavender,[2] sound effects tracks (nine reels in all). The re-edited version was distributed by 20th Century Fox for a period of five years from 25/3/41. (TNA: INF 6/353)

The message behind *Men of the Lightship* was unsubtle: the Germans were by nature barbaric and failed to observe the 'rules of war' and therefore had to be defeated in order for 'civilised' life to continue. It was a perspective which chimed very well with the poster images of the 'rape of Belgium' circulated during the early years of the First World War.[3] The film also had all the hallmarks of many of the later wartime documentaries. It purported to be a documentary reconstruction of a real historical event. The characterisation was based upon apparently real people pursuing fairly mundane jobs and whose lives were transformed by the impact of a war which had been thrust upon them – this was very much in line with the developing self-image of the British as a nation plunged unwillingly into war and having to make the ultimate sacrifice in the face of a barbaric enemy who either did not play by, or perhaps even understand, the rules of the game.

It was all very well to be on the receiving end of German attacks and to accept them stoically as in *Men of the Lightship*, but it was also important that British citizens and, by implication those that supported the British cause overseas in the United States and elsewhere, realised that offensive action against the Nazis was being taken. The importance of the 'hitting back' aspect of this current theme was increasingly magnified after the expulsion of British troops from Norway and France in spring and early summer of 1940 and the subsequent beginning of the Blitz on British cities later in the year.[4] Aside from the occasional naval engagement, the only tangible way of inflicting significant damage upon the enemy was by air. In this vein one of the most successful of the CFU's early productions, both at home and overseas, was 1941's *Target for Tonight*. The images of aerial bombardment portrayed in this film were to become seminal, in that they have been repeated in many subsequent productions about Second World War bombing campaigns from *The Dam Busters* (1955) through *Mosquito Squadron* (1968) to *Catch-22* (1970) and beyond.

In *Target for Tonight*, the story of the exploits of Wellington bomber 'F-Freddie' developed the bombing theme of *The Lion Has Wings*. Its cast of actual RAF aircrew endowed the film with both an aura of credibility and authenticity which in part might explain its box-office success. Looked at with the benefit of hindsight, *Target for Tonight* exhibited a level of naivety which was far less apparent a year or so later in a similar documentary, *Coastal Command* (1942), which tracked the operational events of a Sunderland flying boat, 'T-Tommy'. In Watt's *Target for Tonight*, photographic reconnaissance had identified a 'real peach of a target' and the AOC (air officer commanding) agreed to divert some of the bombers preparing to attack the docks and barracks near the Kiel Canal to the mythical 'Freihausen' marshalling yards which, the audience was told, was on the Rhine about 15 miles north of Freiburg, in the Black Forest. Although the raid on the Kiel Canal can hardly have been in reality a diversionary attack, given that it was some 450 miles further north, it was signalling that the target was well inside Germany, and so bombs would be falling on German soil and in obvious retribution for the Blitz. The take-off sequence built tension in the film as each aircraft powered up its engines and requested permission to take off, accompanied by stirring martial music. Compared to later films of the American bombing campaign against Germany, such as Henry King's *Twelve O'Clock High* (1949), there was no evidence of formation flying. The fact that each aircraft attacked alone was hardly surprising, however, given the inherent difficulties of close flying in the dark.

Target for Tonight used 'real' RAF personnel not only in the crew of F-Freddie but also from the AOC down to the armourers. Despite this element of authenticity, they frequently came across as somewhat valiant amateurs. The dialogue, for example, remained both unmilitary and a little stilted. There was no evidence of radio protocol, the skipper blithely announcing to the crew as they enter enemy territory: 'Hello everybody, let me know if you see something!' Similarly, after successfully dropping their bombs on the target, which was shown as from ground level with locomotives and wagons being blown up, the aircraft was subjected to anti-aircraft fire. *Target for Tonight* was one of the earliest films to refer to this by the German abbreviation 'Flak', as before this the traditional British expression for the weapon was Ack-Ack (Figure 5.1).[5] During the course of this action the wireless operator was injured and consequent interaction between skipper and crew member demonstrated significant contemporary sang-froid: 'Wireless operator has copped it!'; 'Badly?'; 'No, only in the leg'. Following the high point of the actual bombing and anti-aircraft fire, the tension was maintained during the return journey by engine problems and the film cutting back to the airfield where there was much concern about the lateness of F-Freddie. Despite the fog, the shot-up radio and the mechanical problems, the audience can hardly have been surprised to see the Wellington F-Freddie lumber in to touch down. The film concluded with the normal post-raid debriefing with the intelligence officer congratulating the crew and suggesting, 'How about some bacon and eggs?' Despite its essential simplicity of narrative, the film carried a very powerful message, and one which had already been signposted to the audience by an initial visual dedication that emphasised the importance of the Royal Air Force in demonstrating Britain's 'Strength'.[6]

The film title itself was only agreed some two weeks before its eventual release on 25 July 1941, changing from *Night Bomber* to the more evocative *Target for Tonight*. On release it was almost universally acclaimed. The editor of the *Daily Express*, writing to

The CFU's wartime productions, 1940–45

Figure 5.1 There was a price for authenticity: none of the aircrew of F-Freddie in *Target for Tonight* (1941) survived the war

Sidney Bernstein, the deputy director of the MoI's Films Division, commented that, 'I saw *Target for Tonight* today. It is a truly magnificent film, and the *Daily Express* if anything, underplayed it. Just the same I think, after seeing the paper this morning, it would only be right and proper if we were to change the title from the *Daily Express* to "Crown Film Unit Gazette"' (TNA: INF 1/210). The *Express*'s proprietor, Lord Beaverbrook, was equally captivated, also writing to Bernstein: '*Target for Tonight* is a picture which must move and interest audiences not only in this country, but wherever it is shown. It gives an impression of the courage and determination of the bomber crews which can never be effaced' (TNA: INF 1/210, 31 July 1941). Sadly, the majority of F-Freddie's crew would not bask long in all the adulation for, as Nicholas Cull observed, 'none survived long enough to see it' (Cull, 1995, p. 138). However, Flight Lieutenant Percy Pickard, who played Squadron Leader Dickson in the film, did survive until February 1944, when he was killed in his Mosquito fighter-bomber returning from leading the famous Operation Jericho attack on Amiens prison, which secured the escape of captured French Resistance fighters.[7]

Target for Tonight to some extent set the bar as far as CFU productions were concerned. As such, it was important in establishing the reputation of the unit as a key producer of films which encouraged morale and supported the British war effort. It was also significant as one of the first British films which addressed the reality of the bombing campaign against Germany and was a key reference for future feature films of this genre.

Some of the other famous CFU feature films could also be appropriately situated in the anti-German/hitting back category. *Coastal Command* (1942) (Figure 5.2) addressed the anti-submarine campaigns of the Battle of the Atlantic, while *Close Quarters* (1943) looked at submarine warfare from a British perspective. Films which demonstrated that the battle was being taken to the Germans, and later the Japanese,[8] continued until the war ceased. Thus, shorts such as *By Sea and Land* (1944), which looked at the role of the

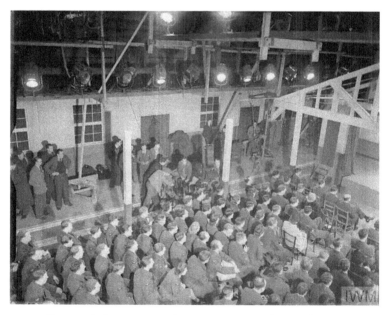

Figure 5.2 Sometimes authenticity was staged: a production shot from *Coastal Command* (1942)

Royal Marines in the battle for Normandy, or, the last of this type, *Broad Fourteens* (1945), actually released after the war had ended but describing the role played by motor torpedo boats in the English Channel, all emphasised attacking the enemy.

As far as the anti-German aspect of this theme is concerned there was a certain ambivalence which seemed to enter the productions around 1943. Jennings' *The Silent Village* was a powerful condemnation of Nazi atrocities. It commemorated the massacre of Lidice (in then Czechoslovakia) in 1942 by transposing the events to a Welsh mining village. Yet, by the following year, in *The True Story of Lili Marlene*, Jennings certainly retained the evil Nazi perspective by emphasising the brutal treatment and incarceration of the song's original singer, Lalli Andersen.

Andersen had made her name on the Berlin and Munich nightclub circuits before the war. However, even though her song about the girl waiting by the barrack gate was extremely popular with the Wehrmacht, its non-martial sentiments and her own friendship with Jewish artists such as Rolf Liebermann[9] brought her to the attention of the Nazi authorities and she was gaoled; even on release after nine months, she was not allowed to sing 'Lili Marlene'.

In contrast, in the second half of the film, Jennings appears far more sympathetic to the ordinary German soldiers, especially those of the Afrika Korps who had adopted 'Lili Marlene' as an unofficial corps anthem. The song itself was, in turn, embraced by their enemies in North Africa, the British Desert Rats. This film certainly seemed to have endorsed or at least reinforced the conventional and popular view that the Desert War was the most chivalric of the entire conflict.[10] Perhaps it was that, by 1944, the Afrika Korps had been defeated, Italy had been invaded and the second front in Europe had opened with the D-day invasion and Jennings felt able to appreciate the common experiences of the soldiers on both sides in North Africa?

Reassurance/appeal to patriotism

Whereas the war in the desert had often been fought in an unforgiving and hostile environment with consequently few civilian casualties or massive destruction of towns and cities, elsewhere conflict was marked by substantial collateral damage. The Second World War was a total war which required, or at least involved, whole populations irrespective of age, gender or ethnicity and, as such, governments on both sides sought to both reassure and mobilise their citizens by the use of film propaganda. Complementary to the hitting-back genre was the reassurance of the home population category; and this made up almost the same number of CFU productions. This, in itself, indicated the contemporary importance the government gave to reassuring the civilian population in the face of dire news and, especially, attack from the air.

Such reassurance was especially important for the government early in the war as, following the evacuation of Dunkirk and the Luftwaffe's failure to destroy the RAF in the Battle of Britain, the Germans turned mostly to night attacks on towns and cities. The British experiences of the Blitz, especially for metropolitan dwellers, tended to suggest that, although blast damage from high explosive was quite significant, the smaller incendiary devices, which were dropped in their thousands, caused major fires devastating whole areas. The creation of firestorms caused by the rapid temperature rise over a large area essentially 'sucking in' air and debris from the surrounding areas became, of course, a feature of the later area bombing of German cities such as Hamburg, Cologne and Dresden. However, apart from isolated examples of firestorms in London during the first Blitz (September 1940 to May 1941), the general impression was that, despite substantial damage to property and infrastructure, civilian casualties remained relatively low. It has been estimated that throughout the whole war some 30,000 Londoners were killed, perhaps half the civilian deaths recorded for the whole of the UK (HMSO: Command papers (hereafter Cmd) 6832, 1946).

Consequently, it was quite reasonable in 1941 for J. B. Holmes and Jack Lee of the CFU to focus *Ordinary People* on the London Blitz. Its expression on screen had to portray a fair approximation of the experiences of those who had suffered the bombing in order to confer the film with a degree of authenticity. Using 'normal' people rather than actors had already become a feature of CFU and its predecessors' productions. This was emphasised in the opening shot of *Ordinary People* with the strapline: 'To the future historian – this film was played by ordinary people of London'.

The CFU's wartime productions, 1940–45

Another common feature of CFU and earlier films was the use of stereotypical characters to reinforce both its message and, perhaps viewed retrospectively, the commonly held view of the stoicism of Londoners under fire. Some versions of the film had a short introduction by the Australian prime minister Sir Robert Menzies, who emphasised that Londoners were regularly suffering the 'senseless and indiscriminate bombing of the half-civilised Hun' – which, of course, harked back to the traditional anti-German sentiments of the First World War and earlier CFU films such as *Men of the Lightship*.

The film opens, and closes, with scenes of an anti-aircraft balloon barrage between which it focusses on a day in the lives of seven ordinary Londoners who were united by their nightly occupation of one particular deep air raid shelter. It early established its London credentials by shots of the Thames and also of the Tower of London, through which the time frame was also created. In this early scene a soldier was shown at the tower blowing 'Reveille' on his bugle; towards the end of the film there was a similar shot, but this time the bugler is sounding 'Sunset', the army's traditional call for the end of the working day. The seven key characters are essentially stereotypes to demonstrate, amongst other things, that traditional class barriers had been reduced, if not entirely abolished. They were all subject to the same bombing and thus there was a message within the film that aerial bombardment was no respecter of social status. The 'we're all in this together' approach of *Ordinary People* set a precedent repeated in other, perhaps more famous, CFU films such as Jennings' *A Diary for Timothy*. In *Ordinary People* the main characters which reflect the various social classes were:

'Tiny' – the inevitably corpulent taxi driver.

Mr & Mrs Payne – the housewife and the factory worker who was also an air raid warden, thus allowing for a wider perspective of somebody engaged in war work and 'doing their bit'.

Miss Ryan – the Bourne & Hollingsworth shop girl who was also a member of the store fire squad.

Frank – the GPO telephone engineer who was always shown with his 'mate', Dougie.

An unnamed judge – perhaps not so 'ordinary' but representing that normal administrative and legal life continued.

Mr Saxby – the local vicar who, in some scenes, provided the 'conduit' which often connected the various individuals.

By counterposing their activities during the day, the film was able to emphasise a number of features of wartime living in London. The key message, of course, was that despite regular air raids not only did life go on as near to normal as possible, but that the war required adaptation and accommodation. This can be seen in the continuation of the court, removed to the basement, alongside a mere short hiatus in the shopping at Bourne & Hollingsworth during a raid. There were also a number of lower key messages which were essentially about both stoicism and mutual support. Mrs Payne, the housewife returning to her bomb-damaged house, refused to contemplate moving to a safer area, explaining that it 'would take more than this [a glass and plaster strewn kitchen] to get me out of my home!' Mrs Payne was also on hand to provide tea and sympathy as well as spaces in the air raid shelter for the bombed-out couple, Mrs Finch and her daughter Doris, from across the road. The neighbourliness might sound a little forced, but again the emphasis was on the need for mutual help and support.

Whether consciously or not, the film also displayed a certain sang-froid in the face of the enemy air raid. After the warning is sounded many refused to go to the shelter. 'Tiny', the cabby, merely dons his tin helmet – it was, 'after all', he said, 'his lucky day' – as do all the men in the shell factory. Perhaps most bizarre of all was the short scene with Frank and Dougie, the GPO telephone engineers, who were engaged in repairing cables within a bomb-damaged building. Frank threw himself on the ground on hearing the whistle of descending bombs and, following the detonation, called after Dougie, who ambled into shot advising that he was not hurt as he had his 'fingers crossed!' The fairly obvious message of *Ordinary People* was that, although the aerial bombardment was destructive of property, the majority of people would survive and the bombs could be effectively ignored in most circumstances.

The recognition in this film that the damage to property would be far greater and casualties far fewer contrasted almost diametrically with that of the earlier *If War Should Come/Do it Now* (1939).

However, the actual survival of the vast majority of Londoners, despite days or rather nights of protracted bombing, contrary to what had been originally expected, contributed to a widely held perception about the Blitz. This attitude, which had been introduced in the cinema as early as December 1940 with Jennings' *London Can Take It!* (later retitled *Britain Can Take It!*), was reinforced in such films as *Ordinary People* and persisted beyond the mini-Blitz in the late summer and autumn of 1944 when the city was regularly attacked from air again, this time with Hitler's revenge weapons, the V1s and V2s. The survivability of the vast majority in the face of aerial bombardment persisted as a feature of most official films until the 1960s, when there was a general realisation that the hydrogen bomb had not only devastating destructive power but also generated lethal doses of radiation.

Even after the German attack on Russia in the summer of 1941, and the lessening of both the aerial onslaught and the possibility of invasion, the government still thought it necessary to appeal to its citizens' patriotism. The subsequent de facto alliance between Britain and the Soviet Union engendered a relatively short-lived but enthusiastic championing of Stalin and the Red Army. An example of this includes the CFU film *The Tale of Two Cities* (1942), in this case London and Moscow. It was a short seven-minute film which exemplified a particular type of CFU production, essentially an edit by John Monck of various newsreels and stock shots bound together by a narration. The authenticity of such a film would be substantiated by a commentary from an expert in the field which, in the case of *The Tale of Two Cities*, was the wing commander leading the RAF wing [probably 151 Wing] which operated a small number of Hawker Hurricanes in Russia at the time in support of the Red Air Force.

The film was fundamentally a direct comparison between the two cities. So there were shots of balloon barrages and listening posts in both the UK and USSR. The commentary emphasised that those in Moscow had learned from the London Blitz experience, so 'Moscow was prepared'. In a contemporary and very pro-Russian review, fellow documentarist Edgar Anstey made the observation that:

> the Russian scenes show Moscow's citizens equalling the fortitude of the Londoners, and the similarities are so close that it is not always possible to decide in which city the camera is located. No doubt it

was part of the purpose of the film to stress this unity in courage of the anti-Nazi front. (*The Spectator*, 5 April 1942, p. 11)

The film contained common scenes of relatively cheerful people chatting, singing and sleeping in underground railway stations to avoid the bombing; the principal difference between Britain and Russia seemed to be the ornateness of the Moscow Metro.

This film was important as an example of the surprising reversal of sentiment which developed in Britain in the aftermath of the German invasion in July 1941. The Nazi–Soviet Pact of August 1939 and the Winter War in Finland (November 1939 to March 1940) had exacerbated anti-Bolshevik feeling in the UK. With the Blitzkrieg assault of Operation Barbarossa, there was almost a complete volte-face as things Russian suddenly became highly popular. Much of this was, of course, both mawkish and, as subsequently revealed in later years, quite naive. Even in April 1942 when *The Tale of Two Cities* was released its sentiments were wildly optimistic. The siege of Leningrad was not to be lifted for nearly another two years and the battle of Stalingrad was still six months in the future. However, the contemporary importance of this film was that it emphasised that other civilians were suffering and that both populations could 'take it'. The short film concluded with a, now traditional, scene of tanks rumbling through Red Square and the exhortation that Churchill and Stalin were 'Defenders of Freedom, Avengers of Humanity!' As will be seen, this was a standpoint which was fairly short-lived, as wartime enthusiasm for Stalin and the Red Army became post-war fear and hostility.

As might be expected in wartime, one aspect of the British government's policy was to reassure the population that 'we're all in this together' and to emphasise patriotism, and many other CFU films can be categorised this way. The vast majority of this type of film were produced and exhibited in the early years of the war when there had been little good military news and the civilian population was suffering from the depredations caused by both the German Luftwaffe and the U-boat attrition of the Atlantic convoys. Sometimes these films were addressed directly to the British audience, such as *India Marches* (1941), which looked at the military contribution from the subcontinent, in this case the Fifteenth Punjab Regiment; or *Letter from Ulster* (1943), about American military training in the province, and *United Nations* (1942), which extolled the fact that Britain was no longer alone in its fight but was now a part of a global military alliance. Other films appear to not only have an intention of reassuring a domestic audience, but also appealing to a worldwide one that Britain and the British could and would 'take it'. So Jennings' *The Heart of Britain* (March 1941), *Words for Battle* (May 1941) and *Listen to Britain* (April 1942), with their stirring evocations of Britain past and present, were aimed at both domestic and overseas audiences.

Participation in the war effort

The previous section's films were concerned with reassuring the civilian population that their sufferings had to be endured, but that these sufferings transcended social class and other divisions so that the entire population was all in it together. However, there was another category of films which encouraged and applauded those citizens who, although not in the armed forces, were working to assist the war effort or were, in the parlance of the times, 'doing their bit'. As might be expected, the opportunities for such employment and activity during wartime were immense and consequently the films produced by the CFU reflected a variety of employment and situations.

An early example of this genre was *Venture Adventure* (1941), a seven-minute short which was essentially a recruiting vehicle for the newly formed Air Training Corps (ATC). The film's somewhat ungrammatical title was derived from the ATC's motto. According to the film, the ATC not only provided an introduction to all things aviation for those boys who wanted eventually to join the RAF, but it was suitable for all the 'healthy, virile and contented youth of Britain' [sic]. Although there were obvious militaristic elements, including the uniforms and marching, the film was anxious to give the impression that with its fitness training and personal discipline the ATC was more akin to a boys' club. It was therefore not just a recruitment vehicle for the RAF but also a sound preparation for adulthood. The overall impression the film gave was of happy teenage camaraderie, demonstrated in the concluding shot of cheerful boys singing the corps song, 'We are the ATC!'

Also in this category, but longer at thirty minutes and following the CFU pattern of utilising 'real' people in a drama documentary format, was Pat Jackson's *Ferry Pilot* (1942), which told the story of two pilots of 15 Ferry Pool of the Air Transport Auxiliary (ATA).[11] To confer additional authenticity, one of the pilots shown in the film would have been reasonably recognisable to contemporary audiences as Jim Mollison, a famous Scottish aviator of the 1930s, but perhaps more widely known then as the husband of the even more famous Amy Johnson.[12] The ATA consisted of civilian pilots, often too old or infirm and definitely not suitable for combat flying, but who were employed to deliver all types of aircraft from factories or repair shops to the operational or training squadrons of the RAF, Coastal Command or Fleet Air Arm. The pilots were recruited from across the globe and, probably in an effort to recognise the United States as a new ally, one of the ferry pilots in this film, Talbot, was an American.

The film followed a day in the operational cycle of an ATA unit with a pool of fifty ferry pilots. It opened with the commanding officer allocating tasks to the various pilots who were then flown by their Avro Anson 'taxis' to pick up their aeroplanes, mostly from factories, and fly them to their required destinations. The storyline focussed upon two pilots, an elderly Briton called Thompson and his younger American colleague, Talbot. Throughout the film the American made complimentary remarks about the British countryside, British aircraft and even a British balloon barrage, all interlaced with standard Americanisms such as 'gee, whizz' and 'back home in Alabama'.

Halfway through the film the storyline was somewhat surprisingly interrupted by two apparently unconnected insertions. Firstly, the two pilots, before picking up the aircraft to deliver, were introduced to two women pilots from another ferry pool. This would seem to be a device to explain and applaud the role that women ferry pilots, such as Amy Johnson, played in the ATA. Cutaways to women pilots climbing aboard another air taxi and then flying off in single-engine planes served to emphasise the contribution that women were making in wartime, even in this fairly esoteric role. Secondly, and perhaps more difficult to explain, the film had a three-minute section in the middle which was entirely of a single Spitfire flown, it was said, by a test pilot. The aircraft performed a series of stunts and manoeuvres, including rolls, loops, controlled stalls and a large amount of inverted flying. It did give Talbot the opportunity to declare, 'Gee, he really knows his stuff!', but beyond entertainment and the eulogy to man and machine, the purpose behind the section is unclear.

After these clips the film resumed its storyline and the two pilots picked up a repaired Armstrong Whitworth Whitley bomber and, following a discussion on the aircraft's various foibles, it was shown taking off with Thomson at the controls and Talbot sitting behind reading an American comic. Unfortunately, they had taken off too soon to be warned of an impending German raid on a town across which they had to fly. The audience was also reminded that, for security reasons, the aircraft had to maintain radio silence. There followed a section showing the Whitley flying over (presumably) England while cheerful farmers looked up from their task of harvesting wheat, all this against a light musical background. This was counterpointed by not only martial Germanic music but shots of German Heinkel bombers heading towards their target. The bombers were protected by Messerschmitt Me 110 fighters and there was a studio shot of a suitably arrogant pilot who noticed the lone Whitley flying on, oblivious to the potential danger. As the Luftwaffe pilot dived to line up his target, his observer was able to utter those words so beloved of British films and comics: '*Achtung Schpitfeuer!*' The German was driven off and was last seen in flames, spiralling down to crash. Despite all this nearby action, neither Thompson nor Talbot saw anything and their aircraft continued on to land at its home aerodrome. The last scene has the two pilots chatting with the commanding officer about the following day's schedule. All of this went to demonstrate that the ATA performed an important task and were of the war, if not directly in the war.

Ferry Pilot has many of the hallmarks associated with the drama documentary productions of the GPOFU and later the CFU. Its authenticity was confirmed by the use of 'real' people performing the same roles they did in their daily lives. Newsreel or stock shots not only from the UK but also, in this case, from German sources was interspersed to both add tension and emphasise realism. By 1942 many of the cinema audience would have, if not seen, then certainly heard the asynchronous throbbing roar of the German bombers' engines, so pictures of British bombers decked out with crosses on their wings (as in *Men of the Lightship*) would have probably been regarded unfavourably. Although the director seems to have given much attention to ensuring that the German planes were real – and even the studio-based German pilot wore a Luftwaffe flying suit – he was less punctilious regarding the continuity of other stock shots. The Whitley took off and landed in an obviously winter countryside, the trees were bare, the sky dour; and yet the cutaways to the happy farmers supposedly watching the aircraft were enjoying the balmy weather at the height of summer.

Films such as *Ferry Pilot* and even *Venture Adventure* imparted important messages to cinema audiences. There were many roles in wartime which, although neither glamorous nor high in the public consciousness, were essential for the successful prosecution of the war. Such films as these either reminded people of this fact or were designed to inspire recruitment into these roles. In the case of *Venture Adventure*, it not only encouraged boys to see the ATC as preparation to become a pilot in the RAF but it also reminded them that there were a range of other essential jobs which were not necessarily flying ones. Further CFU films in this particular category included *The Pilot Is Safe* (1941) about the Air Sea Rescue Services and *Merchant Seamen* (1941) about the important role the merchant marine played in getting supplies to the UK. This last was a theme which was repeated a year or so later with *We Sail at Midnight* (1942); both these films, along with the later, and more famous, *Western Approaches* (1944), acknowledged the terrible losses inflicted during the Atlantic convoy runs. However, probably the most well-known of the CFU productions in this category was Jennings' *Fires Were Started* (1943), the slightly shorter version at sixty-three minutes of the originally titled *I Was a Fireman*, which ran out at seventy-four minutes. As has already been noted, a very few CFU films tend to dominate academic discussion and these particular films fall readily into this category. A detailed examination of them here is somewhat unnecessary as key aspects of the films have already been comprehensively researched, discussed and published by Brian Winston in his 1999 study for the BFI entitled *Fires Were Started* (Winston, 1999).

Looking forward to peace

While the bombings, the depredations, the rationing and the austerity of wartime generated an environment in which the government, through the CFU, encouraged British citizens to accept that such was the price that had to be paid to defeat the Axis powers, it was soon realised that consideration also had to be given to the post-war shape and direction of Britain's society and economy. There was a perceived concern that the public would not accept a return to the status quo ante, especially as the experiences of the failures to build 'homes for heroes' and the Great Depression were fresh in the minds of citizens. According to Hennessy (1992, p. 78) 'from 1943 people began to show a willingness to itemise what was wrong with British society and to suggest ways of putting it right'. Once the danger of invasion seemed to have passed and the Axis powers were on the retreat, British citizens were increasingly focussed on post-war improvements in terms of, usually, more state intervention and better social services. In this they were encouraged not only by the actions of the wartime coalition – such as the publication of the Beveridge Report in 1942 and legislative changes like the 1944 Butler Education Act – but also by the endorsement of expectations for the future as displayed in a number of government-sponsored CFU productions.

A very early example of this category was Pat Jackson's *Builders*, an eight-minute short which was released in 1942. One of the apparently unexpected aspects of the Blitz was that the damage to property was greater than anticipated, whereas loss of life was, fortunately, far less. It has already been noted that, over the duration of the war, some 30,000 Londoners were killed (HMSO: Cmd 6832, 1946); yet in London alone, over 1 million homes were destroyed or severely damaged (Jones, Aucott and Southall, 2013). Consequently, this, alongside the dramatic increase in military building from coastal defences to aerodromes to barracks, meant an upsurge in the demand for construction workers of all types. What was particularly interesting in respect of this category was that Jackson's short film balanced immediate wartime needs with the expectations of a post-war world where builders would turn their hands to erecting schools and hospitals.

As with many CFU productions, the 'actors' were builders themselves; but where this film differed slightly is that it was essentially a dialogue between the unseen narrator, John Hilton, and those on screen. The first line in the film was the narrator's 'Hello, Bob' to which the on-screen builder, looking up from his task, responded, 'Hello, Guv!' There then followed a conversation in which the builder, somewhat half-heartedly, offered critiques of the conditions and problems facing the contemporary industry. The life was apparently quite harsh and the workers often lived in on-site huts as they moved from job to job. The narrator, unsurprisingly, gently chided this and in response pointed out the importance of the work being done. 'You may not be involved in mortal combat' but 'you are building the striking power of the nation'. From the newly constructed factories came weapons, ammunition, planes and so forth. As in other CFU/GPOFU productions, stock shots were used to emphasise and prove these accomplishments. In a further acknowledgement of the sudden reversal of public opinion in respect of Russia, the narrator observed that some of these weapons would be finding their way to the Red Army. Most types of building workers were covered under the Schedule of Reserved Occupations (HMSO: Cmd 5936, 1939) and could be directed from site to site. This was hardly a glamorous existence and it was probable that the overall intention behind the film was to boost the morale of the construction workforce as being the 'unsung heroes' of the war effort.

However, this film was a good example of the blurred lines between information giving and propaganda, as it not only informed the audience that the construction workers were doing 'their bit' but concluded with a section on the future. The narrator announced that, after the war, the money currently being used to build ordnance factories and the like should be used for more peaceful endeavours. He went on to challenge the pre-war economic system, arguing that after the war it 'should be different and better'. For example, he looked forward to an industry which had far 'less cut-throat competition'. By 1942 the central direction of the economy for war purposes had been generally accepted and there was, as this film exemplified, an assumption that this could and should be carried forward to peacetime for the benefit of the entire community.

Within two years, circumstances had changed and the advance of the Allied armies on the Western Front confirmed to many people that the war was winding its way slowly towards its end and that consideration ought to be given to the shape, structure and priorities of the new post-war world. It was in this atmosphere that CFU director Jennings conceived the idea which eventually became *A Diary for Timothy* (1945). It is clear from the initial treatment of this production that he was aware that 'the world and this island are at the end of an epoch' (TNA: INF 6/1917). Although the film was eventually released just after the war ended, at the time of production it was assumed that the fighting would continue a great deal longer. For this reason, this film has been included in this category as one of the last of its type.

The result was a film unusual both in its concept – a diary which addressed a baby – and its production, which went ahead without any form of script. CFU producer Basil Wright agreed to the shooting being done 'off the cuff' and allocated a sum of £300 for the initial research. Having decided that a baby was to be the hero of the film, Jennings spent the summer of 1944 casting around for a mother whose baby was due in early September, on or about the fifth anniversary of the outbreak of the war. Fortunately for Jennings, friends had put him in touch with the chief obstetrician of Oxford, who in turn suggested that he contact Queen Mary's Nursing Home at Eynsham, near Oxford, which provided confinement facilities for the wives of non-commissioned servicemen. Timothy James Jenkins, the son of a soldier serving in the Middle East, was delivered on 3 September 1944. According to Betty Jenkins, Tim's mother, she only became aware that a film was being made,

> when a thin artistic-looking young man came in and strode about the room looking at us from all angles. After a while, he turned to a woman I got to know as his production assistant, 'Well, I'm satisfied, Di,[13] if you are', he said. Then he left. He was quite abrupt. (Purcell, 1995, p. 20)

It was observed in the production notes that 'somehow it never occurred to Humphrey that it [the baby] might be a girl' (TNA: INF 6/1917). Tim's early days, after the nursing home, were spent in the rectory of Nuffield Church, near Henley in Oxfordshire, where his grandfather was the local vicar. This further presented Jennings with not only some interesting footage but also the ability to later make comment upon Tim's 'comfortable' upbringing in rural England.

Although the film focussed on Tim's first few months of life, from the 'tragedy of Arnhem to the hopes of San Francisco' (TNA: INF 6/1917), it was reflected also in the lives of four adults who represented different but enduring characteristics of Britain at that time. The miner, Goronwy Jones, whose dirty and dangerous occupation, combined with the dour and depressing Rhondda village of Ynysbwl, personified traditional labour as well as providing interesting visual images and contrasts. Perhaps socially and economically at the opposite end of the scale, Alan Bloom was an East Anglian farmer, author and filmmaker. Of the four adult 'heroes', Bloom was the only one who was already a minor celebrity in 1944. He had not only bought a derelict fenland farm and drained and reclaimed the land, but he had filmed it as *Reclamation* (1943) in order to show others how it could be done. Whereas the filming of both Jones and Bloom posed little technical difficulties for Fred Gamage, the CFU cameraman, Jennings' third character was Bill Perry, a crack freight train driver for the London Midland and Scottish Railway (LMS). Like Jones earlier with *Night Mail*, Gamage had to arrange an appropriate camera rig. He chose to place a brake van directly behind the locomotive tender to house Jennings and the production crew, while he and his camera were precariously perched on a platform on the tender itself. According to one interpretation of the script, Bill was the one who united the others in the war effort by 'carrying the miner's coal, the farmer's crops and the fighting man's ammunition' (Purcell, 1995, p. 20).

Although one of Jennings' themes was that all these men were heroes in their own way, his last character was actually a decorated airman. Flying officer Peter Roper was a Typhoon pilot who had been shot down over France just after D-day, sustaining a badly broken right leg. His real-life adventures included being assisted by a French farmer and the local doctor, captured by the Germans and eventual release by the invading Allied troops. He was evacuated back to the UK and Jennings was able to film his physical and mental rehabilitation at the RAF hospital in Loughborough. Unfortunately, little is known about his background but, interestingly, Roper was the only character in the film who was always referred to by his full name, including his surname, whereas everybody else was always addressed informally. What this actually signifies remains a mystery.

The film was essentially constructed retrospectively by weaving in the four adult storylines with the background of the progress of the war and juxtaposing these with Tim's early life and development. The actual script for the film was written by E. M. Forster and was narrated by Michael Redgrave. It seems that Forster was enticed by Basil Wright to view a rough edit of Jennings' work and to create a commentary; although it does seem that he had reservations about the project from the very beginning: 'I don't trust my own judgement over films – I am either hypersensitive or obtuse – but I felt sympathetic to the general idea, and admired the sensitive details' (Lago and Furbank, 1983, p. 212). Forster's suggestions for changes appear to have been rejected, but the final cut was moulded as much by his words as by Jennings' visualisation.

The film itself falls into three distinct, but unequal sections, each of which was characterised by its own particular images and atmosphere but linked by the everyday requirements of a baby growing up. As such, it moved from perhaps exaggerated optimism to disappointment to final realisation that the end of the war in Europe was imminent. The introductory section covered the period from Tim's birth on the anniversary of the outbreak of the war until the news broke of the defeat and retreat from Arnhem at the end of September 1944. This was followed by a depressing section in which the direness of the weather was reflected in the problems facing the major adult characters and the obvious resilience of the Germans on the Western Front, culminating in the Ardennes Offensive in December 1944. The turning point of both the film and, by implication, the war came on Christmas day, from which point it was possible to appreciate a deeper concern about the transition from peace to war and the major changes war had caused. These concerns were sometimes expressed openly and directly, while at other times they remained implicit. For example, Alan Bloom, the farmer who combined tradition with new technologies, observed, 'If it hadn't been for the war, I don't suppose we would have done it'. No doubt Bloom was echoing the views of many in his evident appreciation that the war had been, and would continue to be, an agent of massive change in all areas of society.

In the film the essential dynamism of the events and times were focussed around the central character of Tim. The birth of a baby is a dynamic event as well as a tangible commitment to the future – a symbol of hope. So, the film asserted early on that the four major characters, and by implication all those involved, were fighting 'for you, Tim, and all the other babies'. The final shot of the film – a close-up of Tim's face appearing out of the flames which have transformed from the fires of destruction to those of a Victory bonfire – continued this theme. Here the hope for the future was rising phoenix-like from the carnage of war. A more cynical observer might also interpret this sequence as one in which danger still existed and society, personified by Tim, had just managed to escape from the fires this time. Similar images of renewal and renaissance appeared in the film after the Christmas and New Year festivities. Not only does this manifest itself in the somewhat crass pictures of growing plants and to a lesser extent in the building of 'pre-fabs', but more dramatically in the physical recovery from injury of both Goronwy and Roper. Having been damaged by the war, the two are seen undertaking physiotherapy and subsequently returning to their original occupations.

Concern about the transition from war to peace manifested itself in a number of other themes, both ethical and pragmatic, which run through the film. The imminent defeat of Germany brought into sharp focus the structure and nature of the post-war world. Given five years of war and the concomitant anti-Nazi and anti-German propaganda, the post-war treatment of the German people raised important ethical questions. This issue is neatly conflated into one of the sequences and images which Jennings had used in one of his previous films, *Listen to Britain*. The visual references in both films to the 'revival' of the arts may have been slightly exaggerated but it did present an opportunity to address an obvious post-war concern. In both films, Dame Myra Hess, the renowned classical concert pianist, performed Mozart before enraptured audiences. However, by 1945, the narrator, Michael Redgrave, was to observe: 'Did you like the music the lady was playing, Tim? Some of us think that it's the greatest music in the world, but it's German music. That's something you'll have to think over.' Thus, the difficult question of how Germany and the Germans would be treated in the post-war world was raised. Certainly, the transition from demonising a nation to dealing with a defeated and traumatised people would be an inevitable consequence of an Allied victory. So, the closer to eventual victory in a historical sense, the more the film began to examine some of the conundrums likely to face a post-war Britain.

Thus, a radio announcer succinctly outlined the Yalta agreements (February 1945) while a child choir sang its praises to the 'the Red Army and the Glorious Fighting Forces of the United Nations'. Broadcasts of the successes of Stalin and the Red Army on the Eastern Front in the latter part of the film did not anticipate in any way the breakdown of trust between the Allies, which was already a feature of the relationship between the Big Three, Roosevelt, Stalin and Churchill, well before the final storming of Berlin. However, it is probable that for most people in Britain the domestic economy, society and dominant political ethic were more important than the actual structure and organisation of a post-war Europe.

This concern for the post-war social and economic structure was referred to very early in Forster's commentary, as Tim's 'comfortable' birth and situation were contrasted not just with similar children in wartime Holland and Poland but also with those in the 'slums of Glasgow and Liverpool'. Unlike some of the earlier CFU productions, which tended to emphasise, if not the 'classless' nature of the home front then at least an easy relationship of mutual respect between the classes, *A Diary for Timothy* did illustrate class divisions and distinctions with the strong implications that, without a common enemy, these may return to their pre-war state.

This concern was articulated by Goronwy, the Welsh miner and obvious representative of organised labour. In the only 'dream sequence' in the film, his younger self wandered the mountains above a pit village, contemplating a former peace in 1918 which was followed by depression, unemployment and another world war. It raised the obvious question, 'must this happen again?' There was an implied expectation that it must not and that workers such as Goronwy were entitled to better and more secure working conditions and improved welfare services. This perspective was voiced in the next sequence by the contemporary Goronwy outlining to his wife a catalogue of achievements that had been made in the coal industry since the war began – 'an ambulance service, hospitals, canteens and pithead baths, so nothing can stop us after this war!' However, it would seem that mere social and economic improvements after the war would be deemed inadequate if they were not matched by political and ethical considerations.

There was a significant emphasis on the return to political freedom and liberty which peace would bring, but this in turn meant obligations and responsibilities. The narrator intoned somewhat sombrely, 'Part of your bother, Tim, will be growing up free'. It was the dangers of that particular freedom which seemed to exercise Jennings and Forster. Life would continue to be dangerous and the film did emphasise that peace would not mean an end to industrial accidents and the like. However, it would also mean that that eventually Tim, and by implication everybody else, would soon have 'the right to choose, the right to criticise and the right to grumble'. So peace brought uncertainties and dangers which ironically contrasted with the wartime experience of regulations and direction in all areas of life. The ethical and moralistic dimensions of the film were emphasised in an almost plaintive plea to Tim at the very end: 'What are you going to say about it, what are you going to do about it?' Tim is presented with a dramatic choice: 'Are you going to have greed for money and power as they have done in the past ousting decency from the world? Or are you going to make the world a different place, you and the other babies?'

A Diary for Timothy was an important CFU film as it represented a nation on the cusp of change. It was an effective exposition of the concerns of the time; as the war was ending, there was a need to reflect, take stock and ponder as to what would be the shape of the post-war world. Although, along with Goronwy, Jennings and Forster were concerned about the political and social and economic structures, at the end they seemed more worried about the ethical and moral behaviour of the post-war generation. Their tragedy, of course, was that their film was exhibited when that post-war world was a reality. Britain in the late 1940s and 1950s was a mere shadow of what they had hoped for in the film. This was doubly tragic as the other British film of note being premiered that week in November 1945 was, unfortunately for Jennings and the CFU, the Oscar-nominated *Brief Encounter*.

Between the exhibition of *Builders* and *A Diary for Timothy*, the CFU produced an increasing number of films that considered the shape of the post-war world. Most of these lacked the introspection and thoughtfulness of *A Diary for Timothy* and were much more direct in their endorsement of the potential opportunities that peace might provide. So, for example, *Children's Charter* (1945), was a straightforward information explanation of government education policy and the implications of the 1944 Butler Education Act. This, according to the film, would 'give all our children an equal and fair start in life, and one of its most important sections gives every child the right to free secondary education' (TNA: INF 6/363). It would be provided in a new selective system in which children would be chosen at the age of eleven to attend, usually, a secondary modern school which would lead to employment and apprenticeships or, for the more academic child, a grammar school.

Sisal (1945), on the other hand, was essentially a film which harked back to the EMBFU roots, as it reviewed the growing and processing of the cactus-like plant in the East African colony of Tanganyika (Tanzania). It explained the importance of sisal to rope production, which in turn supported the war effort. Although in one sense this film could easily be situated in the war effort category of film, as it clearly demonstrated the efforts being made in one of Britain's colonies, it however concluded with a short section which looked forward to the 'increasing prosperity which peace will bring' when we can all look forward to sisal being used, not for towing or mooring ropes but 'sacks, string, doormats, glamorous summer hats and even the dartboard in the local pub'.

By 1945, and the general eager expectation of imminent peace, some CFU films became almost excessively optimistic. *Transatlantic Airport*, for example, has a feel-good storyline about a British Overseas Airways Corporation (BOAC) flight to and from Canada bringing essential medication for the sick son of a very British stiff-upper-lipped Mr Brown. The film followed the flight crew in their briefing and eventually their safe return to Prestwick with the necessary drugs. By using this life-saving journey as an exemplar, the narrator went on to argue that 'flying will be the biggest factor in stopping future wars'. So increasing transcontinental and, presumably, trans-European flights would enable the peoples of the world to get to know one another and, by doing so, reduce the need, or at least desire, to resort to war. The irony that mankind's hope for the future rested on aviation at a time in history when war had been mainly prosecuted by air attack, as in the Blitz or Hiroshima, seemed to have been lost on the film's director, Michael Gordon.

Miscellaneous

It was hardly surprising that most of the films produced by the CFU between 1940 and 1945 were dominated by the impact of the Second World War. However, despite this, there was at least one film which defied obvious classification. *Myra Hess* was released to the non-theatrical circuit in the summer of 1945. The famous classical pianist was responsible, with Sir Alan Clark, for starting a series of popular lunchtime concerts at the National Gallery that continued throughout the war. As mentioned, Dame Myra had featured in Jennings' films *Listen to Britain* and *A Diary for Timothy*, in both of which there were short clips of her playing Mozart at one of the National Gallery concerts. The rushes which eventually became this new short film featured Beethoven's 'Appassionata', Sonata in F Minor, Op. 57, movement 1, and must have lain dormant in the CFU archive for a few years until, in 1945, film editor John Trumper re-edited the footage to show the entire performance. The film was essentially an edit of four camera angles of Dame Myra playing, without commentary or introduction, and has some of the hallmarks of an early music video. It appears that the film did not have commercial exhibition but was made available to the non-theatrical circuit. It is therefore perhaps best regarded as something of a personal tribute by Trumper to a magnificent pianist who helped to raise the profile of classical music in Britain during the Second World War.

James Chapman concluded his *The British at War* with: 'The images of the British at war presented through the cinema were powerful and dramatic means of constructing the people as united in their common struggle, but in the last analysis those images were perhaps just a heightened version of reality' (Chapman, 1998, p. 254). A review of all the CFU films produced during wartime certainly corresponds with the main tenor of Chapman's conclusion; however, it would also suggest there was a much more complex filmic response to both the conflict and to the development of a commonly accepted national identity. When the range of CFU short productions are considered, it is possible to identify an assortment of themes within that all-encompassing concept of 'national sprit', but it is also evident that these themes were fluid and changed over time to reflect alterations in policies, perceptions and anxieties.

The films being produced by the CFU when the war ended in the summer of 1945 were substantially different from those when the unit was created in 1940. Gone were the blunt anti-German messages and appeal to endurance in the face of adversity, to be replaced by those which looked forward to the post-war world with more or less optimism. A major factor in the importance of the CFU, both at the time and retrospectively, was that through its films it is possible to discern not only the changing priorities of the government, but also the shifting concerns and anxieties of the general population. Thus, the CFU, with its cinema and non-theatrical audience of millions, provided an important confirmation of the policies and attitudes of the time. It was a constant monitor and reflector in a time of immense challenge and change and its films revealed a transformation in the UK.

One of the principal features inherited by the CFU from its predecessors was that many of its productions appeared to be authentic representations of a real situation. Certainly, the unit often went to some lengths to film people in their natural job roles or environment. Sometimes this was enhanced by a respected narrator to confer a degree of authority or even honesty in the productions. This ranged from famous actors such as Laurence Olivier in *Words for Battle* or, as has been seen, Michael Redgrave in *A Diary for Timothy*. Sometimes the apparent authenticity of a film was boosted by a commentary from one of the participants as, for example, a wing commander in *The Tale of Two Cities* or the ordinariness of residents of Cwmgiedd, a Welsh mining village, in Jennings' *The Silent Village* representing the victims of Lidice. This desire for authenticity was not only apparent in the choice of performers but often also in the actual shooting of the films. Locations were chosen to be as realistic as possible and, in wartime, these had additional perils. While shooting the convoy scenes in Jackson's *Western Approaches*, three merchant ships were torpedoed and sunk. If a film required shots of the enemy, it was increasingly likely that the unit would use captured or acquired footage as in *Ferry Pilot*.

A review of the complete canon of the wartime productions of the CFU demonstrates that its films reflected something of the national mood as well as the government's priorities at the time – and as such it is an important, if neglected, aspect of wartime history. Whether this apparent congruence of the productions of the government's principal film mouthpiece and the population at large would survive the entirely different world after 1945 will be examined in the next chapter.

Notes

1. For example, *Kinematograph Weekly* of 14 January 1943 announced the release in its 'New films at a glance' section of: *BBC Brains Trust* – novelty featurette, highly entertaining record of the BBC's most popular feature; *Lenin in October* – brilliant reconstruction of the ten days that shook the world; *Casablanca* – spectacular, breathtaking and intriguing romantic melodrama with colourful background. Story exciting and appealing, characterisation brilliant, thrills big; and *Old Mother Riley, Detective* – fruity, good-humoured low-life comedy with a black market background (p. 21).
2. Lavender refers here to a positive copy of a film printed on lavender-coloured stock, from which duplicate negatives can be made.
3. See, for example, Welch (1999).
4. See Calder (1992) or, for an individual city example of Southampton, Brode (1977).
5. Ack is early radio phonetic for 'a', hence anti-aircraft was A-A or Ack-Ack. The German word Flak, itself an abbreviation of the word *Fliegerabwehrkanonen* (anti-aircraft artillery), was increasingly used, especially by the USAAF's Eighth Air Force from 1942 onwards.
6. In the dedication for *Target for Tonight*, the word Strength has the S both capitalised and emboldened.
7. For more detail of the raid see Ducellier (2010).
8. The CFU did not produce many films on the conflict in the Far East; *Jungle Mariners* (1945) was one of the few exceptions.
9. Rolf Liebermann (1910–99) was a Jewish musician who worked in pre-war Budapest and Vienna. One feature of his music was to incorporate jazz themes into more classical forms.
10. See Bierman and Smith (2003) for a full discussion of this regional conflict.
11. Popularly known as 'Ancient and Tattered Airmen'.
12. There is an irony here which would have probably not been lost on the contemporary audience. Amy Johnson had also been a member of the ATA and had died the year before when the plane she was ferrying crashed into the Thames estuary.
13. Diana Pine was Jennings' production assistant on this film.

6

The Crown Film Unit's post-war productions, 1946–52

The end of the Second World War removed a key focus for both government policy and, by implication, for CFU productions. The primary emphasis was no longer the winning of the war but rather addressing the multiplicity of problems which peace had brought. Although the vast majority of the CFU's films (70 per cent) were produced after the end of the war, these have tended to be dismissed by film historians and commentators. Some reviews of post-war British films have given the CFU short shrift; for example, Neil Rattigan wrote in 2001 that: 'Before it [the CFU] went, it must be noted, it did make a considerable number of post-war films; standard histories of either the British cinema or documentary film fail to note a single one as being of any real significance' (Rattigan, 2001, p. 252). Such dismissive comments fail to recognise the range, variety and importance of CFU productions up until its eventual closure in the spring of 1952. The diversity of the topics prepared for screening by the CFU in the immediate post-war years, addressing the needs of an assortment of sponsors for differing purposes and audiences, demonstrated that, post-war, the unit had increasingly become a multifunctional film production facility rather than, as often described, a documentary company.

VE (Victory in Europe) Day (8 May 1945) had been followed more quickly than anticipated by VJ (Victory in Japan) Day (15 August) and between these two events Britain had rejected its wartime leader, Winston Churchill, and elected, by landslide, Clement Attlee's Labour administration. The end of six years of a conflict which had mobilised Britons across all social classes and regions was both anti-climactic and confusing. At all levels of society there was the obvious question 'and now what?' Although historians have disagreed as to the extent of the overall change that had occurred between 1939 and 1945,[1] it was undeniable that pre-war organisations and structures had changed to accommodate wartime demands; it was, however, unclear whether returning to an antebellum status would suffice in the political, social and economic circumstances that existed both nationally and internationally after 1945.

This confusion extended to the CFU as, during the summer of 1945, it was uncertain to those in the unit whether it would continue to exist. According to Robert Fraser, the director general of the COI, in his first annual report, '[the CFU's] internal self-confidence was shaken by the prolonged uncertainty about its future' (TNA: INF 12/1584). Had they but known, the post-war prospects for the unit had already been the subject of speculation. Responding to the Barlow Report on the future of the MoI[2] (April 1944), the minister of information, Brendan Bracken, was reported as saying,

> it was [his] view that the Ministry of Information should disappear immediately on the termination of hostilities with Germany: that the publicity activities undertaken by the MoI on behalf of other Government Departments should revert to those Departments... We strongly recommend that certain of the activities and techniques which have developed for war needs should be permanently retained even if their scale has to be somewhat reduced... The Films Division is concerned both with production and with distribution... On the assumption that the flow of Government commissions to private production companies for documentary films is sufficiently steady to keep those companies in efficient production, *it may not be strictly necessary for the Government to maintain its own production unit in peacetime*, but there are obvious advantages in so doing. It would be helpful to have some organisation capable of securing effective distribution. (TNA: INF 1/941, p. 2; my italics)

The election of a Labour government in 1945 did not minimise the debate about the future of either the government information services or the continued existence of the CFU. Tom Wildy (1986) and Mariel Grant (1999) have both described the somewhat tortuous twists and turns as the government grappled firstly with the information demands of a wartime economy and then with the equally difficult post-war problems of, especially, austerity and the growing threat from the Soviet Union. There was also a widespread conceptual concern about government control of the distribution of information which was neatly encapsulated by Herbert Morrison, the new lord president of the council, who wrote in September 1945:

> The machinery of publicity which was suitable for war is, however, in a variety of ways, unsuitable for peace. In war, issues are simplified, controversy is in the background and even undisguised Government propaganda is recognized to have its place. In peace the task of a Government publicity service is more difficult and delicate, and in the domestic field its primary function must be to convey to the public the facts, pleasant or unpleasant, which are necessary for the understanding of 'operative' Government policy. (TNA: CAB 78/37)

In essence this highlighted the conundrum which has faced democratic governments since the development of the mass media and a literate electorate, which is 'when does the provision of information by the government become partisan propaganda?' This debate continues to the present day with discussions of what is often euphemistically known as 'information management'.[3] However, in the context of 1945, it was decided that the wartime success of the MoI in coordinating government information should continue, if in a reduced and truncated fashion. So one of the principles agreed by the Cabinet was that,

> There should be machinery for the co-ordination of both overseas and home publicity, so that the different Departments concerned with overseas publicity present a 'common line', which where necessary, is related to home publicity, and so that, as far as possible, publicity at home is consistent and overlapping and conflicts are avoided. (TNA: CAB 134/306)

As Bracken had earlier surmised, the MoI was indeed disbanded and its role effectively downgraded to a non-ministerial department, akin to that of the Stationery Office. The new organisation, which commenced operation in April 1946, was the COI and, now without a minister, came under the purview of the lord president of the council, who at that time was Morrison. Thus, as part of this arrangement, the CFU continued as the government's own film production facility, although essentially now producing films for departmental sponsors rather than on its own initiative. In particular, it had to carry out one of the principal functions of the new COI 'to maintain liaison with all departments on their publicity requirements and to keep them apprised of new developments in publicity techniques' (Grant, 1999, p. 63).

Although this new arrangement introduced some constraints, which are outlined more fully below, the CFU's staff, as ever, interpreted their role fairly liberally. They were, after all, the government's experts in the cinematic field and, despite subsequent dismissive comments such as that of Rattigan given above, were able to use their technical skills to produce films which bear sound comparison with those more famous ones produced during wartime. The award of an Oscar in 1950 for *Daybreak in Udi* was some tangible evidence that the CFU did, indeed, produce films of 'real significance' in the post-war years.

Themes in post-war films

As in the previous chapter, the categorisation of the films produced by the CFU clarified, illustrated and tracked changes in those issues which were of contemporary concern both for the government and to a greater or lesser extent the civilian population. Victory in 1945 had created a much more diverse national and international environment than that of wartime, priorities shifted and developed according to a range of stimuli. Productions tended to reflect changing perspectives, although the delay between pitch and exhibition meant that the immediate publicity needs of government were met by cinema 'flashes' or the more traditional poster or newspaper advertisements, rather than shorts or longer films. The requirement for the CFU to pitch for and produce films acceptable to particular government departments also contributed to delays and confusion, as was early noted by *Kinematograph Weekly*:

> The COI is more in the nature of an agency. The COI does not, in the main, originate film ideas itself; it passes on the desires of other Government departments and arranges for the production of pictures rather as a broker.
>
> This inevitably means delay. If the Ministry of Health wants a picture about diphtheria, it follows that there need to be consultations not only between the COI and the producer, but also with the COI back

to the Ministry of Health. The job becomes a triangle not a straight line. This is unavoidable, and it means that the pictures take longer in the planning stages. (*Kinematograph Weekly*, 9 October 1947)

Despite these difficulties, many of these films not only reflected the important issues of the day but some were of exceptional quality and became archetypes for later public information and similar films.

As with the EMB, GPO and earlier Crown productions previously discussed, a particular film might reasonably be allocated to more than one theme or category. However, the principal criterion for assignment has been a judgement as to the key or primary focus of the film. Sometimes, even though the film is extant and the departmental sponsor known, its allocation to a category is difficult especially when there is no documentary evidence explaining either the purpose behind the film or the nature and response of any audience. An example of this would be Jack Holmes' 1949 film *The People at Number 19*. This twenty-five-minute film was longer than a normal cinema short but, unusually for CFU non-feature films, was classified by the BBFC as certificate A [Adult] and thus deemed unsuitable for children unless accompanied by an adult.

The People at Number 19 was a melodrama sponsored by the Ministry of Health. The topic of the film was not evident from its title and neither did the first few minutes provide any enlightenment, as they merely showed a conversation over the kitchen table between Ken (Desmond Carrington) and his mother-in-law (Margery Fleeson) in which eventually his wife's pregnancy was revealed. His wife Joan (Tilsa Page) then entered the room in an obvious state of high anxiety having just returned from a visit to the doctor. On the mother-in-law withdrawing, there followed a scene of confrontation and recrimination as Joan revealed that she had been diagnosed with syphilis. There was an initial assumption that her husband had been guilty of infecting her, although this was contradicted by his announcement that he had been tested on leaving the army. The unstated implication of this, of course, was that he must have believed that he had at some point exposed himself to potential infection. Subsequently Joan confessed that, in Ken's absence during the war, she had had a one-night stand with somebody who, she now appreciated, must have been suffering from syphilis. The consequent heated discussion revealed popular concerns about the health of the foetus, but Joan had been reassured that, with treatment, all would be well. The final shot of Ken leaving the house to seek new accommodation initially in high dudgeon was tempered by him relenting and encouraging Joan to accompany him. This somewhat anti-climactic conclusion does not accord with the dramatic warnings about the dangers of venereal disease which had been a major feature of the wartime and immediate post-war years. Here was a film which did not moralise about the disease and was not a warning about syphilis and its potential dreadful side effects. It was instead a rather sympathetic and empathetic observation of a domestic situation which must have faced a number of the parents of the baby-boomer generation. Was this a film for general public information or for particular audiences such as medical and social workers? Although ascription to one or other of the categories is problematic on current evidence, on balance it would probably be best to situate it within the public information category for general public education.

The following categorisations have therefore been based upon what evidence is available although this, in most cases, is inadequate for more than a reasonable heuristic allocation. However, there were a small number of films produced by the CFU in the post-war years which deliberately addressed multiple topics. The CFU contributed to two cinemagazines,[4] which were short ten- or fifteen-minute length films containing different items of interest for either a specialist or general audience. The unit produced the first half-dozen *Mining Reviews* (1947–48), which were intended for colliery and mining community audiences explaining issues and developments around such themes as nationalisation, mechanisation and safety. The other cinemagazine series produced by the CFU was *This Is Britain*, which had been produced originally by Merlin Films at the request of the Board of Trade and intended principally for overseas distribution. Merlin produced thirty-six of these magazine shows from 1946 but was unable to continue after 1949, so the final fifteen were produced by the CFU (the series being finally discontinued by the new Conservative government in 1952). The CFU did amend the style of these short films away from random short interest items to content more akin to its tradition. Most of the CFU's *This Is Britain* films addressed a particular theme; for example, *This Is Britain* number 43 is sub-headed *Health* (1950) and contained brief items on cold and influenza research, syringe manufacture and artificial limbs.

While the vast majority of the CFU and its predecessors' productions tended to focus on one major topic, there were of course often minor sub-themes evident as well. The themes outlined below arise from both a review of the films themselves and an appreciation of the context in which they were produced.

1. *Financial problems*: Unfortunately, although one of the Big Three victorious nations, the economic cost of the Second World War to Britain was enormous.[5] In essence the government was faced by a series of severe economic and financial issues associated with rebuilding exports on the basis of often painfully decrepit and outdated industries, a series of foreign exchange crises and, to cap it all, one of the worst winters in living memory in 1947. For the general public the fruits of victory were continued rationing, shortages and exhortations to work harder to not only improve the balance of payments but also because 'Extra effort now means better living sooner' (Crofts, 1989, p. 153).
2. *Unfinished business*: The victory in Europe in May of 1945 did not, of course, end British concern or involvement with Germany. There were many practical issues encompassing the Allied occupation of Germany. Britain had become responsible for all aspects of administration in north-west Germany, including such major cities as Hamburg, Cologne and Dusseldorf. Not only was this a significant and continuing drain on resources but it also raised ethical questions about the treatment of a defeated enemy.
3. *New Jerusalem*:[6] From quite early on during the Second World War the coalition government, and especially its Labour Party component, was concerned with the potential social, political and economic character of the post-war world. As has been seen, several CFU films had already been released envisaging a post-war world, including *Builders* and *Transatlantic Airport*. Clement Attlee's landslide victory at the general election of 1945 was, in no short measure, a result of the electorate demanding that wartime sacrifices should be repaid by significant improvements in living and working conditions. Accommodating these raised expectations in the face of severe financial constraints was a feature of a number of CFU films.

4. *Technological change*: The wartime years had seen dramatic advances in science, engineering and medicine, all of which had contributed to the defeat of the Axis powers. Such developments would be applied rapidly to the peacetime world, resulting in changes in both technologies and the consequent employment opportunities.
5. *Social change*: Almost as obvious as, and probably more profound than, the technological changes were those wrought at a societal level. From the basic demographics of the nation to the expectations of the different social classes, the war had a significant impact. Even at a rudimentary nutritional level the war had been a major influence; according to Harold Smith (1996, p. 7), 'especially for the lower income groups the wartime diet was superior to that before 1939 and contributed to the improved health of the population after 1942. People ate more vegetables, less sugar and fatty meat and ate dark bread from which less of the vitamin content had been removed by milling'. Similar improvements were also noted by Smith in such areas as health, especially maternal and infant health, education and social welfare.
6. *Colonies*: At the end of the Second World War Britain still remained a major colonial power. Defeats by Japan in the Far East, including the fall of Singapore in February 1942 and the later invasion of Burma, may have dented the myth of imperial invincibility and subsequently weakened any desire to remain in control of the Indian subcontinent, but this still left Britain with a large number of sub-Saharan African colonies as well as those in the West Indies, Southeast Asia and Polynesia. These colonies also retained an important role in providing Britain with raw materials for various industrial processes and CFU films reflected the approach taken by the EMBFU.[7]
7. *Red menace*: The comradeship of the wartime allies, Britain, the USA and USSR, did not long survive VE Day, as the division and occupation of Germany revived the old hostilities between what was essentially Western capitalism and Soviet communism. Churchill's 'Iron Curtain' speech was made at Westminster College, Fulton, Missouri in March 1946 and eloquently described the contemporary situation, one which was to pertain for nearly the next half century. By 1951 a new Cold War had already created several potential flashpoints such as the Berlin Blockade (1948–49), the Malayan Emergency (1948–60) and the Korean War (1950–53), any

one of which could have easily morphed into a more general international conflict.
8. *Public education and information*: Given the many problems which the country faced in the immediate post-war years, the government used the opportunity of the continuing agreement with the CEA to produce films which addressed a variety of issues and often reflected earlier productions, such as the regular seasonal concerns of *Christmas Is Coming* (1951), a short animated film for the GPO reminding people to post early for Christmas. Others extolled the beauties of Britain, like *Rhondda and Wye* (1947), which looked at the contrasting landscapes along the two rivers, for national or international audiences.
9. *Specialist audiences*: As the CFU was recognised as the government's principal filmmaking facility, it was hardly surprising that it was commissioned to produce films which were needed by individual government departments. This was particularly the case with training or recruitment films, often with security aspects, such as *Fire's the Enemy* (1951), which encouraged people to join the Auxiliary Fire Service (AFS). Other films were designed and created for discrete audiences such as the farming industry, for which the film *Breeding for Milk* (1947) was conceived. As the title suggested, this dealt with issues specific to those farmers managing dairy herds.

Despite the economic difficulties and the constraints of sponsors' often conflicting demands, the CFU continued to produce films which often interpreted the original briefs in a creative and thoughtful manner. These eventually became exemplars for short films and, especially, public information films in the 1950s and beyond.

Financial problems

Although the CFU produced many films which addressed a variety of topics in the post-war period, the context which almost always underpinned them, and which frequently surfaced, was the parlous state of the British economy. Although these issues relating to austerity regularly appeared in many films there were only a few – about 4 per cent of the output – which directly addressed the economic and financial crises. Some of these films lauded the export achievements of particular industries which, in turn, would improve the nation's balance of payments. The 1951 short *Over to You*, for example, was sponsored by the Economic Information Unit (EIU) and described how British hosiery manufacturers were introducing new technologies, principally from the United States, to improve productivity. Other films in this category were more obviously targeted at improving the nation's understanding of the financial problems. The title of the 1949 short *Dollars and Sense*, also sponsored by the EIU, was self-explanatory and was a review of the balance of payments crisis and the subsequent need to devalue the pound against the dollar in September 1949.

At a more basic level, *Pop Goes the Weasel* (1948) was a slightly tongue-in-cheek explanation of how income tax was spent that was introduced on screen with the unsettling quotation from Tacitus: 'Britons are a people who cheerfully comply with taxation.'[8] The short ten-minute film, sponsored by the Treasury, was a conversation between a Scottish park keeper and a curmudgeonly individual who complained about the level of income tax. Taking him to task, the park keeper explained with both diagrams and the use of coins how the government spent the money. The film was an important reminder to the audience that, although the war had been over for a number of years, the country was still paying for it. According to the park keeper, of every £1 raised in income tax, 9s (45p) went to pay off war debts. The war had been very expensive and the example of one artillery shell costing £2 10s was given, with the overall cost of the war estimated at £162 per second. Despite this debt burden, some of the income tax revenue (7s 9d or about 38p) was allocated to post-war reconstruction of homes, schools, hospitals and many other areas, including 2s 4d (12p) which subsidised food prices. Although the viewer was certainly subjected to a welter of financial statistics in a very short span of time, the key message was that the government's social welfare projects were being introduced, but at a restricted pace as Britain's war debt still accounted for a significant proportion of the government's spending.

The same year the CFU produced a feature-length film on a similar topic called *A Yank Comes Back*. The Yank in question was Burgess Meredith, perhaps better known to later British television audiences as the Penguin in the 1960s series *Batman* (Twentieth

Century Fox, 1966–68). The 'Comes Back' aspect referred to the fact that Meredith had previously made, and starred in, the wartime film *Welcome to Britain* (1943). William Crofts (1989, p. 60) believed that this connection would mean that 'the British public would be deceived into thinking that the film [*A Yank Comes Back*] was made for audiences in the US'. Nonetheless, this is probably unlikely as the original *Welcome to Britain* was made for, and seen almost exclusively by, US military personnel deployed to the UK. However, Meredith did provide an entertaining vehicle by which the government could explain its achievements in the context of severe financial constraints. As the title indicated, the film purports to be the story of a GI returning to, and travelling around, Britain and discovering what had happened since the end of the war. Using stock footage from earlier CFU productions (TNA: INF 6/406) such as *Listen to Britain* and *A Diary for Timothy*, the impression of a traveller visiting all parts of Britain was created by the artifice of a breathless couple of cameramen who regularly discussed on screen where they either were supposed to be or where they were off to imminently. The message of the film was conveyed by informal interviews between Meredith and assorted representatives of various sections of British society – miners, steelworkers, housewives, farmers and so forth. Unfortunately, according to Crofts, 'the real people were given lines to recite and became embarrassingly artificial in doing so' (Crofts, 1989, p. 61). The film did attempt to address the concerns about rationing and other privations as well as to emphasise those post-war successes in science and engineering, such as the ultimately ill-fated Brabazon aircraft or atomic fission. However, when discussing less obviously filmic achievements like improvements in coal and steel production, the inclusion of the dry statistics did not make especially riveting viewing. Meredith's concluding statement to camera sums up the intentions of the EIU-sponsored film:

> Well, this is very difficult, because the way I see it, you've had a bad war, a total war, which has cost you so much in blood and pounds that you should have collapsed afterwards, but you haven't. It hasn't even got you down or hasn't got you confused. It's got a lot of other people down and confused, but it certainly hasn't got you, and that's fooled the experts. And I get the impression that maybe you'll never be as rich as you were, I don't know, but what you have is going to be

enjoyed by more people than it used to, and to me, that's a brave new world, I don't know anybody else that is doing it as well. That's not the kind of thing you can put down on film. In the first place, you see, so few people would believe you and none of the British would, not even if the script was written by Shakespeare and polished up by Walt Whitman, because it doesn't make sense that this old lion should have gotten out of his sick bed, but he has, whether you know it or not, I could hear him all the time I was walking round Britain, I could hear him stretching and practicing his vocal chords, and licking his wounds and any minute now the world is going to hear him get up on his haunches and roar like hell and rush straight at the camera. (TNA: INF 6/400)

Meredith's final observation following his frenetic screen journey around post-war Britain might have been well-intentioned but it does not appear to have been very successful. Writing to the director general of the COI in 1949 about the in-house production of feature films, Ronald Tritton, latterly publicity officer at the War Office but at that time head of the COI Films Division, commented that: 'The[ir] record is simply ghastly – false and feeble and fumbling start after start, wasted money, strained tempers, horribly wasted effort and talent, and on a few films that have been completed, *Cumberland* and *Yank* total distribution flops' (TNA: INF 12/542). Although the state of the post-war British economy was the major determinant of policy, convincing the public through the cinema screen that austerity and deprivation had to continue well into peacetime proved to be a difficult objective to achieve, despite the obvious talents of the filmmakers of the CFU.

Unfinished business

Another theme which continued throughout the immediate post-war years was the future of Germany. As soon as the war in Europe had ended, the CFU dispatched a film crew along with director, Humphrey Jennings, to make a film about conditions in Germany under occupation. *A Defeated People* (1946) was one of Jennings' last films for the CFU (Figure 6.1). It was a thoughtful and reflective production which directly addressed many of the emotions surrounding the defeat of the Nazis. The film commenced with shots of devastated cities bombed into acres of ruins against which voices over are quite vengeful, declaiming that 'they' started the war so 'they' should be made to suffer and pay. The narration, by William Hartnell,[9] stated that 'a lot of Germany is dead'. Moving from the enormity of physical destruction, the film showed the effects that it had upon the people. This included the visually dramatic problems of the displaced persons (DPs) scanning often pathetic messages attached to doors and lampposts, seeking news of missing relatives. As the narrator observed, 'thirty million out of a population of nearly seventy million are seeking someone'. People were also shown existing in the cellars of bombed-out buildings but, as Hartnell explained, the people still had a will to live, and represented 'the indomitable spirit of Germany'. From this point onward the film increasingly explained to the audience that, although victorious, the Allies could not afford to 'live next door to a diseased neighbour'. This meant that the military government had a responsibility to encourage the Germans to put their own house in order. Ironically, the film went

Figure 6.1 A British soldier manhandles an elderly German in *A Defeated People* (1946)

on to identify that one of the most severe problems facing Germany in 1945–46 was caused by the Allied post-war settlement itself. The French demand for coal reparations had meant that much German coal was exported and very little was therefore available to produce steel.[10] Without steel, of course, there were extreme difficulties in any form of reconstruction. What the solution was to this was left in the air by Jennings. However, the medium of film with its widespread national exhibition did enable a complex problem to be placed within the public domain.

Probably of greater concern to a British audience than the economic travails of Germany were the condition and future behaviour of the German people. Here, too, the film seemed initially to be quite hostile to the average German citizen. In food-rationed Britain, the fact that the Germans were existing on half the calorific intake of those in the UK was no doubt seen as poetic justice. Similarly, the physical treatment of the German population by the British occupation forces was shown on screen to be quite robust. There was, for example, a scene on a railway platform where an elderly German was manhandled by British military police. Having made the point that the German population was suffering because of the war they had caused, Jennings counterpoints this with the observation that 'we cannot afford to let them stew in their own juice'. There was an almost elemental fear that a renascent Germany would mean a revived Nazi party. The film emphasised the ongoing and forceful policy of denazification. To demonstrate this point, Jennings introduced a small cameo in which an archetypal Nazi, in full leather coat, was shown being interrogated by a British army officer and curtly returned to the prison stockade. Denazification required that children were educated in a propaganda-free environment, the police acted as representatives of the population and that judges administered the law free from political pressure. Jennings made all these points in sequence both visually and through the narration. The film ended, with perhaps a nod in the direction of his *Listen to Britain*, with a group of children dancing in a circle. However, in *Listen to Britain* the children are counterpointed against shots of a British armoured convoy; in *A Defeated People* they are balanced against a group of judges, swearing to uphold justice without fear or favour. In the first instance, the future must be guaranteed by military force; in the second, it is with impartial law and order.

Overall, the film took the understandable viewpoint of many British citizens who no doubt desired retribution against Germany and yet turned it into a more thoughtful and reflective piece which argued that it was in Britain's self-interest that Germany should be rebuilt. Jennings had, in a very difficult post-war environment, demonstrated some common humanity. The film, echoing this, concluded that the real guarantee for the future was that the Germans would 'grow up sane and Christian, respecting truth and justice'.

The concern about the state and future of Germany was to continue through the rest of the decade. The trials at Nuremburg would have been a regular reminder of the horrors inflicted on the peoples of Europe by the Nazi regime. This, and the fact that Britain maintained a large occupation army in Germany, meant the unfinished business theme regularly appeared in CFU and other shorts and, as such, they are important in that they both reflected British public opinion but sought also to influence it by emphasising the need to rehabilitate Germany and the Germans; an issue which became more pressing as the putative Cold War developed in the later 1940s. Other films in the unfinished business category included *The Way from Germany* (1946) about displaced person's camps and *KRO Germany* (1948) about the problems faced by the Kreis resident officers, the Allied Control Commission's local, normally military, administrators.

Also very much in the vein of German rehabilitation was the 1948 CFU short, *Trained to Serve*. In this ten-minute CFU film, those being trained were the police. Commencing with a brief history of the police in Germany, the film made the point that they had been regarded primarily as the servants of the state. Latterly, of course, it was the Nazi state when, effectively, the police became a feared organ of the Nazi party. As had been shown to the British public in countless newspapers, newsreels and films such as *A Defeated People*, the war had left Germany in a state of total chaos. Part of the rehabilitation and reconstruction process was to implement an effective law and order regime. The responsibility for this, in the British Sector, was in the hands of the public safety officer. His role, as the film goes on to show, was to train the German police, imbuing in them the ideology that they were the servants not the masters of the people. Again reflecting some of the issues in earlier films in this category, a critical aspect of this retraining was to ensure that those with a Nazi past could not be recruited to the post-war ranks. This was especially important, as a key role of the new German police was to identify and arrest those who had quite recently committed war crimes. The film also addressed those criminal activities which would have been readily recognised in the UK as they were often features of a dislocated society and shattered economy. As in post-war Britain, German society faced concerns about the black market, juvenile delinquency and prostitution. The film determinedly pointed out that these were being tackled and, in the context of the latter transgression, women police officers had been recruited and trained for the first time and were shown in the film dealing with girls and young women on the street. Unsurprisingly, given the brief duration of the film, it tended to be both superficial, glossing over the issues quite quickly, and also perhaps a little self-congratulatory. In the British Sector, it averred, everyone is entitled to a fair hearing and trial; and it concluded, a touch sanctimoniously, 'we have given the German police a good start'. The inclusion of this CFU film amongst those given regular theatrical exhibition under the CEA agreement indicated that, even three years after the war had ended, there was sufficient concern or interest in what was happening in occupied Germany. Like the previously discussed financial problems facing the country, the impact of the recent war was an ever-present thread in British policy-making – and this was reflected in the films produced for the COI.

A new Jerusalem

The Second World War itself was also a key factor which influenced domestic politics in the immediate post-war years. The Labour Party manifesto produced for the 1945 general election was entitled *Let Us Face the Future*, but it had an even more telling subtitle: *Victory in War Must Be Followed by a Prosperous Peace*. The underlying message of the document was that the domestic post-war settlement had to be a repayment for wartime sacrifices. The Labour leader, Attlee, initially had some doubts about using the COI to extol the changes the government were making and expected to make. As Grant (1999, p. 61) has noted, he and 'his [Labour] colleagues were certainly anxious lest they open themselves to allegations of creating a state-funded mechanism for the dissemination of party political propaganda'. However, these concerns were put aside as the new government, mirroring the pre-war Conservatives, rapidly appreciated the value of film, especially in promoting both government initiatives and ideas. Sometimes, of course, the intention behind a film did not actually meet the expectation when it arrived on the cinema screen.

One of the best examples of a well-intentioned, but ultimately unfortunate, screen experience was Jennings' last production for the CFU. *The Cumberland Story* (1948) was supposed to be a sympathetic endorsement of the government's policy of nationalising the coal mining industry. The introductory credits immediately identify the goal of the film which had,

> been made with the collaboration of the United Steel Companies and the NUM [National Union of Mineworkers]. It is the story of the pioneering efforts in the reorganisation of the British Coalfields during and after the war and is played by the actual people concerned, particularly James Adam Nimmo, a Mining Engineer and Tom Stephenson, the Cumberland Miners' Trade Union Leader. (TNA: INF 6/385)

The idea underpinning the film was a comparison between the old, uncaring owners of the pits and the new collaborative regime implemented as a result of nationalisation. In order to emphasise the differences, Jennings related on screen the tragedy of the Lady Pit disaster in 1837. A shaft had been driven under the sea off the Cumbrian coast to access a particular seam. Jennings adopted an historical reconstruction approach and, as the narration somewhat pedantically went on to explain:

> His [the Pit Manager] proceedings were deprecated by everyone conversant with the collieries, and a number of pit men left the work through dread of the consequences. Warning was given of approaching danger by heavy falls of roof, accompanied by currents of salt water, but the Manager silenced all fears with asseverations [sic] of safety.

> The matters stood still until 28 July 1837, when the whole neighbourhood was appalled by the breaking in of the sea. A few pitmen escaped by groping their way through the day hole, but 36 men and

boys, with as many horses, together with expensive underground stock, were irrecoverably destroyed, the water having filled the whole of the extensive workings in a few short hours. (TNA: INF 6/385)

Although the dramatic inrush of water into the mine workings was a powerful reminder that mining was, and certainly remained, a dangerous occupation, the reason why Jennings chose to exemplify this with a more than century-old disaster is somewhat unclear. There was much more clarity in the context of the future of the industry for, as the narrator pointed out,

> During the war we carried out experiments which changed the whole atmosphere here and gave us new methods of work to meet underground conditions. In the past, the battles with coal owners tended to divide the miner from mining engineer. Our experiments have shown that the miner himself can become a modern craftsman and he must become one. (TNA: INF 6/385)

Nationalisation and the collaboration between the engineers and the pitmen would, according to the film, not only result in less fractious industrial relations, but would lead to improved output and hence better wages. Much of this would be achieved, unsurprisingly, by greater mechanisation. Thus, the latter half of the film described the cutting of a new seam, this time based on collaboration and the introduction of new machinery. Jennings makes much of the new 'Duckbill' coal cutter and the audience was made aware of the fact, as the pit engineer addressed a miner: 'Now Harrison, this cutter's going to be your toy. The main difference between this and an ordinary long wall cutter is in the haulage gear. You have two drums here, each independently driven by its own set of planetaries...' (TNA: INF 6/385).

Unfortunately, this somewhat stilted and technical dialogue, combined with the detailed description of the sinking of a new shaft, albeit in the collaborative environment of a newly nationalised industry, was not popular with audiences. *The Cumberland Story*, although reduced from five to four reels for eventual theatrical distribution, still cost £58,000, but by 1949 had only received 450 bookings with overall receipts of £1,600 (TNA: INF 6/385).

On release, though, the film received a few favourable notices – such as, for example, Dilys Powell writing in the *Sunday Times* that '[the film] does indeed give the comfortable Southerner a notion of

The CFU's post-war productions, 1946–52

the Northern miner's dangers and difficulties' (8 February 1948) – most contemporaries and subsequent reviewers have been less sympathetic. Harry Watt, also a CFU director, speaking to Elizabeth Sussex in the mid-1970s, complained:

> People were tired and just wanted to forget the war. That's why I still can't understand why in God's name they started to make – and spent a fortune on making – a film about a mining disaster, at the end of the war, when we'd had dying and killing for six years. It seems to me a madness. I've no idea why they did it, but I imagine it was one of the big coffin nails [for the CFU]. (Sussex, 1975, p. 169)

More recent biographers of Jennings have been even more critical – for example, Jackson (2004) concluded 'it was the most boring long film Jennings ever made, and by far the most flawed. [It] is best left to rest, unwatched, in the obscurity of film reference books' (Jackson, 2004, pp. 313–15).

Perhaps the film was doomed from the start. In a horrible example of life imitating art, the release date was delayed until 1948 as on 21 August 1947 the William Pit disaster occurred. A massive underground explosion in the mine near Whitehaven, Cumbria, less than ten miles from the events described by Jennings, killed 104 miners. Although undoubtedly a terrible tragedy the delay triggered a decision which fatally undermined the film. Originally Jennings had been asked by the Ministry of Fuel and Power to produce a film on the 1945 Reid Report for a limited and specialist mining audience.[11] When Hugh Gaitskell replaced Emanuel Shinwell as minister of fuel and power in October 1947, he changed the brief, requesting a film for much wider theatrical distribution about the reorganisation of the mining industry and the problems involved (TNA: INF 6/385). As most of the shooting had already been done, any changes had to be completed at the editing stage. So, in one sense, political interference was in part responsible for Jennings' last and perhaps least successful CFU film.

Despite the pressures of post-war austerity, the government still managed to commission films which both celebrated what had been achieved and looked forward to a brighter future. One of the last in this vein was the 1950 film *From the Ground Up*. This film emphasised the government's achievements by placing them in the context of the future life expectations of the children of Britain. The film commenced with some children in school discussing with their teacher what jobs they wanted to do and these, of course, reflected their perceptions of the future. The film was sponsored by the EIU, as a letter from the unit's H. I. Kinchin on 25 January 1949 to J. D. Forman of the COI Films Division explained:

> I now write formally to ask for the assistance of the COI for the production of a one-reel theatrical film on 'Capital Investment'... at a cost not exceeding £4500... The purpose of this film is to explain as simply and fully as possible the importance to British industry of the national capital investment policy... We feel that this film is of the utmost importance because of the vital necessity for the greatest possible number of people to understand the full implications of the policy and the essential part the present programme has to play in economic recovery. (TNA: INF 6/1338)

The short twelve-minute film went on to extol the successes of the government in such diverse areas as agriculture, coal, steel and engineering, and also in the construction of cities, houses, hospitals, schools and offices. All this was, as the film reminded the audience, achieved because 'we're investing one-fifth of all our resources – the equivalent of nearly one day in every working week – in the making of a new Britain for our children and ourselves. We're rebuilding, modernising, and expanding the whole vast productive machine by which we live' (TNA: INF 6/1338).

The other important messages behind the film were that these developments were an important investment for the future and that the sacrifices of post-war austerity would be reaped by future generations; as the last comment in the film pithily pointed out: 'it's worth denying ourselves now to assure for ourselves and our children a future powerful and plentiful; a country good to live in, good to work in. That's why we're building today – from the ground up' (TNA: INF 6/1338).

As other governments have discovered to their electoral cost, having worthy intentions and investing for the future does not always convince the voters. Such sentiments expressed on film did not seem to make them particularly palatable after five years of austerity for, as a review in *The Scotsman* (4 August 1950) observed, 'both of them [*From the Ground Up* and *Magic Touch*] present their subjects with the accent on the "prosperity around the corner" philosophy; neither, as they discuss progress made in this country since the end of the war, present anything new'.

Technological changes

What was new and often made good cinema-viewing in the immediate post-war years were the developments across a wide range of scientific and engineering projects. Certainly, the pressures of the Second World War had stimulated many significant technical changes, not all of which were necessarily directly military in application. Many of the CFU post-war productions included sections which applauded the introduction of new technologies. As has been previously mentioned, in *The Cumberland Story* Jennings not only addressed the economic and organisational post-war changes in the mining industries, he also presented the availability of new equipment, in that case the somewhat bizarrely named 'Duckbill' seam cutter.

However, there were a number of CFU films – about 14 per cent of the output – which concentrated upon specific improvements and their applications, and these were directed towards general rather than specialist audiences. Despite its unsympathetic review in *The Scotsman* noted above, *The Magic Touch* (1950) gave the filmmakers of the CFU an opportunity to not only explain some of the 'new science' but also enabled them to contextualise it in terms of post-war austerity and financial constraint. This short ten-minute PIF was sponsored by the Department of Scientific and Industrial Research (DSIR) which, as the name suggests, was responsible for the organisation, development and encouragement of scientific and industrial research, and the dissemination of its results. Some research organisations founded by the department had functions defined in terms of a field of science or technology, such as the Chemical Research Laboratory, the National Engineering Laboratory and the Hydraulics Research Station. *The Magic Touch*, however, was about those advances in science which were helping the balance of payments by making the best use of the natural resources of both the UK and its colonies. The film illustrated in rapid succession such novel scientific marvels as seaweed harvested to make medical gauze, swabs and toothpaste, petroleum distilled to make detergents and magnesium for the aircraft industry extracted from seawater. *The Magic Touch*, with its plethora of white coats and laboratories, certainly added to the canon of films featuring the scientist as hero. It predated the mini-boom in the genre in the early 1950s with such fiction films as *The Day the Earth Stood Still* (1951), in which Michael Rennie's alien exhibits special scientific knowledge, or, more prosaically from a British perspective, *The Man in the White Suit* (1951), where the hero, played by Alec Guinness, exploited the comedic potential as an inventor of a unique clothing fibre.

Much more visually dramatic in the immediate post-war years, of course, were the developments in aviation. On the one hand, there was the rapidly expanding commercial market which was represented by the CFU in films such as *London Airport* (1949) about the growth of Heathrow or *The Story of the Bristol Brabazon* (1951), the ultimately ill-fated giant transatlantic airliner. Perhaps more filmic, however, was the new aviation propulsion unit, the jet engine. This single technological advance generated a few CFU films, such as *Faster Than Sound* (1949) and *Eagles of the Fleet* (1951). Also in this category, the title of the 1950 CFU film *The Wonder Jet* gave a fair indication as to both the content and approach to the topic. This film was perhaps most notable in that it included the inventor of the jet engine, Frank Whittle, in an acting role. The somewhat hyperbolic tenor of the production was set at the beginning with the opening words 'a marvel of this century of marvels, with its flaming breath...'. As young children watched the sky, the narrator continued: 'the streaking silver which bespeaks tomorrow'. The film went on to present the development of the jet engine as an example of the British pioneering spirit. Whittle appeared, as his younger self, filing a patent and working in his laboratory in Lutterworth. After the war, in which jets had been involved in combat towards the end, Whittle's invention became a major research area, based primarily at the National Gas Turbine Establishment (NGTE) in Farnborough, Hampshire. The film suggested that this research was 'shattering the limits of the piston age' as there appeared substantial opportunities for the use of jet propulsion in everything from railway locomotives to naval vessels. However, most of all it was in the air that the jet was becoming preeminent. Shots of De Havilland Vampire jets streaking across the sky were cut with film of Whittle, then as an RAF air commodore, emphasising that the future lay with the further development of the jet engine. In a nod in the direction of Britain's export and balance of payments problems, the film assumed that overseas licensing and production agreements would have a significant impact. Thus, British science and engineering would help to rescue the country from austerity as it had, it was argued, during the recent war. Sadly, this optimism proved illusory, as other nations acquired the technologies independently and were able to develop their own industries.[12]

Despite this, *The Wonder Jet* reflected a contemporary national enthusiasm for aviation and the jet in particular, and even established filmmakers such as David Lean encouraged this mood with his 1952 film, *The Sound Barrier*, which also covered the development of the jet engine in a feature film approach. Aviation had become a spectator sport whether in the cinema or, as Michael Paris observed, at a display: 'In 1948, the Farnborough Air Show, the major showcase for the British aeronautical industry, was opened to the public and thousands travelled to Hampshire to enjoy the elaborate high speed flying displays and marvel at the latest developments of British aviation' (Paris, 2005, p. 66).

As far as the new technologies were concerned, the CFU was producing films which both lauded British scientific achievements and reflected those contemporary passions for science and the scientist.

Social change

Perhaps less filmic, but by no means less dramatic, were those changes which had occurred in British society since 1939. Half a century ago Arthur Marwick proposed a useful analytical framework for the examination of the social impact of war by breaking it down into four constituent parts: 'its destructive aspects, its test aspects, its participative aspects and its psychological aspects' (1974, p. 11). Historians have argued about the extent to which the Second World War changed British society, but it is undeniable that there were social changes and these were recognised by the CFU filmmakers and their sponsors in the immediate postwar years.

Although difficult to allocate to one of Marwick's categories, a post-war social phenomenon which had perhaps been unanticipated was the perceived rise in road accidents. The CFU, along with other PIF companies, produced a number of films which addressed this issue. Amongst the earliest of these was the 1946 short *It Might Be You,* the title of which emphasised the perceived seriousness of the problem. The film exhibited a typical CFU two-part structure of firstly factual presentation then illustration by dramatic reconstruction which, depending on the film, was sometimes inverted. In *It Might Be You* the audience is given the cold facts of the issue, in this case by Peter Cushing in hospital doctor role, who advised the audience that up to twenty people per night were being killed on the roads and that most of these accidents were caused by carelessness. He went on state that one out of every six people would become a casualty of some sort of road accident and encouraged the audience to follow the Highway Code. The message of the film was subsequently reinforced in the second half by a very short and somewhat ponderous drama, starring Alfie Bass, which showed the build-up to a fatal accident between a car, cyclists and pedestrians. Although the CFU produced other road safety-type films, such as *Mr Jones Takes the Air* (1946; Figure 6.2), *Worth the Risk?* (1948) and *The Golden Rule* (1950), and these were given widespread theatrical and non-theatrical distribution to schools and so forth, the actual casualties of road accidents in the immediate post-war years were less than they had been in wartime. Of course, many of these had occurred during the blackout, but in 1938, the last full year of peace, there had been 6,648 deaths on the road and some 233,000 overall casualties (Department of Transport, n.d.). Despite the somewhat cataclysmic tone of the immediate post-war CFU road safety films, the annual pre-war death total was not reached until 1960 and the overall casualty rate slightly earlier in 1954. Perhaps these films were either an over-reaction to the problem or they just reflected contemporary popular concern?

Another aspect of considerable social concern both during and immediately after the Second World War was the way children, especially those orphaned or from deprived family backgrounds, were cared for. Pre-war much of this had been undertaken by religious or voluntary organisations, but the inevitable patchwork of provision was quite unsatisfactory. Inevitably children had

Figure 6.2 An example of an early campaign against drinking and driving in *Mr Jones Takes the Air* (1946)

suffered significantly during the war with the dislocations of evacuation and other family disruptions such as the death of a parent. The disturbances of wartime prompted renewed concern about children's education and welfare, which engendered legislation such as the 1944 Butler Education Act and also the 1946 Curtis Report (*The Care of Children Committee Report*, HMSO: Cmd 6922) and the subsequent 1948 Children's Act which required local authorities to oversee the welfare of children. The importance of the CFU films in this category was that they echoed the concern of the public and government about children's welfare and also they advertised and promoted the new provisions. Much of this was, of course, inextricably linked to the changes in social welfare structures as proposed by Beveridge in 1942 and had become, as has been seen in the previous chapter, a recurrent theme in CFU and other company PIFs. The importance of children as an investment and commitment to the future, especially in wartime, could be seen in earlier CFU films such as *Children's Charter* (1945), which had outlined the changes to the educational system. However, post-war CFU films attempted to address the issue of children from both paternalistic and supportive perspectives. As far as the former was concerned, there was an early appreciation that the war might have disrupted traditional social mores leading to a rise in juvenile delinquency, which has been fully discussed by Kate Bradley (2012). The film *Children on Trial* (1946) showed how the approved school [borstal] system addressed the problem of young delinquents, turning them from crime into model citizens. Such behaviour was not, of course, limited to Britain and it was the dislocation caused by the war in Germany which was examined in the 1948 Crown film *Children of the Ruins*.

The other perspective which underpinned several CFU productions in this area were the improvements being made in the provision for deprived and orphaned children that had been highlighted in the Curtis Report. Some films, such as the short thirteen-minute *Caring for Children* (1949), which was sponsored by the Central Youth Employment Executive, were essentially exercises in careers guidance for those wishing to work with children. For those girls such as Pamela Dean, the film's lead, who had to reject both nursing and teaching as they required 'too many qualifications', nursery nursing provided an appropriate alternative occupation. This, despite the fact, as reported by the narrator, that days in the nursery 'revolve around food and lavatories'. Other films, such as *A Family Affair* (1950), made much more direct appeals to support children. This twelve-minute short commenced with shots of happy children playing in the summer countryside in, according to the narrator, 'the endless sunny afternoons'. This was quickly replaced by images of the 'bleak memories of childhood' as described by Dickens. Childhood could, the film explained, mean 'despair, abuse and abandonment'. The 1948 Children's Act had required local authorities to provide for children who were orphaned or whose parents were incapable of supporting them. The film announced that all local authorities now had a children's boarding out officer, whose responsibility was to find homes for the estimated '1000 babies' and even more youngsters. The strongly emotive message was that children needed someone to look after them and provide them with 'the simple joys of childhood'. This was represented by a brief visual reference to a Scottish couple who had fostered six children and retained strong links with them even after they had become adults. The film concluded with the impassioned plea that children 'remember the days when sunlight falls on them' – but there were still many waiting for a home.

Colonies

Although there was a Colonial Film Unit (1939–55) which worked directly for the Colonial Office, the CFU still produced films – about 11 per cent of output – about the colonies in the post-war years. In fact both units worked quite closely together, and many of the Colonial Film Unit productions were edited and completed in the CFU studios.[13] The colonies which featured most, but not exclusively, in the CFU films tended to be those in West Africa, the Caribbean and Southeast Asia rather than the Dominions, and the films, in line with its EMBFU predecessor, viewed them as sources of raw materials and markets for British goods for which, in return, the colonies benefitted by improvements in welfare provision. However, in a vigorous response to the development of the Cold War in the later 1940s, and the accepted need to fight communist infiltration and aggression, the later colonial films included combatting the perceived red menace.

Cocoa From Nigeria (1949) was one of several short films, such as the previously discussed *Sisal* or *Tea from Nyasaland* (1946), in which the titles succinctly summarised the content and were primarily designed to remind audiences of the importance of the resources of the colonies, especially at a time of financial austerity. This film also demonstrated another two of the key CFU approaches to PIFs which could be seen in many other titles across a variety of topics. Firstly, the subject is directly personalised with an individual or family representing the topic under examination and, secondly, other contemporary issues or policies are introduced as supplementary to, but supportive of, the main theme.

Cocoa From Nigeria commenced with shots of cocoa farmer Lawani and his son and another worker picking and shelling the pods to extract the beans. The rest of the process was explained, from fermentation to packing, to eventual transport to the dockside in Lagos and loading onto a freighter bound for the USA. However, in this short ten-minute film, sponsored by the Colonial Office, the benefits of cooperative farming, transportation and marketing were also encouraged, as was an appreciation, less directly, that sales from within the sterling area would benefit the balance of payments.

The second type of colonial films were those which reported on the social and economic developments that had occurred as a result of British governance. It is probably fair to say, however, that the post-war Labour government was less imperialistic but rather regarded these improvements as necessary pre-conditions for eventual independence. Perhaps the most famous of this type of film was the Oscar-winning *Daybreak at Udi*, which was also made for the Colonial Office. This forty-minute conventional drama documentary described the introduction of modern medical techniques and how these often clashed with and eventually supplanted traditional practices. The film commenced with shots of native village elders discussing something in their local language which was then swiftly contrasted with shots of two teachers, portrayed as 'modern Westernised' Nigerians, speaking in English. The focus of the film was on the building of a maternity hospital, under the direction of the local British district officer, E. R. Chadwick, who played himself in the film. Chadwick persuaded the locals to collaborate with him with the interesting encouragement: 'Don't you want your children to benefit from civilisation?' Despite some local opposition, led by a tribal elder named Eze, the maternity hospital was built with local voluntary labour and was then staffed with a British-trained midwife. The hostility of some of the local tribesmen was further shown as they attempted to intimidate the midwife, who responded somewhat vigorously by pouring boiling water over the head of a masked intruder trying to climb through a hospital window. The eventual triumph of the British 'civilising mission' was demonstrated by the successful birth of a healthy child. Subsequently this event was celebrated locally with music and dancing, and the advancement of 'civilisation' was confirmed by the village deciding to build a road which, according to the soundtrack, 'goes for who knows how far'? Thus, the primacy of the civilising mission was substantiated and the metaphorical daybreak realised.

The film was awarded the Oscar for Best Documentary Feature Film in 1950 and the British Academy Film Award the following year, and was received with very positive reviews both in Britain and overseas. The *New York Times* wrote on 2 June 1950, 'actually the people of Umanu were the first to build a maternity hospital and cast out the witch doctors. When the village of Udi decided to follow suit, the CFU organised a script and rushed out technicians from London to record the proceedings.

Unfortunately, the *New York Times* statement was factually incorrect as, like some of the films discussed in the previous chapter, *Daybreak in Udi* was another CFU film which was less than authentic. The National Archives records show that the CFU did actually provide funds for the building of a maternity hospital in the Udi district. There was an agreement, dated 16 November 1948, between the CFU and the village of Agu Obu Owa in south-east Nigeria, about 18 kilometres from Umana, of which the main clause stated: 'it has been agreed that the village of Agu Obu Owa will build a maternity home under the direction of the CFU in the period of not more than three months. The CFU will provide all the materials absolutely free and will also pay the wages of the carpenters and bricklayers employed on this work' (TNA: INF 6/403).

Certainly the villagers succeeded in acquiring a maternity hospital, the building of which was filmed for the documentary. However, almost all the dramatic scenes were conceived and produced and filmed in British studios. The National Archives records (TNA: INF 6/403) contain the employment contracts of the black actors, all recruited from London theatrical agencies. So, for example, the teachers James and Iruka were played by Edric Connor and Pauline Henriques and the doughty midwife by Doreen Renner. As far as the Oscar committee was concerned, dramatic realism had triumphed, if perhaps unknowingly, over authenticity.

There were also a number of other CFU productions that extolled the value of the relationship between the colonies and the UK. For example, *Fight for Life* (1946) was a film about improvements in cattle husbandry in the Gold Coast [Ghana] and *El Dorado* (1951) was about development in British Guiana [Guyana], which contrasted old industries, such as sugar cane, with the new bauxite mines and processing plants. CFU films often addressed several themes within the context of a particular topic, such as the British economy's need for cheap natural resources in *Cocoa from Nigeria*. These films are of historical importance as they not only revealed significant issues of great concern to the British government but they further demonstrated the change in the international climate with the development of the Cold

War. Even in films ostensibly about the colonies, and especially in Southeast Asia with titles such as *Voices of Malaya* (1948), the key message was not just about the production of materials such as rubber but also about the potential disruption caused by what were then known as communist 'bandits'.

Red menace

The comradeship of wartime allies, along with the pro-Russian sentiment of such films as *The Tale of Two Cities*, did not long survive VE Day, as the division and occupation of Germany had revived the old hostilities. As international tension intensified in the later 1940s, CFU films increasingly reflected a much more overtly anti-communist message. So, whereas in *Voices of Malaya* the predations of the communist 'bandits' were somewhat subordinated to the main theme of a confident multicultural society producing rubber for the British market, three years later *Alien Orders* was completely focussed on a full-scale terrorist insurgency, then known as the 'Malayan Emergency'. Undeniably, the title of the film clearly indicated the perspective which was taken.

The original sponsor for *Alien Orders* was the War Office, which had written to the CFU on 26 June 1950: 'It is requested that you prepare a one-reel film entitled *Operations in Malaya* to be taken from the surplus Army travelogue material filmed by the CFU' (TNA: INF 6/996). Although army sponsorship was replaced by that of the Foreign and Colonial Offices over the next few months, the intention behind the film remained: 'Communism has cut at the heart of Malaya. The mines and plantations, her very life blood, are being destroyed by a highly organised, resourceful and ruthless enemy. The film shows how alien orders are being resisted, countered and brought to nought' (TNA: INF 6/996).

Alien Orders was essentially a film created over a short period of time out of footage from a variety of sources including the Malayan Film Unit and even BBC television (TNA: INF 6/996). The film itself opened with shots of Singapore, 'the teeming crossroads of the world's trade' and obviously, from a British perspective, a key strategic outpost. More so because, in those three years, Malaya had become a 'severely troubled continent' and yet it was still the source of three-quarters of the world's rubber and one-third of its tin (TNA: INF 6/996).

Compared with its predecessor, *Voices of Malaya*, while this film still acknowledged the multi-ethnic composition of society in Malaya, it was very direct about the violence. The murder of a leading Chinese politician was the catalyst for the governor, Malcolm MacDonald, to be shown encouraging 'all the races to fight militant Communism'. The rest of the film outlined the actions taken to contain the 'infection', as defeating the communists was deemed necessary for all races in Malaya to prosper. The short sixteen-minute film moved from shots of police trying to 'sift' the innocent from the guilty, to the drilling of a volunteer 'Home Guard', to the introduction of over 50,000 British troops, including Gurkhas, who would fight the terrorists in the Malayan jungles. The film concluded with shots of captured communist bandits and the exhortation, 'This is the enemy. The men who wear the red star [are] preaching the creed of despair'.

Although conflicts in faraway places appeared on British cinema screens in the later 1940s and early 1950s, perhaps more worrying for the general civilian population was an awareness that the weaponry and delivery systems available to the principal opponents in the Cold War had become awesome. The dropping of the atomic bombs on Hiroshima on 6 August 1945 and Nagasaki three days later had killed, maimed or, perhaps most horrific of all, caused long-term sickness to almost half of each cities' inhabitants. The fear, not just of communist infiltration, but of an all-out nuclear exchange became an increasing concern amongst the British population almost up until the collapse of the Berlin Wall in 1989.[14]

This attitude was clearly manifested in the 1951 film *The Waking Point*, which was ostensibly a recruitment vehicle for the Civil Defence Corps. However, this eighteen-minute film had a bleak, pessimistic message which, along with some of the narrative and camera shots, could easily place it in the 'noir' category. The metaphorical darkness was emphasised as the film began in a cinema auditorium where a newsreel was shown featuring communist-inspired violence across the world in places as diverse as Berlin and Korea. From the very beginning of *The Waking Point*, the audience was unambiguously conditioned to accept the contention that another war was not just possible but highly likely. As Gwen

Figure 6.3 Gwen Mercer telling her husband that she expects a nuclear attack in *The Waking Point* (1951)

Mercer, the wife of the key character in the film later said, '[we] should enjoy what time we have left' (Figure 6.3).

The narrative of the film followed the slow conversion of Joe Mercer (John Slater), an ex-wartime civil defence worker who, following a domestic accident in which his children were rescued by the local civil defence volunteers, eventually re-enlisted and became a full-time trainer. The key message of the film was delivered by adopting the traditional artifice of the dream sequence. Joe, exhausted after a day's training at the Civil Defence College at Easingwold, North Yorkshire, fell asleep prior to supper. He was awakened by one of the instructors telling him to get on the bus and return to his area, as war had broken out. The chaotic situation was reinforced by a brief set of shots including a control room with multiple telephonists and a Women's Royal Voluntary Service ambulance driver. Back at his base, Joe was confronted by a large group of citizens all demanding to join the Civil Defence Corps. His colleague verbalised the principal message of the film in that he wished they 'had come when there was still time'. However, there was to be no time, as the sirens sounded, people rushed to the shelters, children were bundled from the streets into houses and the civil defence workers reached for their tin helmets. Joe, outside, looked into the distance and the screen became a gigantic flash, presaging a nuclear explosion. At this point, he is awakened from his dream by a colleague. Walking to the window and drawing back the curtains he saw that life, well, mini-golf on the lawn at Easingwold, goes on as normal. Directly to camera in the final shot he intoned: 'It hasn't happened – there's still time!'

The Waking Point was one of the bleakest films ever produced by the CFU but it is significant in that it reflected the government's concern about the international situation and consequently the need to recruit and train a large number of civilians in rescue techniques. The film was also one of the CFU's internationally recognised productions, winning the award for the 'best civil defense film' at the 1952 Cleveland Film Festival against strong US opposition which included the famous *Duck and Cover* (1951). It reflected a widespread public concern about the possibility, if not probability, of a nuclear attack and pre-empted similar public information films over the next decade or so.

Public education and information

Much easier to explain to the public than the vagaries of economics and the balance of payments – and usually more cinematically interesting – were those aspects of public policy which overtly impinged on the daily lives of British citizens or provided some diverting information or vicarious experience. As might be expected, this category included a wide variety of topics, some of which have persisted in the public information film repertoire up to the present day.

Amongst these recurring themes over the last six or seven decades has been concern about the toll taken by road traffic accidents, as has been discussed earlier with *It Might Be You*. However, other regular topics have been as diverse as Cyril Fletcher's *Postman's Nightmare* (1948), one of the Post Office's annual pleas to post early for Christmas, or various health warnings. In the latter case the CFU produced a number of films which were essentially health advisory PIFs. In 1949 *His Fighting Chance* explained in a reassuring manner what treatments were available for poliomyelitis and, in a similar fashion, one of the later productions was *Surprise Attack* (1951). This latter film was sponsored by the Ministry of Health with the obvious intention of encouraging parents to have their children vaccinated against smallpox. It was a cautionary tale of a small girl who had contracted smallpox possibly, the film implied, from a rag doll bought in a local market. As smallpox was a notifiable disease, the doctor (played by John le Mesurier) was required to advise all the local parents, prompting a rush for vaccination. The film reported that there were eleven cases of smallpox from which four children died. The initial victim, having been incarcerated in a local isolation hospital, survived but was scarred for life. The film concluded with actual shots of the dreadful disfigurement caused by the disease and emphasised that it was essential children should be vaccinated. The film's final message, with interesting prescience, was that, as international air travel increased, so would the likelihood of the spread of diseases not, or no longer, endemic to Britain.

At a far less intense end of the production spectrum were films such as *Football* (1951), a short, descriptive piece about the 1949 FA Cup Final in which Billy Wright's Wolverhampton Wanderers defeated Leicester City 3–1, and *Love of Books* (1951), which reviewed the history of printing and book production. Although some of these films in this category appear rather idiosyncratic, others were produced to meet a particular perceived need. So, *Local Newspapers* (1952) was actually sponsored by the Colonial and Foreign Offices as a means of introducing the concept of a locally based free press to those living in the colonies. The production and distribution of the *Newbury Weekly News* was the newspaper used as the exemplar in this film. The film's introduction exaggerated the isolation of Newbury, as the opening shots are of a bus which, having trundled through country lanes, eventually reached the market square in Newbury. There, within the offices of the local newspaper, the lives of the citizens were reflected on a weekly basis by reporters who had responsibility for such things as local sport, music and drama and 'news of interest to women'. The newspaper was also shown to have an important role in ensuring that justice was done, as it described fully and accurately the proceedings of the local courts. The local newspaper, then, not only reflected and reported on life in the whole district but, in doing so, it was an essential part of British democracy. A free press was, of course, an aspect of democracy that the Labour government wished to export to and instil into the colonies and *Local Newspapers* was a vehicle commissioned to that end.

Specialist audiences

Although a large proportion of the CFU's post-war output was designed for both general theatrical or non-theatrical release through the Central Film Library, a significant number of films – about 22 per cent – were produced for particular and specialist audiences. The Ministry of Fuel and Power, for example, had a regular contract with the CFU to produce some of the monthly *Mining Reviews* which dealt with developments in the industry and were designed for pit workers or those with significant knowledge of mining. The newly nationalised industries quite quickly took advantage of the opportunities offered by the CFU through the COI. In particular, the railway industry regarded the cinema as an ideal vehicle through which employment opportunities could be advertised. *The Railwaymen* (1946) approached the issue from a traditional perspective, introducing the audience through references both to the historical development of the railways and to emotional attraction of childhood when the '[locomotive] driver was the hero of our boyhood'. There then followed a comprehensive catalogue of potential job opportunities available on the railways with some indication of the wage levels which could be expected. For example, a signalman would be paid £4 10s per week for a daily eight-hour shift, with the possibility in rural areas, so the film explained, of a tied cottage and garden nearby. The number of jobs discussed and explained ranged from those on the trains – driver, fireman and guard – to those on the stations – stationmaster, booking office clerk and porter – to those in the goods yard and trackside, including platelayers and shunters. The film appeared to present a realistic impression of the jobs and did not shy away from explaining that many roles were dirty and potentially dangerous. It concluded, with an obvious reflection upon what happened during the 1930s, that the railway industry was 'hard work but steady work with a good record for employment'. However, running at some twenty-one minutes, it was obviously considered to be slightly too long for its potential audience and was re-edited and re-released a year later in a shortened fifteen-minute version under the new title, *Along the Line* (1947).

The CFU also produced films which were both more esoteric and for highly specialist audiences, either restricted by their particular role or profession or because the topic was deemed to be security sensitive. In the former category were films such as *Patent Ductus Arteriosus*, which was produced for the Ministry of Health in 1948 with the intention of advising doctors and other medical professionals about a congenital heart disorder very occasionally found in newborn babies. The following year, in a similar exercise in professional education and publicity, *Early Diagnosis of Acute Anterior Poliomyelitis* was how the Ministry of Health responded to a potential polio epidemic.

In a significantly different specialist context, the CFU also produced training films for the armed forces. *Minesweeping*, a twenty-one-minute film made for the Admiralty in 1946, presented a range of strategies available for the discovery and elimination of naval mines which, following the war's end, remained a danger to shipping. The film showed Royal Navy vessels deploying Oropesa floats to deal with horned or contact mines as well as other means for detecting and disposing of them with acoustic or magnetic triggers. The film went on to show the training of naval officers in mine detection and destruction at the Naval School of Mines, HMS Lochinvar, on the Firth of Forth, Scotland, which, according to the film, used the latest modern training aids – in this case, a slide projector. Similarly, *Aircraft Recognition* (1947), as the title suggested, was designed to train army personnel to recognise and report effectively aircraft types. The other films in this category, which are recorded in the Appendix, are as diverse and varied as are the sponsoring departments. From *Steps of the Ballet* (1948), sponsored by the British Council, to *The People's Palace* (1952), an introduction to Hampton Court Palace sponsored by the Colonial Office, were all grist to the CFU's mill.

Up until its closure in early 1952, the CFU continued to produce films of quality, as the award of the Oscar in 1950 acknowledged. The unit did, however, labour under substantial difficulties during the post-war years. Budgetary constraints restricted some cinematic opportunities and this was often made doubly problematic for the CFU as not only were film sponsors anxious to retain budgetary control but also, occasionally, creative direction as well. This sometimes manifested itself in a quite hostile approach to the filmmakers. In 1948, in a note to the COI over the transfer of books, periodicals and publications from the British Council, an unnamed British Council commentator questioned the need for film not only on a cost basis but also on a lack of editorial control:

> Once the shooting script has been agreed, a film is entirely in the hands of the technical production unit until a rough cut is produced. Alterations can then be suggested and made, but only in most cases, at considerable additional expense (and, of course, two different directors may easily make two quite different films out of the same script). The next stage is the finished product, which can only be accepted or rejected. (TNA: BW 2/381)

It is unlikely that these objections were confined to the British Council; however, despite these attitudes, the CFU produced a range of films which not only reflected the changing social, economic and international environment of the immediate post-war years but, as will be seen, became exemplars for many similar productions in the 1950s and 1960s.

Notes

1 See, for example, Marwick (1974), which argues that the war generated huge changes, whereas earlier Pelling (1970) was far less certain.
2 Sir Alan Barlow of the Treasury was the chairman of the group asked in 1944 to examine the role of the MoI as part of the overall review of the machinery of government to ensure its fitness for the post-war world. For more information see Lee (1977).
3 More recent examples of 'information management' range from Margaret Thatcher's 1985 desire to remove the 'oxygen of publicity from [IRA] terrorists' to news management during the two Iraq conflicts (Newton, 2013).
4 For a detailed discussion and explanation of cinemagazines see Crosby and Kaye (2008).

5 A good summary of the causes, consequences and events of the immediate post-war years can be found in Cairncross (1985).
6 In his speech to the 1951 Labour Party conference in Scarborough introducing the party's manifesto for the forthcoming election, Attlee concluded his résumé of the government's achievements with some lines from William Blake's 'And did those feet in ancient time', more popularly known as 'Jerusalem'. Subsequently many authors and commentators from Bogdanor (2010) to Kynaston (2007) have used the term to describe both the intentions and achievements of the postwar Labour government. The author has therefore continued the device.
7 Goldsworthy (1971) provides a comprehensive and thoughtful explanation of Britain's relationship with the colonies up until the early 1960s.
8 The original quotation can be found in Tacitus' *The Life of Agricola: With an Account of the Situation, Climate, and People of Britain* (various publishers in English since 1763).
9 William Hartnell (1908–75) was perhaps best known to British television audiences as the first *Dr Who*. However, before then he had a substantial film and later television career ranging from *Brighton Rock* (1947) to *The Army Game* (ITV, 1957–61).
10 For a discussion of the post-war European iron and steel industries see Gillingham (1991).
11 *Coal Mining: Report of the Technical Advisory Committee* (the Reid Committee; HMSO: Cmd 6610, 1945). The committee consisted of seven members, all mining engineers with experience in the management of collieries. The recommendations of the committee were divided into methods of working coal, including mechanisation, underground transport, health and safety including ventilation, lighting and power supply, shaft winding, colliery layouts, machinery maintenance, training for new entrants, education in the form of explanations by management of new methods and further education at suitable venues to offer advancement in management, and labour relations.
12 See Edgerton (1996) for a comprehensive discussion.
13 For a detailed discussion of the role and films of the Colonial Film Unit refer to Smyth (1979), (1988) and (1992).
14 For more information see Hennessy (2002) or Shaw (2001).

7

Non-theatrical exhibition and audiences

The EMBFU and its successor film units produced about 375 films over a more than twenty-year period from 1930 to 1952. There is little which could be recognised as a common theme running through these productions other than that they were released under the EMB, GPO and Crown logos. Some were designed for highly specialised and technical audiences, others for the general public. They not only differed significantly in terms of content but also in length, which ranged from five-minute shorts to, during wartime, feature-type films of over an hour. As for format, some were 16 mm, others 35 mm and still others released in both formats; some were silent, although most were not; some in colour, although most were monochrome. Some were recut into shorter films and re-released under a different title; and sometimes the same stock shots were utilised across several different films.

After more than seventy years, evaluating their audience and reception is inevitably fraught with difficulty, although diverse literature exists which supports and establishes frameworks of analysis for the understanding of how films in the past can be judged. At a basic level, films and studios are often judged on financial success; mainly whether the box-office receipts adequately cover the cost of production. The importance of the balance sheet in determining success or failure in the film world has been addressed by Mark Glancy (1992, 1995), mostly in respect of the studio system in the United States. Unfortunately, the application of the profit and loss principle to the EMBFU and its successors would be doomed to failure as the units' costs were customarily paid directly by their sponsors, which were essentially government departments and, most importantly, the films were normally distributed free to exhibitors.

Similarly, an appreciation of a contemporary audience's response to a film, especially one viewed many years ago, is complicated. In 2012 Ian Christie edited a compilation of essays attempting to unravel the complexities of the cinema audience (Christie, 2012). Unfortunately, with minor exceptions, such as the discussion of early British cinema audiences by Nicholas Hiley (2012), the focus of the many analyses tends towards the feature-length film. This in itself is problematic for a discussion of the CFU and its predecessors as most of its productions were 'shorts', with obviously less time to create an impression upon an audience.

Elsewhere, Janet Staiger has written much on the impact of film on the audience and this is most comprehensively explained in her *Media Reception Studies* (2005). Although, once again, Staiger's work does not really identify a coherent analytical framework which could be used to evaluate the myriad reception contexts of the EMB, GPO and Crown films of the 1930s and 1940s, it does recognise a set of factors which cannot be ignored; of these, power and memory are probably the most critical. Referring to the work of Lazarsfeld and Merton (1948) and later von Feilitzen (1998), Staiger noted that the influence of the media can be 'so overwhelming as both to insist on their influence but also to fascinate' (Staiger, 2005, p. 18), but all the time it is important to be reminded that 'it is not power per se that mattered, but in whose hands that power resides' (Staiger, 2005, p. 38). In the case of the EMB and its successor film units, they were essentially part of the government and answered to a particular department. It was only during the years of the Second World War that the unit operated with any real degree of autonomy in terms of initiating topics, as later, after 1945, it had to respond directly to the specific requirements of sponsoring government departments.

Inevitably, too, when addressing any historical event or issue, especially one such as a film showing where there is a possibility of it being experienced by many, then the individual as well as the collective memory must be treated cautiously. 'This is particularly important for reception researchers', Staiger writes (2005, p. 192), 'because we often come across diaries and autobiographical statements and need to be alert to how people string together personal event memories'. This ethnographical aspect requires even further vigilance as retrospection does not necessarily deliver an accurate narrative or coherent analysis.

The variety and complexity of the films produced between 1930 and 1952 make an intelligible and coherent account of reception quite difficult. It is perhaps possible to suggest that government film agencies in other countries provide a suitable comparison. At least superficially Germany's Ufa (Universum-Film Aktiengesellschaf) has similarities being, after 1937, the principal film production unit of the Nazi German state.[1] Ufa was responsible for such famous films as *Dr Mabuse* (1922 and 1933), *Die Nibelungen (The Nibelungs)* (1924), *Faust* (1926) and *Der blaue Engel (The Blue Angel)* (1930) as well as a host of 'perennial potboilers for quick consumption. In addition to this were ballroom fantasies, heavyweight Teutonic dramas and "sophisticated comedies" (German style), operettas and orgies of disaster, Marlene Dietrich and also (a little later) Kristina Söderbaum' (Kreimeier, 1999, p. 5).

However, it was not only in length of operation, nor in the breadth of productions, that the EMBFU and its successors differed from Ufa. Perhaps more importantly, they were much smaller, did not produce large-scale and large budget feature films, and nor did they become as directly subject to central control as Ufa was under Goebbels' Nazi propaganda ministry (Reichsministerium für Volksaufklärung und Propaganda, or RVMP).

Applying any specific framework of analysis to the reception of the productions of these film units is therefore fraught with difficulties for the reasons outlined above. A key distinction between the films and their audiences was that some were released onto the commercial cinema circuits and others went primarily for non-theatrical exhibition. However, there were occasions when films were distributed by both methods, although this was usually sequential in nature. Ralph Elton's CFU fifteen-minute *Workers' Weekend* (1943), for example, was introduced into the cinema circuit in October 1943 and then available for non-theatrical exhibition a month later (*Documentary News Letter*, 1944, No. 2, p. 18). Similarly, those films which had been seen by cinema audiences were later available through the Ministry (later Central Office) of Information Film Library for non-theatrical exhibition. Even this fairly elementary method of distinguishing between films and their reception on the basis of exhibition was heavily nuanced.

Non-theatrical exhibition

During the decade or so before the war the non-theatrical circuit had been developing apace and sponsors such as the GPO and Empire Marketing Board and others maintained libraries for the, usually free, distribution of normally 16 mm films to interested agencies and organisations. An early advocate and pioneer of non-theatrical distribution was John Grierson, who commented in 1936 that this type of exhibition was 'more important and more solidly founded than the ordinary cinema'. He went on: 'the church is interested. So (are) the gas, electricity, motor car, railway, tea, cocoa, soap, chemical and pill industries... from these organisations every day and week flow out to the theatres of the new: to church halls to meeting rooms, discussion clubs, school rooms and college rooms throughout the country' (*Today's Cinema*, 1936, p. 2). A feature of the inter-war years, for example, was the rise of the local film society where loaned films were shown and discussed. The Manchester and Salford Workers' Film Society activity was reported in the *Manchester Guardian*:

> Of particular interest is the announcement that several of the films made by members of the GPO Film Unit, who were previously associated with the Empire Marketing Board have been booked including *Industrial Britain* made by John Grierson and *Contact*, a film of air travel made by Paul Rotha. (*Manchester Guardian*, 11 September 1934)

In a comment about the potential for audiences, the paper went on to say, 'the opportunities in Manchester of seeing the experimental work of these young directors are very small, yet they are the only makers of films in this country who are attempting an advanced technique'.

For the purposes of this study non-theatrical exhibition describes those myriad venues in which EMB, GPO and Crown films were normally distributed free and shown to a range of people. The non-theatrical audience, according to *The Factual Film* (Arts Enquiry,

1947, p. 12), was composed 'generally of people gathered together for study or discussion, but not primarily for entertainment'. In line with the characteristics of this particular audience, the COI Film Library classified its non-theatrical lending policy in 1946 as follows: 'The Library does not lend films for showing in ordinary programmes at public cinemas; nor for any shows for which an admission fee is charged; nor for inclusion in shows of an advertising nature' (TNA: INF 12/677, Nov 1946).

The following year it categorised the types of organisation which borrowed, free of charge, from the COI Film Library (TNA: INF 12/279, 1947), providing support for the essentially non-commercial aspect of this type of exhibition (Table 7.1). This classification could be further refined in terms of the medium of exhibition, the audience and, in a limited manner, whether the showing occurred in wartime or in the periods from 1930 to 1939 and 1946 to 1952.

Table 7.1 Categories of COI Film Library borrowers, 1 September 1946 to 17 April 1947 (%)

Schools, colleges, etc.	28.8
Churches, missions	14.7
Forces, including ATC (Air Training Corps)	3.2
Central government departments	5.0
Local authorities, excluding educational	3.5
Hospitals, Red Cross	3.0
Film societies	2.6
Film companies	0.7
Factories and commercial firms	6.4
Private individuals	8.1
Social bodies, including Scouts, Guides, miners' welfare, etc.	12.8
Educational organisations, workers' educational associations, cooperative societies, literary societies	11.0

Mobile cinema vans and the 'celluloid circus'

Although some commercial companies and public utilities had developed a pre-war means of distribution of essentially public information films, it was the use of film as a political propaganda medium which was a major factor in the arrival of a new type of mobile cinema, one which was not confined to a darkened factory canteen or scout hut. Zoe Druick (2012) has offered a fuller discussion of the use of cinema vans both in the UK and overseas. As the name suggests, these were vans equipped with projection and usually sound facilities, and they could be set up almost anywhere as the power was often produced by a mobile generator. In a television and internet age, it is worthwhile considering the impact of seeing moving pictures close to home or work and, certainly, in much reduced numbers the cinema van lasted until well into the 1960s in the UK. Although a proportion of the non-theatrical exhibition of EMB, GPO and Crown films occurred in places where projection equipment already existed, some would have been shown by means of a cinema van.

As has been noted earlier, the mobile cinema van was pioneered principally by the Conservative Party, which had been anxious to exploit the opportunities film provided for political propaganda. Their value in this context was confirmed in a post-war internal party memorandum by D. Clarke (secretary to the Conservative and Unionist Film Association) on its transformation into the more directly named Film Propaganda Committee. He wrote:

> Before the war the Association operated 12 public daylight cinema vans and also made available to the constituencies public address equipment, loudspeaker vans and similar facilities. It was charged with the responsibility for producing propaganda films, many of which were made by its own unit [British Films Ltd formed in 1930]… It maintained contact with newsreels for arranging interviews for Party Leaders and similar purposes. (Conservative Party Archive, 17 October 1945)

The future prime minister, Neville Chamberlain, was obviously impressed by the use of cinema vans, confiding to his diary as early as 1931:

> It is very remarkable how they can get publicity when meetings fail. During the LCC [London County Council] elections on two nights

when large halls were booked and good speakers brought down, only 50 people turned up. On these same two nights speakers going round with the vans reckoned they addressed audiences amounting in the aggregate to over 3000 each night! (Quoted in Hollins, 1981, p. 322)

The 'roadshow' approach had also been adopted by the EMB and subsequently continued by the GPO. It is difficult to determine the size of the audience and estimates vary; so, in 1936 for example, it has been suggested that the films were seen by over half a million children and some 25,000 adults. This was, of course, far less than Grierson's contemporary annual estimate of over 4 million.[2] However, he was describing the totality of non-theatrical exhibition. Notwithstanding, when war broke out, cinema vans seemed to the MoI to be an appropriate method of exhibiting those short public information films produced by the CFU and other companies in support of the war effort (Figure 7.1). In a somewhat incestuous manner, just after the war, the CFU film *Shown by Request* (1946) described the role, purpose and function of the MoI/COI Films Division in wartime and, by implication, in the immediate post-war reconstruction drive. As the soundtrack described it, 'People had to be kept informed, many of them had to be trained quickly to do new jobs. When the scheme began there were 50 of these vans. Each of them could carry films, a screen, a projector and sometimes a portable generator. For the films had to be taken to their audiences – to wherever people happened to be gathered together in the upheaval of war' (TNA: INF 6/382, 1946).

In September 1941, the *Documentary News Letter* had colourfully described the operation as the 'celluloid circus':

> It is a business of one night stands and then on to the next village next day. Sometime it will be a 'midnight matinee' between shifts at an armaments factory; sometimes it will be a 'fit up' in a barn for a group of new agricultural workers... in the afternoons the mobile units keep engagements with Women's Institutes and Townswomen's Guilds to show films about food and wartime housewifery and in the mornings shows are given to children at schools with special films about the Empire, our Allies and life in Britain... Town social clubs, adult educational groups and church societies all have their visits from the MoI's units, see films about the war, discuss problems raised and learn how to adjust themselves to wartime life. (TNA: HO 186/1456)

Figure 7.1 An early cinema van (Southwark Local History Library and Archive/ Medical Photographic Library/Wellcome Images)

The mobile cinema vans were organised into fleets across twelve regions in the UK and the local MoI regional film officer had the responsibility of coordinating their allocation and scheduling in accordance with local needs and requests (Figure 7.2). In addition to this, the local film officer was also expected to arrange showings for specialist audiences in local cinemas, but outside normal opening hours. As the *Documentary News Letter* further explained:

> On a Sunday afternoon you may find ARP (Air Raid Precautions) workers going to the local cinema where they will see films of special interest to them; or you may find on a Wednesday morning that your local cinema has opened up with a programme of films of special interest to women, so they can learn something more of wartime housekeeping. (TNA: HO 186/1456)

The speed by which this system was implemented nationally and the size of audiences which viewed the myriad MoI-sponsored films was quite impressive.

Figure 7.2 Mobile film show car leaving London's Senate House (c. 1943)

Although it is impossible to discriminate between actual CFU films and others produced by such documentary companies as Realist or Strand in the figures in Table 7.2, a significant proportion would have been those released under the Crown logo. This assumption can be supported from the annual film release data which was published in the same cinema renter's journal, *Kinematograph Weekly*. Although by no means comprehensive or complete in its listings, it is indicative of the balance of non-theatrical production companies. For example, in 1945, according to *Kinematograph Weekly* on 10 January 1946, of the 60 films released for non-theatrical exhibition fifteen (25 per cent) were clearly identified as CFU productions. The summer of 1945 also marked the end of the war and the election of a majority Labour government. It might have been thought that, with the coming of peace and a new administration facing tough economic decisions, there would a real appetite for reducing the production or distribution of public information films. In fact, Herbert Morrison, the new lord president of the council, declared to the CEA in the autumn of 1946 that:

> [although] he appreciated the ordinary desire that the lot of propaganda would come to an end with the war, it is still necessary to disseminate information in regard of the major operation which was involved in the transition from war-time to peace-time conditions. (*Kinematograph Weekly*, 12 December 1946, p. 7)

Table 7.2 MoI film audiences, 1940–44 (adapted from *Kinematograph Weekly*, 28 December 1944, p. 29)

Details	September 1940–41	September 1943–44
Mobile vans	50	150
Number of shows	20,688	67,000
Total audience	3,130,374	11,500,000
Average audience	150	170
Shows arranged in cinemas	573	1,700
Total audience	331,557	1,000,000
Average audience	646	550
Estimated total audience	3,461,904	12,500,000

The mobile van with its projector or the utilisation of the local cinema to show non-theatrical productions were not the only ways for public information films to reach their audiences. Another form of transport which was pioneered as a mobile cinema, albeit far less successfully, was the railway train. There was certainly an initial enthusiasm, though, which was even endorsed in 1927 by Grierson, whose presence on the train was revealed by the *Manchester Guardian*:

> Kinema films were shown with perfect success yesterday on a train travelling at over 60 mph. The experiment, undertaken by the Empire Marketing Board in conjunction with the LNER (London and North Eastern Railway), demonstrated the complete practicability of the 'train kinema'... The train, a 'special' bringing members of the Imperial Agricultural Research Conference back to London on a 500 mile tour of England and Scotland, left Edinburgh at 10.35am... To enable the members to see certain technical films which could not be shown to them otherwise a guard's van at the rear of the train was fitted up as a theatre. Chairs were ranged in rows of four along one side and the films were projected on the other. In this way 40 people together saw the show in comfort, and four shows were given... The motion of the train had little or no effect on the projection, which was remarkably clear and steady. The films included specimens of rapid motion photography, in one of which, produced

by British Instructional Films, the growth of a nasturtium was shown at a speed 20,000 times greater than the actual rate of development... Major Walter Elliott, Under-Secretary for Scotland and chairman of the Films Committee of the EMB and John Grierson, film officer of the Board, travelled with the party. (*Manchester Guardian*, 24 October 1927)

Unfortunately, the experiment was not as well-received as the newspaper asserted; despite that, it was briefly revived by the LNER in June 1935 with, this time, a custom-made cinema coach on the London to Leeds mainline service. By November of that year the movie coach had travelled about 63,000 miles and received a total audience of over 16,000 people. However, the experiment was slowly phased out as passengers complained that the noise, heat and motion negatively affected their cinematic experience. Whether or not any GPOFU films were ever shown in this way is unknown.

By far the largest of non-theatrical venues were the myriad institutions and groups which had their own, normally 16 mm, projectors. On their request, films were sent to them by post, free of charge. This facility, more than almost anything else, determined the breadth of exhibition of films from the various government film units. The origin of this film lending library was one of the first innovations of the EMB which, in 1927, established the Empire Film Library, then housed in the Imperial Institute in South Kensington, London. Alongside the library was a cinema in which most of the films created by the EMBFU and later the GPOFU were shown to generally non-fee-paying audiences. The library itself continued in various iterations, ending as the Central Film Library after the Second World War. An indication of the importance of both the library and the in-house cinema was revealed as early as 1933 when Grierson mentioned in the final EMB annual report that, in the last year of operation, the number of annual film bookings had risen from 947 to 3,706, with a potential viewer increase from 300,000 to 960,000. As mentioned earlier, the cinema at the Imperial Institute had garnered an audience of 161,000, of which 67,750 were schoolchildren. This development expanded dramatically over the next decade or so. It was estimated by *Kinematograph Weekly* (28 December 1944) that the audiences for Central Film Library despatches between September 1940 and

September 1941 were 2,200,000 and that this had increased to over 7,000,000 for the year ending September 1944. Although it is unclear how such audience numbers were determined, it is clear that many people were viewing the EMB, GPO and Crown films at non-theatrical venues. Combining the three published non-theatrical exhibition methods for the latter date resulted in an audience of around 20 million which, even with probable multiple viewing, was quite substantial.

Much of the success of non-theatrical exhibition was a result of an effective storage and distribution system. It was a significant operation which required the storage, despatch and return administration of a large number of films. At a stocktaking exercise in 1946–47, for example, the library held 1,221 film titles and had despatched 81,550 prints (TNA: INF 12/279, 1947). As the years progressed, the pressure on storage and demand caused increasing concern to such an extent that, in order to prevent demand outstripping supply, senior officers in the COI's Films Division circulated the following instruction to the library and regional officers on 25 July 1949:

> It is already evident that the demands which will be made on the CFL during the coming winter will be too great to be handled and that, as last winter, a limit will have to be placed on the number of applications to borrow which can be accepted. The ceiling was fixed last year at 11,000 titles per month – with certain exceptions – all applications which are received after the limit had been reached were turned down. (TNA: INF 12/677)

Not only was there a demand for the films but they appear to have been well received, as a selection of letters of appreciation sent by a very diverse range of organisations in 1941 indicated. The Film Library had letters from, amongst others, the YMCA (Farnborough Branch), the Institution of the Rubber Industry, the Institution of Electrical Engineers, Dickie, Paterson & Riddick Bacon Curers of Ayr, the Borough of Erith, the Lincoln Cooperative Society, the Southall and District Spotters Club, the National Savings Movement, the Southwell Diocesan Association for Moral Welfare and the 2nd Battalion, Cambridgeshire and Suffolk Home Guard (TNA: INF 17/33 1941).

The value and importance of these films were summed up in a letter from the chaplain at RAF Hereford, dated 25 April 1941, in which he wrote:

> It has always been a real help to me personally to give the men something of interest on Sunday evenings as this camp is some way from the town and there are always many who cannot leave camp because of duties. With the longer evenings and putting forward the clock, I have decided to stop these evening showings during the summer, but I shall hope to start again in the autumn. (TNA: INF 17/33, 1941)

The library received a similar endorsement ten days later from Michael Sherwell (Films Organiser), Friends' Ambulance Unit, London Hospital, Whitechapel, who wrote: 'I wish, at the end of the winter season of film shows in the East End shelters given by the Friends' Ambulance Unit, to thank you very much for the assistance you have given through the loan of the films for these shows' (TNA: INF 17/33, 1941).

Other domestic non-theatrical exhibition settings

An assessment of the reception of EMB, GPO and Crown films is further complicated as there were other domestic non-theatrical exhibition settings which were of importance. Inevitably, the films produced by the two former film units were exhibited in situations which were endorsed by their respective sponsor. EMBFU productions tended to be circulated to schools and occasionally appeared at local EMB exhibitions which, according to the 1933 annual report, occurred in places as diverse as Abertillery and Worcester. The GPO approach was similar in that it offered shows at larger post offices throughout the country. The programmes, which normally consisted of films, posters and talks, travelled as a self-contained unit, with a dedicated showman who would bring with him everything he needed. In the mid-1930s nine units incorporating projection and sound equipment, screen and projectionist, travelled the country presenting such shows. The standard procedure was to select a site, then fix a date and advertise through leaflets in post offices in the area and/or posters and announcements in the press. This approach proved successful, with an estimated 3 million people seeing GPO presentations in 1935. The GPO also exhibited its films using mobile cinema vans. In 1938, for example, the GPO programme of films announced that:

> Six projector units have been touring the country during the past winter. Apart from London, which has a full-time service of projector units, 72 provincial towns have been visited and displays given by arrangement with the Education Authorities at some 1,250 schools. In the evenings displays are given to adult audiences. (TNA: PO 108/396)

Occasionally the GPO hosted a major exhibition to advertise its services. Thus, in October 1935, the *Manchester Guardian* reported, somewhat backhandedly, that:

> This afternoon the Lord Mayor and members of the council visited the post offices in Spring Gardens to watch a programme of films made by the GPOFU under Mr John Grierson. So great has been the demand for tickets between now and January 15,000 seats have been reserved for members of firms and societies… The films are not pretentious, but in their simple and direct method they produce an effect which might be compared to that of a good descriptive report in a newspaper. (*Manchester Guardian*, 1 October 1935)

That the principal purpose of the events and the film shows was a public relations exercise can be seen by an article in another local newspaper, the *Somerset Standard*:

> The Frome Cooperative Hall was crowded on Tuesday and Wednesday evenings on the occasion of a visit from the GPO Sound Film Unit. The unit is one of several touring the country bringing to the public notice in a new and fascinating way the ever-increasing services offered to the public by the GPO. The programme opened with *Calendar of the Year* followed by *Cable Ship*. Also shown were *Fairy on the Phone, The Saving of Bill Blewitt* (humble fisherfolk of Mousehole, Cornwall), *Tschierva* and finally *Night Mail*. (*Somerset Standard*, 12 November 1937)

A few of the GPOFU's productions were not designed for general public consumption but rather as training or information films for GPO staff, such as *Messenger Boy* (1937). As the title implies, this was essentially a recruitment film showing the tasks and responsibilities of the role to potential recruits.

Similarly, after 1940 the CFU was commissioned to produce films for specialist audiences of either a civilian or a military nature. Amongst the former were the Ministry of Fuel and Power's (later the National Coal Board) *Mining Reviews*. One of the most important of these specialist films was produced for the medical profession with the somewhat unprepossessing title, *Early Diagnosis of Acute Anterior Poliomyelitis* (1949). Since the introduction of the Salk vaccine in the mid-1950s, and the eradication of polio from Europe, it is perhaps difficult to appreciate the anxiety generated by what was then popularly referred to as infantile paralysis, an infectious disease which, as the name suggests, affected predominantly children and young adults. The late 1940s were characterised across the Western world by a sudden increase in the numbers being diagnosed. In 1950 nearly 8,000 children in England were identified with the disease which, irrespective of the consequent disability, had a mortality rate of around 15 per cent (Public Health England, 2012). As the *Daily Mirror* pointed out in a piece in opposition to the closure of the CFU in 1952:

> Remember the polio scare a couple of years ago? The figures at one time were very frightening. Every doctor and every laboratory was mobilised to attack the disease… The film Unit at Beaconsfield finished (the film) in four weeks. Immediately afterwards the COI's hundred mobile projectors throughout Britain were showing the film in hospitals and clinics and surgeries… This is what the Ministry of Health said about it yesterday: 'The film was a great help in the early diagnosis of the disease. It was shown to hundreds of doctors and nurses when the information in it was vital in the campaign against the disease'. (*Daily Mirror*, 5 February 1952)

Whereas most CFU films were for general release and a few for particular professions – or, as in the case of *Early Diagnosis of Acute Anterior Poliomyelitis* or the earlier *Patent Ductus Arteriosus* to meet specific urgent needs – a few others had a very restricted and even top secret audience. As Ronald Bedford explained in a *Daily Mirror* piece entitled 'Why an MI5 man watches Miss Pine':

> The films show stage-by-stage developments of Britain's top-secret harnessing of the atom and the perfection of 3000 mile an hour rockets among them… Green-eyed, brown-haired Miss (Diana) Pine, 5ft 4in tall and in her early thirties, is the director of the special

Crown Film Unit producing them... Yet when I asked to see one, so that I could see how your money and mine was being spent, I was told, 'Certainly not. No such permission can be granted!' (*Daily Mirror*, 16 February 1950)

These secret films, such as *Harwell Assembly* (1952) which dealt with a new atomic reactor process, appear to have been sponsored by the various armed services and related ministries and were designed to be shown to selected audiences with significant security clearance credentials. Despite his apparent pique at the slight, this obviously did not extend to Bedford, and consequently both reception and complete identification of these CFU films remains almost impossible to discover.[3]

Slightly easier to discuss are those films which, although classified, were more generally available to the military. These were often inserted into film shows which were given in a variety of military environments and venues from the more traditional NAAFI canteen to the troopship or base camp on active service. The extent of the NAAFI operation was quite significant. According to a 1943 report on Entertainment for the Forces (TNA: T 161/1163), the NAAFI controlled 132 garrison theatres and camp halls. It also provided and maintained 117 mobile cinema vans and, during 1943, had been responsible for 48,913 film shows to an audience of 27,212,405. The importance of films to troops both overseas and being deployed there was officially recognised. In 1949 the notes of a meeting between the War Office and the Army Kinema Corporation (TNA: WO 32/12553) reported that:

> a large number of passengers, especially in outward-bound troopships, consist of youths who have previously led a sheltered and parochial life. Posting overseas and the radical changes it involved comes as a great shock to them and at the start they tend to be very homesick. It's more than necessary to soften the break and to provide as many of the facilities as possible which they are used to at home.

These facilities, of course, incorporated regular film programmes which, apart from the main feature, 'normally include a travel short, an interest short, a cartoon and a newsreel' (TNA: WO 32/12553). Even as late as 1951, *Kinematograph Weekly* was reporting (3 May 1951, p. 10) that '16 million went to Army kinemas [obviously multiple attendances] and that the Army Kinema Corporation has

32 film libraries and some 1800 film projectors which are used and are fully maintained'.

Films were also produced for specific units and sections of the military. Many were inevitably produced by the respective service film units but were often edited and finished at the Crown studios in Beaconsfield, while others were direct CFU productions. In this latter category, the self-explanatory *Introduction to Aircraft Recognition* was produced for the Royal Observer Corps and *Minesweeping* for the Royal Navy. These films were incorporated as a compulsory part of a military training schedule and any assessment of their reception is intrinsically bound up with reactions to the training as a whole.

The CFU was producing films during the period of the slow revival of post-war television broadcasts and, perhaps unsurprisingly, a few productions found their way onto television screens. At 3.30 pm on 10 October 1950, for example, the BBC broadcast the CFU film *Making Engines* (1950), which was one of the *Is This the Job for Me?* series and described working in heavy engineering in a tractor factory (BBC Genome Project). Given that the number of television licences in 1950 barely exceeded 350,000, the actual audience was probably quite small, although the potential for such school-orientated programming would become clearer over the next few years.[4]

Overseas non-theatrical distribution

A much larger non-theatrical audience for EMB, GPO and especially Crown films were those living overseas. This intention to use film as a means of disseminating information about the UK was appreciated quite early on, as *The Observer* reported in December 1932. It announced that TIDA was working with the EMB to 'show films at the Copenhagen Exhibition and, following that, throughout Scandinavia. We are arranging to show them in America and other parts of the continent' (*The Observer*, 18 December 1932). Perhaps unfortunately, however, this initial enthusiasm for the EMB's overseas film work was often excruciatingly patronising, as J. Russell Orr observed in *Sight and Sound* in 1932. 'To the ignorant and to the mentally underdeveloped,' he opined, 'visualization is the strongest form of appeal and we are not surprised that medical, agricultural and veterinary officers find their meetings crowded when they show the natives their own people striving to attain a higher standard of life'.

Although the GPOFU continued to produce the occasional film for TIDA until quite late in its existence, including Cavalcanti's *The Chiltern Country*, overseas exhibition became more effectively organised when the MoI took over control of the CFU and created a specialist department which organised distribution covering,

> the Dominions and Colonies, the Americas, the Middle East, China and the neutral countries. In the Middle East distribution has been handled through the Ministry's Cairo office and in the United States through the British Information Services, in most of the countries it has been handled through British embassies and consulates. (Arts Enquiry, 1947, p. 15)

Films were regarded as an essential part of propagandising the British cause during the war and of projecting soft power and influence after. In order to support this, the Foreign Office distributed CFU and other films with significant largesse. In December 1946 a report prepared for the Foreign Office (TNA: INF 12/129) listed the most recent showings. These included:

1. Argentina – 400 non-theatrical shows given during October to an audience totalling 200,000.
2. Australia – average of 50,000 children each Saturday morning.
3. France – film officer reports for November 516 feature bookings and 1,977 shorts bookings.
4. Italy – over 100,000 people at non-theatrical showings in October.
5. Mexico – over 2,000 non-theatrical shows were given during October to over 1,000,000 audience. Besides the Department of Education, which has 12 mobile vans with 16 mm projectors, many other societies and clubs collaborate in showing COI films.

Those films selected for non-Anglophone countries were normally dubbed into the local language before distribution through Foreign Office channels. It is, of course, difficult to estimate the size of this overseas audience; however, in April 1951, following discussions with overseas representatives, the COI argued that it exceeded 100,000,000 annually (TNA: INF 12/129). This was probably an overestimate but nonetheless it does indicate that COI, and hence CFU, films were viewed by a substantial audience overseas.

It must also be remembered that, for the lifetimes of the EMB, GPO and Crown film units, Britain was an imperial power with significant colonial responsibilities. Consequently, the non-theatrical distribution and exhibition mechanism, along with occasional theatrical releases, was seen as an important vehicle by which national policy and propaganda could be disseminated on colonial and also international stages. This was particularly important during wartime as, according to Valerie Bloomfield (1977), the films made for the colonies then were created to tell the 'British story', whereas when the war ended it was rather to make the colonies better known to the British public. Although, inevitably, many of those films were made by the CFU's partner in the MoI's Films Division, the Colonial Film Unit, and had such worthy titles as *Empire at Work* (1940) or *Our Indian Soldiers* (1942), others were produced directly by the CFU. Some of these, such as *The Story of Omolo* (1946), *Sisal* and *The Eighth Plague* (1945) were specifically re-edited into silent versions in order to be more readily appropriate to the limited projection equipment in sub-Saharan Africa (TNA: INF 12/127, 1948). Rosaleen Smyth's study of the Colonial Film Unit (1992) makes occasional reference to its Films Division partner, the CFU, and outlines comprehensively the issues involved with filmmaking, distribution and exhibition in, mainly, colonial West and East Africa. Using the evidence of the 1944 *Mass Education in African Society Report* (TNA: BW 90/58) she endorsed,

> the great popularity of films and acknowledged that they were the most popular and powerful of all visual aids... The report also recommended that documentary films be used to extend the horizons of villagers and help them adjust to 'changing political, economic and social conditions'. Films could explain new types of organisations like trade unions and cooperatives and new techniques and processes like crop rotation, sanitation and brick kilns. (Smyth, 1992, pp. 163–64)

Like its predecessor the EMBFU, the CFU not only produced films which had an educational value, as outlined above by Smyth, but also films which reflected contemporary colonial concerns, especially in the post-war period. One particular anxiety was the rise of insurgency, mainly in Southeast Asia, and *Voices of Malaya*, for example, with its strong anti-communist message would have been an important weapon in the local colonial propaganda armoury.

Over the twenty or so years after 1930, countless millions gathered in front of hastily erected cinema screens in factory canteens, village halls, in the bush in West Africa or maybe in front of the many cinema vans in military bases, car parks and on street corners to be informed, instructed and maybe even entertained by EMB, GPO or CFU films (Figure 7.3). That this was appreciated is shown by the positive response of many organisers. What the audiences themselves thought is less clear and, at this distance in time, more difficult to ascertain. Many local histories and personal reflections on contemporary life mention regular village hall cinema shows but, apart from the occasional main feature, particular films, especially PIFs, are ignored. A typical illustration of this includes the recollections of the villagers of Cumnor, Oxfordshire, recorded by John Hanson in 1992. They remembered that 'by the end of the war there was a cinema every Monday night in the village hall, with a newsreel, film and a serial called *The Scarlet Man*. It was run by

Figure 7.3 A Ministry of Information film show in a works canteen (1944)

Mr Hopkins of Cowley, who also made black and white silent films of weddings, which could be shown the next Monday night'.

Similarly, the villagers of Kingston Bagpuize, Berkshire, recalled the local history society:

> Mr Kirby used to come to the old village hall in Longworth twice a week, Wednesdays and Saturdays. In the end he used to put reserved on our seats because we were always there but when the hop-pickers came you couldn't get a seat. It wasn't fair. That's how we got to see all the films. When the Americans were here we had films on a Sunday where Rimes Close is now. We used to see all the films – there wasn't anything else to do. We used to pay about 1/-. We also used to have square dances there.

Unsurprisingly, there is more evidence as to audience and reception in the other main distribution avenue for government films – that of the commercial and theatrical exhibition circuit.

Notes

1 Kreimeier (1999) is a comprehensive and thoughtful account of this major European film production house from 1917 to 1945.
2 Both estimates from Swann (1983), p. 27.
3 *Harwell Assembly* was not added to the open access COI Library until 1958. This coincided with the meeting of Soviet, US and UK experts in Geneva to discuss the implications of atmospheric nuclear tests and pave the way for subsequent test ban treaties. Who watched the film over the previous six years remains a mystery.
4 For more information on the development of children's television see Oswell (2002).

8

Commercial and theatrical exhibition

From the early 1930s Grierson had tried to get theatrical distribution for EMB and, later, GPOFU productions, constantly approaching Wardour Street distributors. While he never wavered in his belief that there was a commercial market, sadly his success was limited. On the positive side, he did manage to convince one of the commercial cinema chains, Gaumont-British, to take a small number of EMBFU films and add soundtracks in preparation for theatrical exhibition. The so-called Imperial Six were *The Country Comes to Town*, *Industrial Britain*, *King Log (Lumber)*, *The Other Half of the World*, *Upstream* and *O'er Hill and Dale*. Gaumont-British advertised in the trade papers that 'they would be released fortnightly commencing January 22, 1934' (*The Era*, 22 November 1933). There is some evidence that they made appearances as part of the supporting programmes in local cinemas. The *Edinburgh Evening News* on 17 January 1934 published an advertisement for the New Picture House in Princes Street, which was showing John Barrymore and Diana Wynyard in *Reunion in Venice* and the supporting programme of *Industrial Britain*. In Bristol the same EMBFU film was part of the programme supporting *Day of Reckoning*, starring Richard Dix and Madge Evans, at the Embassy (*Western Daily Press*, 12 June 1934). Although at least some of the Imperial Six were exhibited commercially, they do not seem to have troubled the cinema audiences sufficiently to warrant published comment. The only other EMBFU production that can be confirmed to have been exhibited commercially, albeit very briefly, was the almost universally execrated *One Family*.

During the pre-war years, theatrical exhibition was less important for the GPOFU, as the Post Office had a sophisticated national publicity machine through which the films were shown locally in post office buildings or in rented venues for special showings. Exhibition was also enabled nationally through the central library loan system. However, a few GPOFU productions, mostly of the best of Britain type, managed to access the commercial circuit. At the Hippodrome in Bath in February 1938, *Farewell Topsails* was in the supporting programme for, firstly, *Old Mother Riley* starring Arthur Lucan and, later in the week, *Lives of the Bengal Lancers* starring Gary Cooper (*Western Daily Press*, 1 February 1938). The same paper, on 30 September 1938, advertised the News Theatre in Bristol showing *Slacks Appeal* starring Niela Goodelle, with part of the supporting programme including the thoughtful *We Live in Two Worlds*. What the documentarists thought of their oeuvre sharing the bill with *Molly Moo Cow* and *Porky's Building* has not been recorded.

The opportunities for the commercial exhibition of EMBFU and GPOFU productions during the 1930s were severely limited by the lack of suitable films. Unfortunately, there were two other issues which worked against them: one legal and the other attitudinal. Firstly, the protectionist 1927 Cinematograph Films Act required that a quota of those films shown had to be British in origin. As mentioned earlier, the importance of the quota 'quickie' in the development of the British film industry has been discussed elsewhere (Dickinson and Street, 1985; Swann, 1989; Glancy, 1998) but it had little or no influence upon the exhibition of the government film units' productions, other than, perhaps, entrenching the general view of cinema owners in their general pre-war hostility to British film, and to documentary in particular. As *Kinematograph Weekly* explained to its readers in 1940:

> Fifteen years ago the critic who extolled a documentary picture was regarded by the showman as something of a crank. And the showman's estimate of the British entertainment public was instinctively right in so far as the word 'educational' was concerned. Audiences resent being instructed or preached at, they plank [sic] their money down to be amused. (*Kinematograph* Weekly, 1 August 1940)

This commercial versus artistic merit debate may have softened briefly during the war, but as early as January 1945 it had raised its head again. Under the banner 'Why documentaries fail', Sub. Lieut. Tom Massicks, RNVR, delivered a fairly vitriolic piece in the renters' journal:

> When the 'masterpiece of dramatic realism' wearing the box office hat of a smash hit at the premiere houses comes to the little kinemas of the industrial cities; the little kinemas' box offices take precious little money that week… Call it 'escapism' if you will; but they demand of a feature film that it should amuse or entertain. Entertainment in this sense occasionally involves 'having a good cry'. If the programme fails to amuse or entertain but tries to educate or elevate in the pretence of entertaining, they are resentful. They feel that they have been tricked, and they take good care to warn their friends to stay away that week. (*Kinematograph Weekly*, 11 January 1945, p. 90)

Implicit in this is the paradox in assessing the reception of EMB, GPO and Crown films in that critical contemporary success did not always appear to translate into box-office receipts.

However, once the country was at war, the cinema owners seemed to have had high expectations of the government documentary shorts. In January 1940, *Kinematograph Weekly* was able to divulge in an exclusive to its readers under the banner headline 'Government to sponsor its own films': 'We are able to reveal today the sensational and exclusive news that the Government itself intends to foster British films by producing FEATURES AND DOCUMENTARIES [sic]' (11 January 1940, p. 1). The operational details of what eventually became the Five Minute Agreement were later detailed in a MoI memorandum written by Russell Ferguson of the Films Division in November 1940. He explained:

> An arrangement has just been concluded by the MoI whereby a series of twelve 5 minute films for miscellaneous propaganda purposes shall be shown in the theatres of the country at a rate of one per week, each film appearing simultaneously in 1,000 cinemas. Broadly speaking each film will be shown for a week in the first run houses, thereafter a week in the second run houses, thereafter for a week in the third run houses and by the end of the fourth week the film will have covered most of the 4,000 cinemas in the country. (TNA: INF 6/205)

These MoI 'shorts', many of which were produced by the CFU, were therefore effectively guaranteed national exhibition, if not always a sympathetic audience. However, although the arrangements outlined by Ferguson above appeared comprehensive, there was at least one major drawback from a cinema owner's perspective. In the context of the weekly 'short', rather than a more normally distributed feature film, according to a Mass Observation report, 'The exhibitors have apparently no foreknowledge of the nature of the MOI film which they will receive for showing the next week until they take it out of the box on the Monday morning of the showing' ('The distribution of MoI films', 22 February 1941).

This meant that the short could neither be advertised in advance as part of the weekly programme nor could a decision be taken as to the film's suitability for inclusion in the daily schedule until it had already been shown. Unfortunately, too, the problems associated with producing a high-quality film on a regular weekly basis resulted in many complaints and the agreement being modified in 1942 to one fifteen-minute film every month, a policy which continued into the post-war period.

A further potential constraint on exhibition during wartime, as before, was the BBFC, which was ably, if occasionally eccentrically, supported by municipal watch committees. A flavour of the random approach of the guardians of local morality can be seen by the response to various horror films in 1936. According to Tom Johnson (1997, p. 130),

> The Hands of Orlac (1935) was banned by the Northampton Watch Committee on 2 March. Individual horror movies would be banned by individual authorities with regularity throughout the year. The Raven (1935) was next to go when the local censor in Rotherham refused its exhibition.

The advent of war now meant that films not only had to conform to contemporary morals and mores but also to security requirements. Thus, any film which appeared on British cinema screens – and by implication any British film which appeared abroad – could, 'only do so if it had secured the approval of the British Government, and in so far as the specific official body responsible was concerned, this meant the Ministry of Information' (Taylor, 1981, p. 7).

During wartime, then, the domestic commercial exhibition circuit was required to show essentially three types of CFU productions. Firstly, there was the sixty-to-ninety-second trailer, essentially a 'flash' and usually in support of some government initiative such as national savings, war on waste and so forth. Secondly, there were the five- and fifteen-minute shorts which normally addressed a current issue or concern. In this category would be films such as *Lofoten* (1941), a five-minute film,[1] which described a much-needed, if minor, military success and the fifteen-minute *The Children's' Charter* about the implications of the previous year's Butler Education Act. Finally, there were the feature-length films, often drama documentaries which were for general release and expected to be the A, or at least B picture in double-feature programmes. In this category were the probably more famous CFU productions such as *Target for Tonight*, about the beginnings of the bombing campaign against Germany, *The Silent Village*, Jennings' homage to the victims of the Lidice massacre translated to a Welsh mining village, and *Western Approaches*, which brought home the horrors of a U-boat attack and the subsequent days adrift in a lifeboat in the Atlantic.

With the ending of the war in 1945, and the abolition of the MoI and its replacement the next year by the COI, the Films Division and the CFU lost the opportunity to initiate film production and subsequently all CFU films were sponsored by individual government ministries and departments. Despite this change in organisational structure, the new Labour government continued the short film exhibition arrangements. The cinema owners, however, appeared to be somewhat ambivalent about this requirement. On the one hand, there were obviously those who appreciated that government information films as produced by the CFU could be valuable in the immediate post-war reconstruction drive. So, in November 1945, *Kinematograph Weekly* could advise its readers:

> There is still an emergency in this country and exhibitors can help by showing those short films which carry the right propaganda message. It is up to us as good citizens to help the Government in its reconstruction work to the limit of our ability. (*Kinematograph Weekly*, 29 November 1945, p. 8)

However, the key words in the previous quotation seems to have been 'right propaganda' as, within a week of publication, local branches of the CEA requested that 'Rehabilitation films must not carry propaganda' (Leeds CEA, reported in *Kinematograph Weekly*, 6 December 1945, p. 33). By the turn of the year, they were suggesting that individual exhibitors should determine the political content of any government film which, needless to say, proved to be a stillborn expectation (*Kinematograph Weekly*, 3 January 1946). It is probably sufficient to observe that the post-war relationship between the government and the commercial film exhibitors was somewhat strained. This was not entirely down to the quality or content of CFU productions but rather to the renters' desire to reduce or abolish the Entertainment Tax, and also by the 1947 attempt to impose a 75 per cent import duty on American films (see Jarvie, 1986) which disrupted film programmes in Britain. Despite this, the short film agreement was amended and reconfirmed in 1947, as was noted in a Cabinet minute:

> An arrangement has been made by the COI and the CEA whereby the members of the latter organisation show one 10-minute film made by the COI every month throughout the country... This enables us to have 12 films a year shown in over 3000 cinemas, which is a far wider distribution than any normal commercial film could ever get. (TNA: CAB 124/1005, file no. 1421/7)

Therefore, both MoI and, later, COI films, many of which were produced by Crown, had an open access to the commercial cinema circuits from 1940 right through to 1951 when the agreement was terminated by the CEA.

Public response to these shorts seems to have been generally positive in the early years of the war. A Mass Observation report from July 1941 (MoI Films no. 779) records that 'people's opinion of MoI films is very considerably higher than their general opinion of Government advertising'. It goes on to report that the twenty-three films mentioned by the Mass Observation reporters were produced by four different film units and the ratio of praise to criticism was significantly higher for the CFU. The actual figures being:

Crown	4.2:1
D&P (Denham & Pinewood)	0.6:1
Ealing	1.0:1
Strand	1.0:1

In other words, people in this, albeit limited, sample were four times more positive about CFU productions than its closest rivals. Also, of course, at a time of great anxiety people sought out information to give meaning and understanding to their personal situations and, in this context, the cinema, and the CFU, was a natural magnet. Furthermore, by the outbreak of war the British people had certainly developed the cinema-going habit. It was, according to *The Factual Film*, for 25 million people:

> a once a week habit. A warm comfortable and at times palatial building with gaudily impressive decorations and, in some cases, cafes and restaurants. It has an obvious attraction for people in search of warmth and company, people who are uncertain how to spend an afternoon or evening, who want to get out of the rain or the cold, or enjoy the licence of a darkened hall. (Arts Enquiry, 1947, p. 151)

Even the normally sceptical cinema owners were perhaps a little surprised by this early apparent enthusiasm, as *Kinematograph Weekly* reported on 1 August 1940: 'At last the documentary film is coming into its kingdom. The Ugly Duckling of kinema, its inheritance is yet to be complete, but its status can no longer be ignored.' It should not be thought that, even in these early days, audiences were all enthusiastic, or even sympathetic to the MoI films included in the regular cinema programmes. Daphne Cokkins from Dorking wrote to the *Picturegoer Film Weekly*:

> In my opinion the Ministry of Information shorts defeat their own ends. Such films may cause hot-blooded Italians to leap to their feet crying, 'Let us sweat and die for our country!' They have the opposite effect upon Britishers... We've got patriotic spirit enough; we don't want to have patriotic heroics blared at us from the screen.
> (*Picturegoer Film Weekly*, 7 September 1940)

This might have been a minority view in the early months of the war for most audiences, but the novelty of the inclusion of the MoI shorts seems to have worn off quite soon as far as the cinema owners were concerned. Perhaps underpinning this was a philosophical conundrum: as commercial operators they were required to include films in their daily programmes which, although distributed free to them, were not necessarily suitable for generating a paying audience. Certainly, by the following summer *Kinematograph Weekly* (17 July 1941) was headlining 'MoI shorts shelved by exhibitors'.

It went on to support this claim with a number of examples, including 'one of the biggest kinemas in the West End shows its Government propaganda films only at 10 o' clock in the morning' whereas 'at a number of businesses in south London the films are not shown in the last programme of the evening'. The article went on to offer an explanation for this failure to show the MoI shorts in every programme:

> The Ministry was not only turning out inferior films but their own distribution was careless. The town audiences who had to sit through films intended entirely for the country audience, such as a film about Silage, do not easily forget the five minutes of boredom they had to endure. Can you blame them if they reach for their hats when a 'Ministry of Information film appears on the screen? (*Kinematograph Weekly*, 17 July 1941)

It seems quite clear that cinema owners quickly became disenchanted with the five-minute shorts and that this was a significant push factor in the 1942 agreement to move to monthly fifteen-minute films, which were supposed to be of better quality and distributed more effectively to the appropriate audiences. This change seems to have reduced, if not entirely removed, the complaints from the cinema owners and, through them, the audiences. On reviewing the incorporation of shorts into the daily cinema programmes towards the end of the war, *Kinematograph Weekly* was able to report: 'The MoI policy of issuing one monthly 15-minute film to commercial cinema… has resulted in a higher quality production. Of these the two-reeler *By Land and Sea*, the Crown Film Unit's film about the Royal Marines, has been the most popular' (*Kinematograph Weekly*, 19 April 1945, p. 8).

It is not clear from the article how the film's popularity was determined, but by December 1945 the cinema owners had undertaken a survey of their own which did support the continuation of shorts into the post-war period – the balance in favour was more than double at 61 per cent to 24 per cent (*Kinematograph Weekly*, 20 December 1945, pp. 71–72). It was generally accepted that the shorts should continue after the war as, according to *Sight and Sound* (1944, vol. 13(50), p. 50), 'the tasks of reconstruction which await us will need to be brought home to the 300 million weekly filmgoers just as the problems of the war have been explained to them through the screen'. So the shorts continued after the war and became, for the owners, a minor irritant in their subsequent battle with government over the British film quota as well as the Entertainment Tax which had to be paid on each admission. The tax was, in part, blamed by the exhibitors for the main problem facing the industry in those immediate post-war years, which was that the British public was slowly losing the cinema-going habit. From the financial year 1948–49 to that of 1950–51, cinemas recorded a reduction in attendances of nearly 200 million, from 1,480 million to 1,292 million (*Kinematograph Weekly*, 11 September 1951, p. 6). The reasons underpinning the disappearance of the cinema-going public after the Second World War have been addressed elsewhere by Docherty, Morrison and Tracey (1987), Pronay (1993), Geraghty (2000), Harper and Porter (2003) and others. Suffice to say that nowhere has the MoI short, nor the CFU itself, been advanced as reasons for this dramatic and continuing decline.

What this audience, albeit declining by the time of the closure of the CFU, thought about these films is obviously difficult to assess at this distance in time. However, it is reasonable to assume that the normal cinema-goer in Britain between 1940 and 1952 would have been exposed to a number of MoI shorts and trailers, a proportion of which would have been produced by the CFU. To establish the critical success or failure of each particular film and its overall reception is highly problematic. There seems to have been an understandable tendency for both audience and exhibitors to amalgamate the films together as, for example, in the survey reported above, which merely asked the respondents to react positively or negatively to the continuation of MoI shorts (*Kinematograph Weekly*, 20 December 1945).

Some appreciation of the reception of CFU films in the commercial cinema can, of course, be gleaned from reviews published contemporaneously in national and local newspapers as well as in journals and magazines. However, the relationship between audience attendance at, and reaction to, a particular film is inevitably complex, especially when this is muddied by film advertising and reviews. In the former case, Janet Staiger (1990, pp. 20–21) noted that:

Historical, theoretical and empirical studies indicate that advertising comes in mediated form to the consumer, that the consumer is an active (if not fully conscious and unified) interpreter of that discourse, and that effects are a result not only of the ad's construction but also of the consumer (i.e., constructed self-image, unconscious desires, knowledge and ideologies).

However, this advertisement mediation factor could only have been an issue in respect of a few of the CFU's productions – those few which were released as feature films with preliminary publicity as with the examples given (Figure 8.1).

The vast majority of the CFU productions released through the commercial cinema circuit in the UK were shorts, which were almost never pre-advertised to the public and rarely featured on any cinema programme bill. However, there would, of course, be promotion by word of mouth and by the impact of the occasional published film review.

Figure 8.1 *Target for Tonight* (1941), US cinema poster

It was quite rare to read newspaper reviews of the MoI short films as these were evidently almost always supplementary to the main feature in a cinema programme. However, there are some limited examples which give a flavour of contemporary critical opinion. Some of these emphasised both the excellence of the production values as well as the intrinsic worthiness of the message. So, in 1942, the *Yorkshire Post* was able to report:

> A Crown Film Unit documentary *Builders* is one of the best this alert company has ever turned out. Short, simple, hard-hitting as a pneumatic drill, it brings to the screen the immediate actuality of the war effort as it is understood and practised by ordinary people in a way that has to be seen to be appreciated. (*Yorkshire Post*, 31 March 1942)

The words 'actuality' and 'ordinary people' are recurring themes in many of these reviews and it is important to accept that there is a significant temporal filter; to a more media savvy audience in the third decade of the twenty-first century, many of the films might appear somewhat crass or naive. However, if a film was described as 'authentic' then, at that moment and for that audience, it probably was in some way. Similarly, the contemporary reviews often reflected the partisanship of the newspaper more than a critique of the actual films themselves. Thus, the following year the *Daily Worker*, the official newspaper of the British Communist Party, was able to review the CFU short *Workers' Weekend* as follows:

> Some time ago the workers in a North of England factory decided to complete a Wellington bomber in 30 hours in their time off. They did it in 24½ hours and the bonus went to Red Cross Aid for Russia. This is a composite portrait of the workers on the job... This is an unbelievably tense and exciting film. The growth of the plane as the minutes race by is pictured in all its sections. There is too, the deeper implication – the love and pride of the job that is inherent in all workers, and which, unfettered, could build a new Britain in record time.

Reviews of the CFU's shorts continued after the war, although infrequently, and were nonetheless generally supportive. So Donald Zec of the *Daily Mirror*, under the heading 'Ballet gets weaving in this film', produced a complimentary notice of the short *The Dancing Fleece*:

If I awarded the Oscars I'd give one to the CFU for *The Dancing Fleece*. It tells the story of wool, in ballet. Instead of the whirr and clatter of looms and the usual clogs and shawls, we see the dancers of the Sadler's Wells Ballet pirouetting the warp and the weft. (*Daily Mirror*, 23 January 1951)

Not all the reviews of shorts were written by dedicated film reviewers; sometimes the subject of the short determined who produced the notice. For example, as mentioned, a key problem in the immediate post-war years was the perceived increase in road accidents and the government became anxious to improve the nation's attitude to road safety. In order to support this policy the CFU produced, in 1948, a short entitled *Worth the Risk?* In line with the film's topic and content it was reviewed for *The Times* by the motoring correspondent, who commented:

> *Worth the Risk?* is the Government propaganda film offered to exhibitors for August and will be distributed free to some 3500 cinemas throughout the country next week. The film follows the cinema tradition of being larger than life, with the result that the 'good' motorist is shown blinding [sic] round main road curves on the wrong side at an impossible speed, and it is difficult to believe that he has succeeded in doing this 'year in year out' without having an accident (or at least a sobering narrow shave) before his spectacular meeting with a lorry – a sequence which is shown with properly frightening vividness. (*The Times*, 7 August 1948)

The importance of the short in getting across a message of national importance was certainly a factor which motivated the opposition to the closure of the CFU, announced by the new Conservative government in 1951. So a *Times* correspondent was able to comment about another short:

> *A Family Affair* was released a year ago and has already been given over 12000 times in cinemas and elsewhere. It is addressed to the general public to encourage the adoption by suitable foster-parents of the 20000 orphaned children which are at present in the care of the nation. This most moving film has already been highly successful in encouraging new foster-parents to come forward. (*The Times*, 19 February 1952)

Inevitably, most of the contemporary newspaper and magazine reviews of CFU films seem to have been generated instead by the relatively small number of feature-length films which can normally be categorised as drama documentaries. These were often amongst the most famous of CFU productions and have subsequently spawned, as discussed in the introduction to this book, a literature of their own, featuring in monographs (Winston, 1999) or in the autobiographies or biographies of, mainly, their directors (Watt, 1974; Logan, 2011). Most of these feature-length films were produced during wartime and were usually initiated directly by the CFU or MoI. The opportunities for producing films of a similar type or length after the war ended receded substantially when the MoI was replaced by the downgraded COI and its film arm, the CFU, was only able to create films if they had been sponsored and financed by particular government ministries or departments which were themselves strapped for money by expenditure cutbacks.

As mentioned above, an interesting aspect of many of the contemporary reviews of CFU feature films is the frequent assertion of 'authenticity'. This may seem a little naive when the records indicate that sections of some of the most famous films were created in studios with mock-up sets that were often quite artificial. So, for example, the shooting of *Coastal Command* was delayed as, according to a letter dated 5 November 1941 from the CFU to the Ministry of Food,

> The CFU is constructing in Pinewood a film set representing a section of a service aircraft [Short Sunderland flying boat]. They have to simulate rows of small rivet heads, which appear in the original. For the purpose there is nothing more suitable than large grey continental lentils which would be glued and painted over. Permission is sought to purchase 7lbs of these. It is unlikely that the whole of the 7lbs would be used, but as the lentils are not of uniform size then some selection would be necessary, any balance would be handed over to the canteen. (TNA: INF 5/86)

It is not recorded whether the subsequent meals were satisfactory.

An aspect of the authenticity of CFU films which often provoked contemporary comment was that they frequently used non-professional actors, preferring individuals selected from the ranks of the appropriate occupation or military unit. It was perhaps this unusual casting approach which was a key differential in the critical success of some of these films.

One of the earliest reviews of the GPO/CFU film *Men of the Lightship* certainly supported this observation:

> The effect of the film depends upon the skill with which the crew are made to seem real people in a real situation, and once again the employment, not of professional actors but of men who might well have had the experience – in fact men of Trinity House and the Royal Navy – turns out to be inexplicably a better means of attaining reality than any skilled imitation. (*The Times*, 25 July 1940)

Furthermore, Dilys Powell, writing about *Target for Tonight* in the *Sunday Times*, also emphasised the contemporary belief in the value of the apparently authentic in film:

> I have long been persuaded that the most effective film propaganda is a good feature film which makes no attempt at direct argument but which, by its intrinsic truth, or charm, or beauty, persuades the audience to a certain way of thinking... Harry Watt's *Target for Tonight* turned out to be, not only exactly the line needed, but by far the best war flying film since the war began, and I am not forgetting Hollywood... All this first part of the film is calm, orderly, controlled; the plans are laid with minute accuracy; it is only in the audience that the undercurrent of excitement makes itself felt... The film is a superb unemphatic statement of the work of Bomber Command; it makes the usual fiction film about the handsome pilot and the blonde look, in the classic phrase, like a ha'porth of cat's meat. (*Sunday Times*, 17 July 1941)

Less flowery in its praise but striking a similar note was the review in the *Yorkshire Post*:

> The grimness of the flight home is accentuated by glimpses of the RAF station's tense anxiety, until finally, in a thick fog, F for Freddie makes a successful landing. RAF personnel and Harry Watt, director for the CFU, have made *Target for Tonight* a piece of vivid reality. (*Yorkshire Post*, 17 September 1941)

Although not the first feature film produced by the government film units, *Target for Tonight* to some extent set the standards or at least expectations for a wartime drama documentary as far as some reviewers were concerned. Many of the CFU's subsequent wartime drama documentaries upon which much of the unit's popularity rested were generally well received by the press.

A sense of the developing critical response to the CFU's feature films in wartime and post-war Britain can be gleaned from some of the reviews of a selection of the other more famous films often identified as key works of certain directors. While *Target for Tonight* ably demonstrated the cinematic impact of a single aircraft and its crew, when this model was repeated a year later in Holmes' *Coastal Command* it received almost identical plaudits in the press. According to Reg Whitely in the *Daily Mirror*:

> This is another of those very interesting CFU productions, a seventy minute film which provides a fascinating peep behind the scenes of a less spectacular and often underrated branch of the RAF... A story told with simple realism and embellished with no heroic frills – the story of the exploits of T-Tommy, a Sunderland flying boat. (*Daily Mirror*, 16 October 1942)

For Powell, however, this film was not quite up to the standard of *Target for Tonight*: 'that is all, that and the unemphatic playing, the casual dialogue and the vigilant untheatrical faces. Holmes may not have an ability quite equal to Harry Watt's for handling non-professional actors, but it is good enough, it will do' (*Sunday Times*, 18 October 1942). Interestingly, the *Yorkshire Post* seemed to be still confused about the nature of reality in documentary films:

> Stripped of the artificiality and embellishments of a fictional film *Coastal Command* grips the interest by its authenticity and straightforwardness. It is a plain tale of plain men doing a vital job of work guarding convoys, sinking submarines, crippling raiders and fighting German aircraft. Drama is lightened by the laconic humour of the crews; pictorially the film is of the first order and the music, especially written by Dr Vaughan Williams, gives greater depth to a fine piece of work. (*Yorkshire Post*, 24 October 1942)

It seems unlikely that anybody could be baffled into thinking that the feature-length wartime drama documentaries directed by Humphrey Jennings could be anything other than fiction. He had used his creative skills in the direction of such films as *Fires Were Started* and *The Silent Village*. The former, also released in a shorter version called *I Was a Fireman* (1943), was essentially a homage to the work of the National Fire Service during the Blitz. Once again the CFU used non-professional actors, as the *Daily Express* reported:

Star of yesterday's production was pre-war taxi driver, Fred Griffiths, 31 years old of Englefield Green, Surrey, driver of a heavy unit in the worst of the 1941 blitz. 'Blimey, they'll want me for Hollywood next! I've a lovely scene in the picture with my own boy, David, – kid of seven he is, and my old woman. It's a fight scene and he hit me so hard the blood came out of my face' [sic]. (*Daily Express*, 30 May 1943)

That particular aspect of authenticity was appreciated by other sections of the press:

> 'Fires were started' was a familiar phrase in the news bulletins of the time (NB – now past!), but not even those who had fires raging on their own doorsteps, so to speak, could realise the extent of the organisation and the amount of work and courage which went to the combating of them... The film follows the tradition of the Crown Unit in telling of heroic events in a matter-of-fact manner... The night does not pass without its tragedies, but the ammunition ship sails in the morning and the Crown Film Unit completes yet another film which shows its genius for interpreting the services to the world without emotionalism, vainglory or false modesty. The idiom is difficult, but the Unit is its master. (*The Times*, 25 March 1943, p. 6)

Ironically, the next of Jennings' major drama documentaries was highly emotionally charged and slightly outside the usual choice of topics. *The Silent Village* was a direct homage to the villagers of Lidice, now in the Czech Republic, who had been massacred by the Nazis in reprisal for the assassination of Reichsprotektor Reinhard Heydrich in June 1942. Jennings' film envisaged this happening in a Nazi-conquered Wales. He did, however, retain the unit's policy on actors, as seen in the *Daily Mirror* report of the film's world premiere:

> Miners in the village of Cwmgiedd, near Swansea, changed their clothes in a hurry yesterday and took their wives and families to the pictures in the neighbouring small town of Ystradgynlais. It was no ordinary cinema entertainment they went to see. They watched themselves on the screen – and afterwards received the congratulations of hundreds of people. (*Daily Mirror*, 29 May 1943)

More reflective in its review was *The Times*, which opined:

> This imaginative record is one of the most powerful exercises in intelligent propaganda yet witnessed on screen. The Crown Film

Unit made it, and the Unit is expert in the means of expressing fundamentals by means of colloquialisms.

Too many films have been made which, however honest their intentions, distort in effect the reality of what is happening on the Continent – this is a record that does not pretend to heroics but which explains, with tight-lipped emotionalism, some of the consequences of being 'protected'. (*The Times*, 10 June 1943, p. 6)

Although *The Silent Village* can be seen as unusual in that it is entirely fictional, the contemporary reviews place it clearly within the CFU mould. More conventional in its selection and consideration of its subject matter was Pat Jackson's *Western Approaches*. As *The Times* review stated:

There have been many films made of ships going down and men struggling in the water or suffering in lifeboats, but *Western Approaches* has the immense advantage of being both authentic and austere... There are no professional actors in *Western Approaches* and the Atlantic is allowed to unroll in its own story in terms of effective Technicolor. Those who appear in it, men of the Navy and the Merchant Service make the mintage of men shine brightly, and if only for that reason *Western Approaches* would be a memorable film. (*The Times*, 10 November 1944)

Although *The Times* review has, once again, emphasised the absence of professional actors, this is not to suggest that this particular policy was without criticism. Admittedly written some thirty years after the war, John Mortimer, who worked for the CFU as a scriptwriter, penned a stinging, if witty, condemnation of the use of laymen in *The New Statesman*:

Another reason for the extreme artificiality of our films was that it was part of the documentary credo never to use actors. 'The Man in the Street' had to be played by the actual man in the street, with results which varied from embarrassing timidity to outrageous overplaying. Documentary films never learned the first dramatic lesson, that naturalism is only possible by the use of extreme artifice... 'People' in our films were confined to that wholly mythical figure 'The Man in the street' – or the worker at the assembly bench, or the landgirl in the turnip field, or the pilot at the 'Roger and out' apparatus. (Mortimer, 1979, p. 6)

Crown did, of course, occasionally use professional actors, including some very famous ones in either film voiceovers or cameo appearances. For example, Laurence Olivier narrated *Words for Battle* and John Gielgud appeared briefly as Hamlet in *A Diary for Timothy*. The screen appearance of recognisable actors during wartime in CFU films was quite rare. *Two Fathers* (1944), starring Bernard Miles and Paul Bonifas, in which an English father of a downed pilot commiserated with a French father of a woman in the Resistance, was almost unique in this category as having 'named' film stars in the credits.

War has always been a major topic for the film industry; on the one hand, it is dynamic and exciting and, on the other, frightening and horrific. The end of the Second World War had a curious impact on the reception of one CFU drama documentary, Jennings' *A Diary for Timothy*. Jennings was doubly unfortunate in the timing of his film. Not only had the war in the Far East ended far more quickly than was expected, but, as mentioned, the film had the misfortune to be premiered on the same evening, 23 November 1945, as *Brief Encounter*. Although technically well-constructed and now regarded as one of Jennings' major films (Logan, 2011), it was given somewhat of a rough ride by contemporary reviewers. Perhaps it was no longer appropriate for the zeitgeist; perhaps the coming of peace posed too many problems and uncertainties to reflect on those last days of war? This was succinctly summed up in *The Times* review, which thought that,

> by ignoring the bomb which destroyed Hiroshima, the detonation of which was heard within the time limit this film lays down for itself, it shirks the issues it well-meaningly attempts to raise... Idealistic and intelligent as it is, it seems to be at sparring distance from, rather than at close quarters with, its theme. It is not only the atom bomb which makes *A Diary for Timothy* seem a little out of date. (*The Times*, 24 November, 1945)

A Diary for Timothy effectively marked the end of feature-length drama documentary production for the CFU. Post-war expenditure constraints and the move from being an initiating production unit to one which only dealt with commissioned work meant that most films would not only be restricted to a maximum of thirty minutes or so, but that there was little appetite amongst sponsors for films which had general morale-building intentions. Ironically, by way of a postscript, Jennings did produce another CFU drama documentary of thirty-seven minutes' duration for the Ministry of Fuel and Power on the nationalisation of the coal industry. The response to *The Cumberland Story* summed up the rapid decline of that particular aspect of the genre. The admittedly unsympathetic *Kinematograph Weekly* (4 September 1947, p. 81) concluded its review: 'and the film ends on a triumphant note, with the nationalisation of the mines. "Now the battle of the miners is over," declares the miners' leader, "and the pits belong to all of us." At which I heard a titter of laughter here and there in the house.'

Although the production of the CFU's feature-length drama documentaries were essentially restricted to the war years, their theatrical success was not just confined to the UK. They were an important part of the British overseas propaganda effort that also had the important role of generating income from being shown, principally, on the US commercial exhibition circuit. There, according to *The Factual Film* (Arts Enquiry, 1947, p. 87), the British information services 'works a rota system with the eight major American distributors, whereby each company distributes one feature and two short films in each twelve months. In this way *Desert Victory* (a 1943 Army Film Unit production but edited by CFU personnel) reached some 12,000 cinemas in the USA'. Certainly the impact of the American market was by no means negligible. It was estimated, for example (TNA: INF 1/632, Sept 1942), that *Target for Tonight* grossed more than $100,000 from its release in the United States. As early as the summer of 1940, distributors sympathetic to the British (and later Allied) cause had eased the distribution of MoI films onto the American circuit. In order to maximise the impact of some of these films they were re-edited for the United States. By way of illustration, CFU productions *Men of the Lightship* and *Merchant Seamen*, although distributed on different US circuits, were both re-edited and re-dubbed by Alfred Hitchcock (TNA: INF 1/632). Such films did give American audiences an insight into the battle being waged on the other side of the Atlantic and may have been a factor in ensuring that the British government had a sympathetic hearing in Washington even before the Japanese attack on Pearl Harbor on 7 December 1941 pushed the USA into the war.

There was also the occasional example of a film being produced specifically for the American market. *Patients Are In* (1945), for example, was commissioned by the American Division of the MoI for distribution in the USA. This short film showed daily life in an American Field Hospital in Cirencester, dealing with the casualties being flown in from western Europe battlefields. As such, it demonstrated to their countrymen that these wounded soldiers and airmen were receiving excellent medical care and, in a sense, and without the obvious satire, it was a precedent for the later movie and television series *M*A*S*H* (1970 and 1972–83).

It is beyond doubt that between 1940 and 1952 many people watched films produced by the CFU. The context and environment in which they were both seen and shown differed significantly from palatial London cinemas to factory canteens, from mobile cinema vans on street corners to troopships heading towards conflict zones and from downtown Los Angeles to a small bush hospital in Nigeria. Given the complexity of exhibition and the widely differing and changing audiences, CFU films do not sit easily within any conventional analytical framework. However, from a reception perspective, each member of any particular audience would have taken something from the film away with them, whether that be a new technical skill or an appreciation of life in Britain. The depth, influence and effectiveness of these factors on the individual differed dramatically and, given their complexity, are impossible to quantify.

There is some evidence to suggest that cinema audiences in the UK were positively disposed to the early CFU productions, perhaps as a way of seeking comfort in an increasingly hostile and negative war environment. Following the entry of the United States to the war, and the improving military situation, the desperate need to seek out reassurance diminished and, with it, some of the enthusiasm for CFU films. Having said that, even when the war ended and the nation was faced with a long period of austerity, the government, exemplified by Herbert Morrison, still felt that there was a place for the CFU shorts to be shown to a generally sympathetic national audience.

However, these five-, ten- or fifteen-minute shorts are not to be found amongst the more famous films produced by the CFU. There are just a very small number of feature-length films which have had a disproportionate influence on the audience and general perceptions of the unit. Films such as *Target for Tonight, Coastal Command, Fires Were Started* and *Western Approaches* became box-office successes in the cinema. These films were reviewed in the same way as any commercially produced pictures and have subsequently received academic interest to the exclusion of almost all the others.

Success at the box office was, of course, a key requirement for the cinema owners and exhibitors, and their fluctuating support for MoI films from 1940 to 1951 has been examined above. After 1946, with audiences on the decline, the exhibitors became more discriminating in deciding which MoI films to show in their programmes, even though they were normally supplied free. The cinema owners had already proved that they were not without influence on the actual productions themselves. Their hostility to the five-minute short had become apparent quite early on, thus ensuring that the government moved to the better quality, if less frequent, fifteen-minute film.

That the CFU films were often regarded highly by their various audiences is undeniable. In particular, much of the early praise revolved around the apparent authenticity of the productions. The frequent employment of non-professional actors supposedly imbued the productions with a sense of reality. However, perhaps the most telling endorsement of the reception of CFU films were the accolades received from the film industry itself. Not only was the unit recognised in the UK by the award of best documentary by BAFA (British Academy Film Awards) for *Daybreak in Udi* in 1949 and *The Undefeated* in 1950, but Hollywood had also awarded an Oscar to *Target for Tonight* in 1942 and *Daybreak in Udi* in 1950. So the impact of the films made by the government film unit had indeed been generally recognised.

Note

1 Seven minutes including titles, credits, etc.

9

The end of government filmmaking, 1951–52

The closure of the CFU came quickly after the Conservative government took office at the end of October 1951. The new financial secretary to the Treasury, John Boyd-Carpenter, had concluded that, despite making 'beautiful films', filmmaking was not a necessary function of government and was also commercially non-viable. Of course, whether Boyd-Carpenter appreciated that one of the major aspects of public information films was that they were not usually created to produce a profit at the box office, but rather to make a message, normally a government one, palatable to an audience, is not clear. It was not as if the demand from various departments was declining. In fact, the reverse was the case as the annual production figures below testify:

- 1946 – 16 films;
- 1947 – 14 films;
- 1948 – 20 films;
- 1949 – 19 films;
- 1950 – 27 films;
- 1951 – 29 films; and
- 1952 – 18 films (post-production completed after unit's closure).

The financial secretary to the Treasury might have acknowledged that the films produced were 'often of high artistic merit'. There were the obvious plaudits to support this view, notably the Oscar for *Daybreak at Udi*. The majority of the films produced by the CFU from 1946 onwards were not dissimilar in quality to those made in wartime. They had provided clear advice and information for specialist audiences, such as *Early Diagnosis of Acute Anterior Poliomyelitis*, which enabled those in the medical profession to learn about the post-war threat of infantile paralysis. Or, for a more general audience, but retaining the medical theme, *Surprise Attack* had encouraged vaccination in the face of a worrying smallpox outbreak.

Unfortunately, though, Boyd-Carpenter's assertion was not entirely true anyway, as during the post-war years there were a small number of films which have become symbolic of a creative malaise in the unit. Occasionally this was down to just bad luck. Would Jennings' *A Diary for Timothy* have been so universally panned if the war in the Far East had not been so dramatically terminated by the dropping of the atomic bombs on Hiroshima and Nagasaki? Had the war continued for at least another eighteen months or so, as had been reasonably expected, the film would have been more in tune with the continuing wartime restrictions and behaviour. As it was, its introspection and thoughtful observations failed to resonate with the new environment of peace.

Bad luck, though, could not disguise the opprobrium heaped upon the later Jennings' production, *The Cumberland Story*. Much of this came from the documentarists themselves, as Harry Watt's critique had pithily observed: 'I've no idea why they did it, but I imagine it was one of the big coffin nails' (quoted in Aitken, 1998, p. 169). Had it just been one major film which was a disaster that might have been overlooked, but this was followed quickly by *A Yank Comes Back*. This film was a prime example of a creation by committee, as not only was each sponsoring department represented by a welter of on-screen statistics but the wooden acting by real people reciting their lines, and the obvious artificiality of the sets, prompted a response from Ronald Tritton, director of the COI's Films Division and the man in overall charge of the CFU, that the film looked and sounded 'phoney'. It was neither a commercial nor critical success.

By then Jennings had left the CFU to join Wessex Films, although, sadly, his time as a documentary maker was cut short by a fatal accident while filming in Greece in September 1950. Grierson, too, had made a brief reappearance as CFU controller of films in February 1948 having been somewhat ignominiously ejected from Canada some months earlier as part of the fallout from the Gouzenko Affair.[1] This was the only occasion in the unit's short history that the 'father' of the documentary movement had some direct influence in the operation of the CFU. Despite Grierson's appointment, he was unable to ignite the creative 'fire' of wartime as the unit now had to respond to the often mundane demands of its sponsoring government departments. A random selection of films produced in 1949 includes *Heating Research for Houses*, *Pigs on Every Farm*, *Beet Sugar* and *The Good Housewife in Her Kitchen*; these titles would seem to indicate that public information films were now more specialised and focused. This restriction on subject matter, combined with the parsimony and regulation of the Treasury, were no doubt instrumental in convincing Grierson to seek alternative pastures. A possible explanation for this flight of talent from the CFU was addressed later by Basil Wright who, speaking in the 1970s, saw the situation in terms of the cyclical rise and inevitable decline of a famous arts movement. 'You start by being wild men,' he observed, 'then you become established, and then you become old fashioned. Just like the French impressionists were first of all regarded as raving lunatics, then they were popular, and then they became old fashioned (although their effect is seen to this day on railway posters and hoardings and that sort of thing) I think by 1946, 1947 we were over the peak' (quoted in Sussex, 1975, p. 175). Certainly, new recruits to the unit were less than enthusiastic about what they found, as John Taylor, who had left Realist Films in 1946 to join the CFU as a producer, observed, 'It was a very difficult time, really, because Crown had fallen to pieces. There was a big boom in the commercial industry, and practically all their best people had left. Well, they all had! There was no one left. When I went there, I think they had eight directors on the establishment, and four scriptwriters. And only one director had ever made a film, and none of the scriptwriters had ever written a script. They were completely new people. None of them had really done any film work at all!' (quoted in Sussex, 1975, p. 165). This comment is perhaps somewhat exaggerated, but it does describe a malaise in the creative side of the unit. Of course, wartime had enabled the CFU's production staff to indulge significant independence in the choice of topic to be filmed and also in the way it was addressed. The post-war world was one of both restrictions and austerity and, from a creative perspective, a return to the days of the GPOFU when the subjects of the films to be produced were primarily determined by the needs and concerns of the sponsor.

Not only were there some issues with the creative environment within which the CFU now operated but it, and its predecessors, had triggered several powerful enemies. These included sections of the commercial film industry, the Treasury and parts of the Conservative Party.

The commercial film industry

Although opposition to government-produced PIFs, with their variable quality, might be expected from the cinema owners, whose prime concern was encouraging attendance by the paying public, it is perhaps a little surprising to note the increasing hostility of fellow documentary producers. Their main objection was that the CFU, and previously the GPOFU, always received sympathetic treatment from the government. By the later 1940s, industry opponents of the CFU often regarded it as a heavily subsidised and questionably talented group. In 1949, in its submission to the French Committee on the Cost of the Home Information Services, the Association of Specialised Film Producers drew attention to the fact that, by reason of high overhead expenses, the costs of films produced by the CFU had exceeded the cost of films produced by the documentary companies (TNA: CAB 124/74). This criticism continued a corrosive process up to and after the general election of 1951. In a similar vein, Edward Cook of the Big Six Film Unit wrote to the new financial secretary of the Treasury, Boyd-Carpenter, on 8 December 1951, complaining, 'since the war ended I have made 68 industrial documentary sound films at an average cost of 17/7 per foot. The Select Committee on Estimates heard evidence that the average cost of documentary films made by the CFU was £3 8s 4d a foot… There was a considerable waste of money in this direction' (TNA: Treasury GS 49/019A). The impression that the CFU was protected by preferential treatment from normal commercial economic variables did not enamour it to many other documentarists outside the new Beaconsfield studios.

Opposition came, too, more predictably, from the cinema owners. There is no doubt that the Labour victory in 1945 posed the exhibitors with somewhat of a dilemma. True to its commercial instincts, the CEA had campaigned quite vigorously for either a reduction in, or abolition of, the Entertainment Tax which added cost to the price of cinema seats – although the CEA itself was perhaps perceptive enough to appreciate that this issue would not feature significantly in the 1945 general election. So, somewhat wistfully, *Kinematograph Weekly* advised in a leader entitled 'Investigating candidates' that, 'it may be said that the public at election time is interested in larger issues than the Entertainment Tax, but the average exhibitor could hardly be criticised if he gave his otherwise uncoloured [sic] support to a candidate who pledged himself to help the industry' (*Kinematograph Weekly*, 14 June 1945, p. 4). A fortnight later the same journal announced, 'The General Election is now over. The film industry today knows with whom it has to deal in the fight for the reduction of Entertainment Tax. The fight is on!' (*Kinematograph Weekly*, 28 June 1945, p. 4). The issue of the tax, although buried in the Labour landslide, continued to be an undermining feature in the relationship between the exhibitors and the government up until its demise in 1951. Even as early as 6 September 1945 the CEA was campaigning against the tax, arguing in a front-page leader of *Kinematograph Weekly* that, 'slackening of work in many centres has resulted in less spending money, and already Kinematograph receipts in a number of districts have decreased. This means that the present rate of ET, which in prosperous times could have been borne without undue hardships in busy centres, now assumes much more serious proportions'.

However, perhaps of more immediate concern in the aftermath of war was that documentaries, and especially the MoI shorts, which before June 1945 could be justified under the banner of 'national' public information, were now being commissioned by a conventionally political government, no matter how non-partisan the outputs might appear. This caused some debate within the CEA as an editorial in November 1945 came out in favour of the continued showing of MoI (and hence CFU) productions because, 'there is still an emergency in the country and exhibitors can help the authorities by showing these short films which carry the right propaganda message. It is up to us as good citizens to help the Government in its reconstruction work to the limit of our ability' (*Kinematograph Weekly*, 29 November 1945, p. 8). It could, however, be argued that this was just bowing to the commercial pressures exerted both by the general assumption of the swing of the public mood towards the left combined with the apparent continued popularity of the MoI/CFU information shorts. Grierson, writing in December 1945 in *Kinematograph Weekly*, offered a graphic warning to both filmmakers and exhibitors: 'We have to realise the significance of the almost universal shift to the Left and the implications of the technological and social revolutions which are taking place in the farthest corners of the globe... We have, in short, to realise the part we shall be required to play in giving men the kind of mind and spirit that will bring the world to order. This involves a new measure of understanding and a will to use the medium more *directively* than we have done in the past' (*Kinematograph Weekly*, 20 December 1945, p. 63). This mood seems also to have been reflected in the continuing public demand for documentaries as part of the 'normal' cinema programme. In late 1945 *Kinematograph Weekly* commissioned a survey on film entertainment which had asked the questions: 'Do you like documentary shorts of the type introduced during the war? Should they continue?' (*Kinematograph Weekly*, 20 December 1945, pp. 71–72). In reply, 61 per cent of the respondents said yes, although most of those qualified their agreement by asking for less propaganda and more factual treatment; 24 per cent did not want documentaries and the remainder were indifferent. Certainly, some of the two-reelers produced towards the end of the war by the CFU, such as the film about the Royal Marines, *By Land and Sea*, had been received well both critically and by cinema audiences. Unfortunately, the post-war world did not lend itself to such dramatic content and films such as *Sisal* and *Tea from Nyasaland* were less than popular with audiences. Despite the anodyne topics of many of the shorts, a significant number of CEA members seemed to have been concerned that there was too heavy a propaganda message. During a letters debate in *Kinematograph Weekly*, Mr Kern of west Scotland had pointed out that 'the wartime arrangement with the MoI to show "shorts" had no period put on the agreement and that it would be left to us (the CEA) to terminate the agreement at any time' (*Kinematograph Weekly*, 5 January 1946, p. 5). Negotiations between the government and the CEA on the extension of the agreement continued throughout 1946 and were concluded early the following year. From the government's perspective it was a confirmation of the existing arrangements. So the joint secretaries of the Home Information Services Committee, Messrs D. H. Boon and A. K. Gore, advised its members in February 1947 that:

> An arrangement has been made by the COI and the CEA whereby the members of the latter organisation show one 10 minute film made by the COI (CFU) every month throughout the country... This enables us to have 12 films a year shown in over 3000 cinemas, which is far wider distribution than any normal commercial film could ever get. In addition, the arrangement also covers the distribution of 'trailers'. These short 'flashes' of about one minute's duration are used by Government Departments to carry messages to the people. They are used for recruiting publicity, for fuel saving, for road safety, and for many other purposes. (TNA: CAB 125/1005)

On the surface the acquiescence of the CEA to an identical arrangement post-war is remarkable, particularly given the political reservations of many of its members and the continuing 'sore' of the Entertainment Tax.

It could be, though, that they were bowing to unspoken political pressure manifested both in the quote from Grierson and the economic exigencies occasioned by the ending of American aid and the bitter winter weather of early 1947. However, opposition to the government and its film policy was already evident as, in early December 1946, *Kinematograph Weekly* revealed to its readers that 'compulsory acquisition by the Government of 500 Kinematographs, mostly from the big circuits; a Government owned and controlled renting organisation to handle independent British films, and Government acquisition of studio space to encourage and facilitate the making of British films (are) the most spectacular recommendations in the report of the film sub-committee of MPs of the Labour Party which was presented to the Party's Trade and Economic Committee at a meeting in the House of Commons on Tuesday night' (*Kinematograph Weekly*, 5 December 1946, p. 1). Although this course of action never became government policy, the exhibitors certainly perceived that there was a very real threat that they could be compulsory-purchased out of existence and therefore acquiescence to showing COI films was a very limited sacrifice in the circumstances. However, by 1950, the CEA had recovered from its timidity and, along with the Newsreel Association, was threatening the government with a series of demands. These included control over film laboratory processing, limiting the theatrical circulation of official film and, optimistically, the 'power to censor all official film to safeguard against any abuse of the national spirit of the (COI "shorts") agreement' (Wildy, 1988, p. 100). As a result of the rising opposition amongst cinema owners to the requirement to show COI films, the agreement was terminated and the semi-captive audience for CFU films disappeared forever.

The Treasury

From very early on, by far the most dangerous and determined opponents of the government films units were the civil servants within the Treasury. Post-war optimism had very shortly collapsed when the scale of the economic crisis forced the government to refocus on public expenditure and the means of reducing it. Inevitably, government film production would, along with all other services, come under scrutiny. As early as the autumn of 1948, the Treasury established the Review of the Crown Film Unit, led by A. G. D. Collis of the Treasury's Organisation and Methods Division, with the remit to 'examine the organisation of the CFU and to make recommendations on organisation, costing and production procedures necessary to maintain an effective control over production expenditure' (TNA: T219/144). Its conclusions echoed many of the findings of its predecessor, the Boxall Report. What it revealed was what many in Whitehall had long suspected the CFU had operated with both ad hoc and cavalier methods and systems often inherited from its predecessors.

Amongst a range of negative conclusions, perhaps the most damning, in light of what was to happen eventually, was the actual cost of film production. In a striking echo of the Boxall Report, some eight years earlier, Collis discovered that:

> In the year to September, 1948, CFU completed and delivered 25 films totalling, in all, approximately 50 reels... The yearly charge for salaries and other expenditure, to March 1948, was £194,000, but this amount should be increased by at least £13,000 in respect of the services which are not actually paid by the Central Office... This

The end of government filmmaking, 1951–52 229

indicates that the cost to the Government per reel of film produced by the CFU is over £4100. A sample of eleven representative films made by contractors in 1947 – 8 of a type which could be made by CFU, showed an average cost to COI of £2830 per reel. This obviously raises the question of the profitable continuance of CFU at all, but since factors other than cost are also concerned, the question has not been taken up in this report. (TNA: T219/144, para. 6)

Unfortunately, it was not just that the accounting procedures had been somewhat haphazard but there were also criticisms to be found in the manner in which operating expenses were incurred and monitored at every level. Collis was particularly scathing about the differences between the treatment of the support staff and the 'creatives': on the one hand, 'The constructional staff, i.e. plasterers, carpenters and studio hands are paid on an hourly rate and fill in time sheets every day showing on which jobs they have been employed and how much has been spent on that particular job', while, on the other hand, 'production and technical staff do not fill in time sheets except when they wish to claim overtime... In this connection it might be commented that time keeping by the production and technical staff is not good. This does not, however, prevent persons who arrive at the studios at or after ten o'clock in the morning, submitting overtime sheets if they stay late in the day' (TNA: T219/144, para. 33). The knife was twisted a little further as he went on to observes pithily: 'although it's extremely difficult to obtain the true figures for idle time, an analysis of the August wages and salaries figures between direct and indirect costs indicated that, with the current programme, only two thirds of the time of the directors, assistant directors, continuity staff, unit managers and Art Department and one half of the time of the Camera and Electrical Departments and only one seventh of the time of the constructional staff, was spent on direct production' (TNA: T219/144, para. 36). Collis' critique was so detailed that he even included the operation of the CFU's transport section and the dire state of stock control which, he inferred, presented opportunities for pilfering.

Apparently, much of the accounting and operational issues were the direct result of a confused organisational structure. Simply described, the principal issue was that the various roles and responsibilities had never been clearly defined. This meant, for example, that 'there is little effective control over the accurate maintenance of time sheets and in fact the production and technical staff are not required to keep the time sheets at all. Even where members of the staff complete a detailed time sheet, the detailed allocation to particular jobs appear to bear little relationship to the actual work done. Although it is clear to everyone that there has been a high percentage of idle time in the last twelve months this is not shown in the costing records' (TNA: T219/144, para. 12).

It was not even as if the Collis Report, like so many before and since, got buried in the morass of civil service prevarication and ineptitude. Within a year it was to feature in a major supporting role, underpinning the conclusions of the Committee on the Cost of the Home Information Services (TNA: CAB 124/1005) which essentially required the CFU to either cut its costs or raise revenue. That the government's film services were at risk from a political perspective was evident as early as December 1948 when the lord president of the council, Herbert Morrison, wrote to Prime Minister Clement Attlee:

> I am myself seriously concerned at the rising cost of Government publicity, and I share the Chancellor's view that the time has come to call a halt and that estimates for the financial year 1949–50 ought, if possible, to show some reduction. A gross figure of £16.7m is certainly not beyond public criticism. In that connection I have ordered the D-G COI that the estimate of the Department for next year must, at all events, keep within and should, if possible, show some reduction on the figure for the current year. (TNA: PREM 8/1064)

Therefore, at a senior government level, even the Labour administration was beginning to have serious concerns about the cost basis upon which the CFU operated. How far this information trickled down to the filmmakers of the CFU and subsequently influenced their actions remained a moot point.

The Conservative Party

If Labour politicians were concerned about the expenditure supporting the CFU, then the incoming Conservative government, for which cutting public expenditure was more ideologically acceptable, would find it an easy target. As early as 1941 the Conservative-leaning *Daily Express* had noted that, 'The Crown Film Unit consists of a dozen or so young enthusiasts. They wear red ties and they talk a lot. Largely for these two reasons they are deeply suspect [sic] by authority' (*Daily Express*, 25 September 1941). Although the dissolution of the CFU was not directly promised within the Conservative Party's election manifesto for the general election of 1951, suspicions of its motives were long held and therefore its future was likely to be under review. Some twenty months beforehand, at the 1950 general election, the Conservative manifesto had clearly stated, 'there is also plenty of scope for retrenchment – to give only a few examples – in public relations, *Information Services* [my emphasis], excessive control over local authorities, the county agricultural committees, Government travelling, etc.'.

Opposition to the film unit and to government information films in general had been growing within the Conservative Party since its massive defeat at the general election of 1945. Such an apparent rejection of Churchill's wartime endeavours tended to stick in the craw of Conservatives, and it was hardly surprising that they very soon began to cast around for scapegoats. Many alighted very quickly upon the 'ingenious and a little sinister productions of the documentary makers' (M. Neville Kearney quoted in Short, 1983, p. 72). Furthermore, as Nicholas Pronay has suggested, 'going to factories, working men's institutes, church halls, adult education classes and the like at regular intervals, and thus being projected not in an entertainment context but in a context designed to lead "structured discussion" afterwards (documentary film) was, in fact a classic Soviet type, Agitprop operation... It gave firm resolve to the Conservatives to abolish the Crown Film Unit whenever they returned to power, especially since the Labour Government had not only retained it in existence but, under Basil Wright, used it for much the same purpose' (quoted in Short, 1983, p. 72). The charge is perhaps a little ironic as, just before the war, Grierson, writing in *Kinematograph Weekly* (hardly an agitprop organ!) had complained that 'Whitehall has permitted the very dangerous constitutional situation to arise in which the (Conservative) Party machine has tended to act more and more and more as Whitehall's public relations instrument in regard to the film trade. One cannot wonder that the film trade no longer distinguishes very clearly between National and Party service' (*Kinematograph Weekly*, 12 January 1939). What was sauce for the goose was evidently not sauce for the gander!

It seemed to have been generally assumed by some in the Conservative Party that the documentary movement in general was irredeemably biased towards the political left and the dirigiste economy. That this view might have been given some traction could be seen by such articles, even in the exhibitors' journal *Kinematograph Weekly*, which announced in December 1944: 'British documentary films in post war – creating a better informed and better educated nation'. The piece commenced: 'The film as a powerful aid to the democratic ideal is insisted upon in an informative broadsheet, sponsored by the Political and Economic Planning Society. While recognising the post-war potentialities of the documentary film, the sponsors of the Society deplore the possibility of its development being controlled by the profit motive and urge that the basis of a sound Industry can only be effected by Government action' (*Kinematograph Weekly*, 28 December 1944). This perception of the documentary movement as 'tainted' appeared to continue well into the later 1940s. In 1947 the movement's most notable publicist, Grierson, just prior to his return to the UK to take over as controller of film at the COI, was writing in *Kinematograph Weekly* that the role of the documentary filmmaker was to be a 'necessary force for public understanding and public order... The condition of our (creative) freedom lay in fact in the capacity to be so expert in the public issue that our need of Whitehall was matched, in normal human terms, by Whitehall's need of us' (*Kinematograph Weekly*, 11 September 1947). Furthermore, some notable members of the film and allied industries occupied the Labour benches in the Attlee administration, including Ben Levy, the playwright, Tom O'Brien, general secretary of the National Association of Theatrical and Kinematograph Employees (NATKE), Eric Fletcher, chairman of ABC, and John Reeves, secretary of the Workers' Film Association. Of course, this is not to say that the industry was not represented on the Conservative side, as frequent contributors to debates were E. P. Smith of the Screenwriters' Association, Walter Fletcher, an independent exhibitor, and Beverley Baxter of Gaumont-British Pictures. This fear of Labour dominating the arena certainly persisted up to, and including, the general elections of 1950 and 1951. Conservative Central Office was certainly convinced, as the party agent G. Davies commented: 'film propaganda provides one of the most effective means of conveying the Party's message to the electors' (Conservative Archive; uncatalogued).

However, whether this fear of Labour dominating or manipulating the documentary film was really justified is open to question. Certainly, senior members of the party attributed their electoral success to film as, according to Paul Rotha, '[Stafford] Cripps once said to me, "I think that the showing of the British documentary during the thirties and during the war years (was) a contributory factor to this enormous 1945 result in the election"' (quoted in Sussex, 1975, p. 32). It is certainly true that the new government began to use the CFU to produce PIFs which explained their new policies, although how far these became strongly partisan was a moot point. In terms of types of film these ranged from 'traditional' Griersonian drama documentaries to straightforward 'informationals', interspersed with the occasional animated piece. *Town Meeting of the World* (1946), for example, was a record of the first meeting of the United Nations held on 6 June 1946 in Westminster Central Hall, London. The film showed the Attlee's keynote address cut against brutal images of concentration camp victims, battle-scarred veterans and other horrors of the war. Attlee exhorted his fellow statesmen to set aside their private national interests in favour of the common good. In doing so, security, justice and freedom, all based upon universal economic prosperity, would deliver the world from the perils of the fear of war. *London Airport*, on the other hand, related the story of the development of what is now Heathrow, with its importance for international trade and communication. Many of these films were fairly straightforward apolitical reportage. Similarly, the drama documentary *It Might Be You*, directed by Michael Green using professional actors, was one of the first in what has become a recurring theme for PIFs. Peter Cushing, the young hospital doctor, addressed the audience directly, advising them that the new road systems being planned required greater caution, especially given the large number of postwar traffic accidents. The film concluded with a salutary tale of carelessness which resulted in one young man dying, another losing an arm and a young woman being badly bruised.

A review of the post-war catalogue of CFU films does appear to show that the Labour government was at pains to avoid using the COI film machinery too obviously for party political purposes. On the eve of the 1950 general election, for example, Morrison had the opportunity to champion the CFU, but his endorsement was hardly effusive. 'You asked me about the future of the CFU in your letter of March 28,' he wrote to the Conservative MP Ronald Bell. 'There is no intention of disbanding the Unit or interfering with its work in any way... It was, however, announced by the Central Office towards the end of last year that this year's programme was shaping in such a way as not to require the continuous employment of all those working (for) Crown' (TNA: INF 5/32).

It would seem, then, that the hostility to the CFU manifested by the Conservative Party on ideological grounds rested upon the twin presumptions that it presented a significant potential for use in party propaganda but also that its existence conflicted with the views taken by many leading Conservatives. Thus, for example, Duff Cooper, speaking in the context of the CFU's sponsoring department: 'I believe the truth of the matter to be that there is no place in the British scheme of Government for a Ministry of Information' (quoted in McLaine, 1979, p. 280). Certainly, opposition to the CFU seems to have been, in the main, subsumed into a greater hostility towards the COI in general. Indeed, when the Salisbury Committee on the Government Information Services was established a few days after the general election in 1951, one of its first targets was to recommend, if not the closure, then a significant reduction in the role of the COI.

The announcement of the closure of the CFU in early 1952, only a few weeks after the election of Churchill's Conservative government, came with such speed and remorselessness that it seemed to justify the documentarists' claims that this was a political vendetta. As the *Manchester Guardian* reported:

> M J A Boyd-Carpenter, Financial Secretary to the Treasury, amplifying the Chancellor's statement that expenditure on Government information services in 1952-3 would be reduced by at least £1.2m below the 1951-2 figure (announced) that production of the films by the Central Office of Information (COI) would cease. This would involve closing down the Crown Film Unit and giving up its premises in Beaconsfield. (Furthermore) distribution of films by COI mobile

vans would be discontinued, as would other performances paid for by the COI. Films from the COI Library would still be available on loan, but a system of charges was under consideration. (*Manchester Guardian*, 30 January 1952)

This rather curt dismissal of the film unit was even more galling to those at Beaconsfield in that it came in the form of a written parliamentary answer and did not dignify their passing by a Commons' statement. Little did they realise that the instruction given by Boyd-Carpenter to Sir Robert Fraser, the director general of the COI. a fortnight before was even more blunt. 'The Crown Film Unit is to be disbanded. Please arrange to give appropriate notice to all staff forthwith. No new films will be started. Please let me know as quickly as possible what film work is in actual progress, how far it is advanced and what is your recommendation as to its future' (TNA: GS 49/019A).

This was not to say that there was no opposition to the ending of general government filmmaking – although public concern over the health and subsequent death of King George VI meant that it was initially quite muted. Inevitably, the most vocal opponents of the closure were those with a vested interest in the CFU's continuation. As early as 14 January 1952, Ralph Nunn May, the CFU general manager, had written to R. A. Butler, the new chancellor of the Exchequer, making a desperate plea to avert the strongly rumoured execution:

> There are, alas, few things of which it can be truly said that Britain has the best in the world. The CFU has an unchallengeable position as the best short film unit in the world. In war it proved itself a vital weapon; and in peace a skilful and adaptable instrument making films of many different kinds for almost every department; making them all well; and not only doing a thoroughly practical and useful job, but winning awards the world over for the quality of the films – in itself no bad thing for British prestige. There is now a danger that, as a result of the economies very rightly imposed on government spending, the Unit might altogether be abolished. That would be a profound pity; and would, I'm sure, later be regretted. An authoritative word now to the effect that with due regard for essential economy, the Unit should, in essence, be kept in being, would bring steadiness and clarity to discussions that may otherwise be swayed by something like panic. I hope that it is not asking too much that this word should be given. (TNA: Treasury 0549/019A)

Despite this appeal to patriotism, which was a common thread in the arguments used by many of the opponents of closure, the words fell upon deaf ears. Roger Manvell of the British Film Academy expressed similar views in a letter to *The Times* on 18 July 1952: 'Everywhere I went in the USA I was asked why the famous CFU had been closed down. This it was implied, was a great blow to British prestige, especially at a time when the maintenance of our prestige matters greatly to America.' More concerted opposition was expected from the trades unions involved and George Elvin, the general secretary of the Association of Cinematograph Technicians (ACT), rallied the unions involved and coordinated a meeting of union leaders[2] with Boyd-Carpenter on 24 March 1952. Unfortunately for the union side, the financial secretary to the Treasury remained unmoved by their arguments. The minutes note that: 'The FST [financial secretary to the Treasury] explained that the Government had decided to make a substantial reduction in the use of film as a medium of information; this was not because of any dispute about the merits of Government films made in the past, but simply because they were an expensive medium' (TNA: T 219/121). There is no doubt that the government expected opposition would come from these fairly predictable quarters, but it might have been a little bemused in the concern expressed by the United States Mutual Security Agency (MSA). In the burgeoning Cold War world, the US was anxious that at least part of the COI's film operations should remain intact. A Mr Sirkin was despatched from the MSA Productivity Film Program for a private meeting with senior civil servants at the Treasury. The minutes explain: 'the US was not unduly troubled by the abolition of direct Government film production or of the CFU, because their own experience as sponsors showed that there were satisfactory alternatives. But distribution, which they had also explored carefully for various reasons, was another matter entirely. They did not themselves know of any suitable equivalent of the Government's film distribution service, and they were doubtful whether any commercial alternative which might be built up could be as economical' (TNA: Treasury GS 49/019A). Unfortunately, like other previous interventions, the government ignored its ally and banker's request.

So crocodile tears, but few others, were shed as the government consigned the CFU to history. The COI's office circular was brutal and to the point: 'The CFU will be disbanded and the mobile projection service abolished. There will be no more home theatrical distribution and narrow limits placed on home film production' (TNA: COI Circular 3/52).

Notes

1 The Gouzenko Affair was one of the first post-war 'red scares'. Igor Gouzenko defected to Canada in September 1945 and revealed an extensive Soviet spy and 'sleeper' network which had the aim of accessing nuclear secrets. Grierson was involved peripherally as his secretary had been named as one of the Soviet agents. However, his reputation was unfortunately compromised and he chose to return to the UK.
2 The union delegation included Elvin, Geddes, Thomson and (Miss) Wilson from ACT; Thursby and Varney from the Electrical Trade Union (ETU); Mingay from NATKE; and finally Mayne from the Institute of Professional Civil Servants.

10

Legacy

On learning of the closure of Crown, Ken Cameron, the senior sound editor, as he casually recalled during his BECTU interview with John Legard on 14 November 1988, felt 'desperately sorry to see that [it] was closing' and resolved 'to do something about it'. The 'it' in these circumstances was to establish the post-production company Anvil. It was hardly surprising that those who worked in the CFU sought employment in areas and organisations which recognised their particular talents and skills. In fact, during the lifetimes of the government film units they had a fluctuating membership – of never more than 200 – with individuals dropping in and out and moving between other similar film units. However, as the COI's director general Robert Fraser noted in an appeal to Mr A. Johnston of the Treasury, 'Not less important than its own direct production has been its role as the parent of all British documentary, and as a training ground for young producers, directors and technicians for the UK film industry' (TNA: INF 12/691).

Inevitably the more famous individuals, such as Humphrey Jennings, have attracted greater research and comment, but the work of the government film units was essentially that of teams of skilled practitioners and technicians. As one of Jennings' most recent biographers, Philip Logan (2011) has recorded,

> the final cinematic representation [of Jennings' wartime films] relied upon the contribution of each member of his team... Ken Cameron's recording then mixing of sound attempted to achieve not necessarily a natural rendition of sound but the creation of 'soundscapes'... Chick Fowle's black and white photography would attempt to capture the appropriate visual texture for images. Joe Mendoza advised on suitable types of music to accompany sequences. This creative

process could stimulate the memory and create forms of authenticity and truthfulness which may have an imaginative impact on the observer. (Logan, 2011, pp. 342–43)

The creative symbiosis to which Logan refers above had an influence upon many who worked in the units, and it was not unexpected that they subsequently achieved success in a wide variety of roles. What they had learned, experienced or developed would often underpin their ensuing careers. Sometimes they directly acknowledged that foundation and at other times it must be inferred. Unfortunately, tracking, describing and evaluating all the lives and employment histories of everybody who worked for the units would be a herculean task and is beyond the scope of this book.

It should perhaps be stated early on that the legacy of the film units has an international as well as a domestic aspect – in Brazil, for example, where cameraman Chick Fowle had been recruited in 1950 by Alberto Cavalcanti to assist in the development of the new Vera Cruz Studios in São Paolo. Fowle was to provide the cinematographic expertise which underpinned the development of post-war Brazilian cinema as he was the main cameraman on several films, some of which won international acclaim: 'According to Cavalcanti, Fowle was the only genuine success of the imported talents, and he was engaged as the cinematographer for Vera Cruz's first feature film, *Caiçara* (1950), directed by Adolfo Celi and produced by Cavalcanti' (Rist, 2014, p. 257). Fowle went on to shoot a number of films in South America, including *O Cangaceiro* (*The Bandit*, 1953, directed by Lima Barreto), which won the best adventure film award at the Cannes Film Festival in 1953, and a decade later *O Pagador de Promessas* (*Keeper of Promises*, directed by Anselmo Duarte) won the top prize in 1962, the Palme d'Or. The pervading influence of the CFU could also be seen in contemporary reviews such as that in *The Spectator* (10 September 1953, p. 10) which commented, somewhat affectedly, on *O Cangaceiro*: 'the film is photographed by Chick Fowle, who was for long a leading cameraman in British documentary and whose work here has a characteristic silky luminosity'.

Secondly, if imitation is the sincerest form of flattery, then there were certainly international examples of countries developing national film production organisations which were very reminiscent of Crown in particular. Although Crown's sister government film production organisation, the Colonial Film Unit, survived the Conservative cull at least until 1955, the units had worked reasonably well together; indeed, Crown actually completed a number of films for the Colonial Office, such as *Cocoa from Nigeria*, *El Dorado* and most famously *Daybreak in Udi*. From the early 1950s the remit of the Colonial Film Unit had changed away from making films to establishing national film units in those countries working towards independence. Countries as diverse as Nigeria or Malaya developed their own national film units modelled on the example of the CFU and began producing films which celebrated local achievements and were designed for local, rather than imperial, audiences.

However, one of the greatest legacies of the government film units was the effect they had on British films in the 1950s and early 1960s. Not only was this the result of the later filmmakers being the adolescent cinema viewers of the 1940s, but it was also hardly unexpected since many of the technicians behind the camera and in post-production had 'graduated' from the CFU film school of Pat Jackson's recollection. During his BECTU interview in 1991 he confirmed that he and his colleagues regarded the training aspect of the GPOFU and subsequently Crown as extremely important: 'there was nobody to teach us, we had to teach ourselves'. He also explained that Crown's approach contrasted to that of Grierson, which he described as 'pamphleteering', whereas the CFU, he argued, emphasised 'the use of story [and] the presentation of your story in dramatic terms', which was more in line with the approach of commercial filmmakers.

These unit 'graduates' appeared across all aspects of British filmmaking in the subsequent years. Some, such as Ken Cameron, who had also explained in his BECTU interview in 1988:

> I say this with all modesty, I was terribly reluctant to see this [CFU] Sound Department going because we'd built it up into quite an efficient Sound Department and we were getting a lot of outside work, like Group 3 and other things. [Also] foreign versions [of COI films] meant that practically every documentary had to be made in about 15 or 16 different languages, which meant translation, commentary, dubbing, a very big job.

This reluctance to see his skills dissipated by the closure of Crown encouraged him, along with three other ex-CFU members, Richard Warren, Ralph Nunn May and Ken Scrivener, to establish Anvil Productions. Working initially out of the Crown studios in Beaconsfield, this outfit provided audio facilities for both documentary and feature films in the 1950s and beyond. So successful was Anvil that in 1956 it acquired a controlling interest in Realist Films. Realist had been established in 1937 by Basil Wright and had subsequently produced documentary and similar films to that of the film units. There had been a regular transfer of staff between the two film units with the inevitable cross-fertilisation of ideas and methods, although its final subsuming into the Anvil operation is indicative of the continuing successful legacy of the government units. Realist continued to produce documentary and short films up until the 1970s, including such diverse topics as *Electro-magnetic Waves: Part 1 – Discovery and Generation* (1964), *The Bagpipes* (1969) and *HMS Pinafore* (1972), the latter as part of a series on Gilbert and Sullivan works.

Also continuing to practice in a similar area of work, but primarily in the public sector, was Stewart McAllister (1914–62), the often-mercurial film editor who had worked closely with Jennings on most of his CFU films, from *Words for Battle* to *A Diary for Timothy*. McAllister joined Edgar Anstey's British Transport Films (BTF) as senior film editor, subsequently increasingly taking directorial roles. McAllister brought some of the government units' standards and production processes to such films as *Berth 24* (1950), a quite long (at forty minutes) look at the turnaround of a freighter on the Hull to Gothenburg route, or the shorter (six minutes) but more whimsical *I Am a Litter Basket* (1959), featuring a talking litter bin urging railway users to be more litter-conscious. McAllister had also encouraged his young protégé at Crown, John Legard (1924–2017), to join him at British Transport Films. The CFU legacy continued when Legard went on to become the editor-in-chief at BTF, producing films in a similar vein, such as *The Nine Road* (1976), a story about the Number 9 bus route in London between Mortlake and Liverpool Street, and *A New Approach to Hong Kong* (1982), about the building of a railway line from Lo Wu on the Chinese border to Kowloon on Hong Kong harbour.

The prominence of high-quality production values alongside a coherent storyline told in dramatic terms were key aspects of many of the units' productions which translated easily into to a range of films. As a director, Jackson, for example, claimed to have pioneered use of the subjective camera in the 1942 film, *Builders*:

> I was asked to make this film on building an ordnance factory and we went to Bedford and just covered ourselves in mud, filth and slime! And I thought, 'This is impossible – how on earth are you going to make a subject of building an ordnance factory interesting?' And so I was in despair about that and I thought, 'Well the only way to do it, is to really use the subjective camera, and the camera will be somebody who is going to visit them and talk to various people. It was the first use of subjective camera, actually. (1991)

Not only were the government film units' influence important for production techniques and standards, but also their films often predated aspects of what are thought of as later genres. This anticipation of future cinematic trends had been noted as long ago as 1972 by Allan Lovell and Jim Hillier, who maintained that there was a direct link between so-called Free Cinema and the work of John Grierson and Humphrey Jennings. Free Cinema had been established by Lindsay Anderson, Karel Reisz, Tony Richardson and Lorenza Mazzetti in 1956 as a putative pressure group with the main aim of establishing the right of directors to creatively interpret society. As such, according to Lovell and Hillier, they were clearly influenced by the documentary filmmakers, especially Jennings, who 'captured the interest in film as an art' (Lovell and Hillier, 1972, p. 138).

However, it could also be argued that the influence of Crown, in particular, on subsequent films, especially those that are sometimes referred to as British New Wave films, was more subliminal but no less important. For example, as has already been seen, Jack Holmes' 1949 CFU film *The People at Number 19* addressed venereal disease, a highly controversial topic in the late 1940s. Holmes' perspective is relatively free from either sentimentality or prurience, instead concentrating on the impact of the infection within one small working-class family. The mise en scène anticipated somewhat literally the 'kitchen sink' or social realism films of a decade or so later. Holmes situated almost the entire action of the film within a small kitchen with the entrance and departure of the various characters determining the direction and flow of the storyline. This approach is certainly adopted and developed further in scenes in such New Wave feature films as *Saturday Night and Sunday Morning* (1960, directed by Reisz) and *Billy Liar* (1963, directed by John Schlesinger). *The People at Number 19* was not an isolated example of a CFU film of this type, as the same approach, with a similar mise en scène and confrontational storyline but this time dramatising family problems associated with mental health, can be seen in Leacock's *Out of True* (1951).

It was not just in this type of staging that EMB, GPO and Crown anticipated later films, but also a case can be made for their impact on the development of certain specific genres. Thus, *The Magic Touch*, with its plethora of white coats and laboratories, certainly added to the canon of films featuring the scientist as hero. It predated the mini-boom in the genre in the early 1950s with such films as *The Day the Earth Stood Still* or *The Man in the White Suit*, which had ex-CFU man, Terry Bishop, as second unit director. The latter film, a comedy drama, starred Alec Guinness as the scientist who had invented a fibre which was both stain-resistant and indestructible. Unfortunately, the resulting cloth would have been the death knell for both textile workers and factory owners and the film ended with Guinness being chased from the town by an angry mob. Of course, the most famous of the British scientists as screen hero in the 1950s was Barnes Wallis, played by Michael Redgrave in *The Dam Busters*.

The most obvious connection with fictional film genres can be seen in the war-based feature films that were produced in some numbers in Britain during the 1950s. This link was most apparent in films such as *The Wooden Horse* and *Appointment in London* which were directed by ex-CFU men, Jack Lee and Philip Leacock respectively. Both men made use of location shooting, eschewing the then standard practice of the British film industry to remain within studios, and they were also shot in black and white. This approach was later adapted by other directors in a conscious manner, as John Ramsden has pointed out:

> It was also a deliberate policy in at least some cases where colour or a wider screen were a real option, as for example in *Dunkirk* (directed

by Leslie Norman, 1958) or *The Dam Busters* (directed by Michael Anderson, 1955); in such cases, the traditional look was consciously adopted so as to make post-war films look like films made during the war years, deliberately obscuring the passage of time, and continuing the visual merging of documentary and fictional traditions that was a notable feature of 1939–45 film-making. (Ramsden, 1998, p. 37)

Of course, this also enabled directors to splice in actual combat and contemporary footage quite easily, an approach utilised earlier by the CFU in such films as *Ferry Pilot* and, somewhat later, *Alien Orders*.

The importance of combat footage, whether actual or fictionalised, became an essential element of many British war films in the 1950s and has been examined in no little detail by several historians, including Ramsden (1998, 2003), Eley (2001), Rattigan (2001) and Murphy (2005). However, for the purposes of this study, what was important was the debt they appeared to owe to the documentary movement and to the CFU in particular. A brief review of the highest-grossing British-made films in the 1950s certainly demonstrated the domestic popularity of the genre. According to Murphy, '*The Dam Busters* and *Reach for the Sky* were the top box-office films of 1955 and 1956 respectively, and *The Cruel Sea* (1953), *The Battle of the River Plate* (1957), *The Bridge on the River Kwai* (1957) and *Sink the Bismarck!* (1960) were equally successful' (Murphy, 2005, p. 205).

Take *The Dam Busters* as a case in point. The debt it owed to its predecessors, especially *Target for Tonight*, has been acknowledged by both Rattigan, who described it as 'the linear descendant of *Target for Tonight*' (Rattigan, 1994, p. 149) and Murphy (2005, p. 219) who argued that it 'was a dry run for *The Dam Busters*'.

It is therefore somewhat surprising that in his otherwise comprehensive and thoughtful BFI monograph, *The Dam Busters*, Ramsden (2003) singularly ignored its CFU predecessor, despite their many similarities. Once the section which addressed the development of the 'bouncing bomb' is discounted then the comparisons with the earlier film are manifest. The storylines followed the same sequence: the briefing for the raid with the inevitable 'jokey' behaviour of the bomber crews, probably necessary to relieve obvious anxieties; the take-off into the night and the journey over enemy territory; the raid itself and the German response, then the tortuous and hazardous return, and finally the debriefing and the essential bacon and eggs. All of this was cut at regular intervals with scenes of the operations control room staff who were monitoring the progress of the aircraft. If the mise en scène which accompanied this sequence was similar in both films then so, too, were many camera angles and approaches. The tension-building close-ups of the bomb aimers in both films was an example, as was the result of their actions with the detonation of the bombs. In both cases this, by modern CGI standards, was rather naive but no less effective.

Not only did Ramsden omit any comparison with the CFU's *Target for Tonight* in terms of its filmic quality but he also missed similarities in the production process. At least one member of *The Dam Busters*' production team had worked briefly with Crown. The film editor Richard Best (1916–2004) had also been an uncredited film editor on *Malta G.C.*, a CFU production in conjunction with the service film units. However, in a less serious vein, Ramsden also described an unfortunate occurrence during filming:

> The actors had been given use of the officers' mess [at RAF Scampton, the original Dam Busters airfield] for the duration of the filming but 'Flight Sergeant' Robert Shaw was denied admission on the grounds that he wasn't an officer. After an embarrassing row, the actor-NCOs were allowed in, but only if they removed their uniform jackets, surely a mess rule unique in the history of armed forces etiquette. (Ramsden, 2003, p. 51)

Ironically, some fourteen years earlier, Harry Watt and Jonah Jones had a similar experience. During the filming of *Target for Tonight* they were summoned to an important meeting at the Air Ministry. A lengthy and disrupted night-time journey to London at the height of the Blitz found them the following morning in the office of an RAF wing commander who proceeded to admonish them for failing to wear jackets and ties in the officers' mess at RAF Mildenhall where the flying scenes were filmed. They were advised in no uncertain fashion that, unless they conformed, the particular courtesy would be removed (Sussex, 1975, pp. 129–30). This was at a time, of course, when the government was asking citizens 'is your journey really necessary?'

Such examples of military protocol, however, enabled Ramsden to argue elsewhere that there was a contrast between the earlier

CFU films in their representation of social classes and those war films of the 1950s, such as *The Dam Busters*, which,

> do not celebrate the union of classes and regions that was so characteristic of such wartime films as *The Way Ahead* (directed by Carol Reed, 1944), *Millions Like Us* (directed by Frank Launder and Sidney Gilliatt, 1943), or *Fires Were Started* (directed by Humphrey Jennings, 1943); rather they tend to revert to the stock officers-as-heroes and other-ranks-as-comic-figures that was more characteristic of films of the 1930s. The reviewers were particularly hostile on just this point, but a modern viewer can hardly disagree: Peter Baker complained of *Sink the Bismarck* that 'the characters are almost unbelievably typed – the wooden, muddling British officer types; the matey, tea-swilling lower deck cockney types'. There were certainly exceptions to this approach, but not many, and even such quality films as *The Dam Busters* clearly leave leadership in the hands of senior officers and the scientist Barnes Wallis. (Ramsden, 1998, p. 56)

The differences between the social class cohesion of the wartime CFU productions evident in such scenes as the pilots' mess in *Ferry Pilot* and, more obviously, in *Ordinary People* can be overstated, especially in the context of an operational military unit. It perhaps ignores the fact that the majority of the contemporary audience in the 1950s had acquired an understanding of service life either directly or vicariously and that screen representations, especially of actual events, ought to have at least a veneer of contemporary reality. Ramsden perhaps unconsciously overlooked the fact that in the military there is a strict distinction between the officer corps and 'other ranks', which continues to exist today.[1] In the Second World War there were, after all, many 'temporary gentlemen' who had been recruited from social classes and situations without a tradition of supplying officers to the forces. The rank-based segregation was not primarily evidence of social class divisions, although it did of course frequently echo and reflect them; but more, it reflected the exigencies of command in which life and death decisions have to be made.

While Crown produced a small number of feature-length films that, like *Target for Tonight* and *Western Approaches*, received both critical and reasonable box-office success, most of the unit's output, especially in the post-war years, can easily be placed under the heading of public information films. The CFU PIFs covered a wide variety of topics and were sponsored by an equally diverse range of government departments and organisations. Sometimes the subjects were highly specialised and designed for particular audiences – such as *Patent Ductus Arteriosus* for the medical profession and *Pigs on Every Farm* for the agricultural community. These and many similar films produced by the CFU and other film companies, such as Realist, became the basis of the training film sector. Ex-CFU staffers appeared in the credits of a number of these after 1952; so, for example, twenty years later, Fred Gamage was the cameraman on the somewhat esoterically entitled *Remotely Operated All-Hydraulic Support* (1972), which was produced for the National Coal Board to introduce miners to a new piece of equipment.

The government film units' approach and successes proved to be a model for some filmmaking organisations and the demise of Crown created a vacuum which others exploited. The demand for film amongst public sector organisations continued long after 1952. Crown's last year of operation was its most successful in terms of actual productions, having made twenty-nine films. This demand for training and public information films encouraged the development of film units, often leavened with ex-EMB, GPO and Crown staff, both within and working directly for government departments such as, for example, the aforementioned British Transport Films.

Alongside the training films were those which were less occupationally specific but usually intended as general careers guidance for a younger audience. Amongst the final films completed by the CFU in 1952 were *Making Boots and Shoes* for the footwear industry, and *Light Repetitive Work* which introduced young women to opportunities available in factories. It should be noted, from a social history perspective, that these films revealed the contemporary strict gender division in employment. Indeed, the former film emphasised that access to job roles and opportunities in the industry were actually determined by gender. Although it was some five years after the closure of Crown that the BBC and the new Independent Television began regular transmissions designed for schools, CFU productions certainly anticipated this.[2] As has been already mentioned, during the afternoons of the early 1950s the BBC did indeed broadcast some Crown films in the *Is This the Job for Me?* series.[3] These broadcasts were often repeated as, at that time, there was no facility for domestic recording and all programmes had to be watched live. How many actually watched these films directly transmitted rather than borrowed from the COI library and viewed by means of the school projector is a moot point given the actual number of television licences in the early 1950s. It was, of course, highly likely that these films were included in broadcast transmissions not so much for their vocational relevance, but rather to ensure that the potential television-buying public would at least be able to see something on screen when visiting their local retailer.

The government film units developed a consistency of style and production values in non-theatrical PIFs which were both reflected in similar output from other commercial companies such as Realist and Verity and which lasted well into the 1970s. Although vocationally specific films have been discussed above, valid cases could equally be made for a variety of different topic areas for particular audiences from local government administration (*Houses in Town*, 1951) to factory design (*Layout and Handling in Factories*, 1951).

Film shorts were a regular feature of cinema programmes during the 1950s and 1960s. Shows often consisted of the main feature with either a 'B' film and/or a short or animation or newsreel. The short tended to be fairly anodyne – often a travelogue or tribute to a particular British achievement or other. These had, of course, been a feature of early EMBFU productions, such as Marion Grierson's 1933 *So This Is London*. In this vein, Crown later produced *Royal Scotland* (1952), essentially a scenic review of places in Scotland with royal connections, and *Trooping the Colour* (1950) as well as *Into the Blue* (1950), about British aviation successes such as the Comet or the jet engine. Following the closure of Crown the staff would be found producing similar films. Thus, Jonah Jones filmed *Foxhunter: Champion Jumper* (1953), about one of the most famous show-jumping horses of all time, and another CFU cameraman, Fred Gamage, shot *Oxford* in 1958 for Greenpark Productions on commission for the COI, described later by Anthony Neild as,

> part travelogue and part infomercial, both for the University itself and the city in general. Yet Williams [the Director] is determined to throw in the odd artful moment, show off some ambition and remain quiet when necessary: at times we get some wonderful compositions

and striking tracking shots, at others we simply serve as a fly-on-the-wall, gaining an interesting behind-the-scenes glimpse at this institution. (Neild, 2011)

How far the director Derek Williams was advised by his more experienced cameraman is, of course, open to question. Similarly, Ken Cameron, the CFU's principal sound recordist, worked on *Under the Caribbean* in 1954, a film which introduced British audiences to the thalassic world of Hans and Lotte Hass, later famous for their BBC television documentaries on life under the sea. As had been the case with earlier government films, many of this type of PIF were also made available to overseas exhibitors, especially in the colonies.

It was the nature of theatrical exhibition that, in the years before the general availability of television in Britain, enabled the government to disseminate a particular message in a short and readily accessible manner to a wide audience. It is therefore hardly surprising that many of Crown's post-war PIFs were essentially advisory. The topics addressed by these films could be many and various and usually reflected the concerns of the moment; sometimes these were immediate and yet at other times they were recurring. In the latter customary category there were, for example, the PIFs which addressed road safety. As has been seen, *It Might Be You* was an early CFU example in this classification and this was one of the monthly COI films distributed to cinemas throughout the country. It was followed two years later by *Worth the Risk?* which strengthened the road safety message. The topic was subsequently reinforced at regular intervals, first in the cinema and then on television. Such examples would include *Ambler Gambler Twins* (COI, 1977) and, increasingly, concerns about the incidence of drink-driving, such as with *Fancy a Jar, Forget the Car* (1982).

Also in this recurring category were the health advisory PIFs. Sometimes these provided mainly informational details of changes in government policy or practice, and occasionally they addressed immediate threats. A periodic issue was the need to recruit blood donors and the CFU had produced the short *Wanted for Life* (1951) to encourage people to volunteer to donate blood. This became a continuing theme in the ensuing decades, with the COI producing a range of films including *Blood Donors: The Spinners* (1976) and *Blood Donor – Jenny Jones* (1983). In an early response to an immediate and developing health threat, the CFU had produced *Surprise Attack*, which encouraged parents to have their children vaccinated against smallpox when the disease had recently reappeared in the UK. Fortunately, until the coronavirus pandemic of the early 2020s, when such shorts as *Hands, Face and Space* (2020) were released through both broadcast and online outlets, the government has not usually found the need to invest in nationally exhibited PIFs. The exception to this, of course, was the response to HIV/AIDS[4] in the 1980s, which did trigger perhaps one of the most famous recent PIFs, *Don't Die of Ignorance* (1987), broadcast on television as well as being exhibited in cinemas. Today, given the diversity with which the population now consumes media products, the most recent PIFs in the early 2020s concerned with combating the Covid-19 pandemic[5] were released on a multitude of platforms, including the internet.

As far as the combination of advisory and informative films was concerned, it is possible to demonstrate the lasting legacy of the government film units by examining over time a particular topic which addressed both an important public concern and a key aspect of government policy. In structure, filmic devices, social observation and contextualisation, the GPO and CFU films sponsored by the British government about the possible impact of an aerial assault between 1939 and 1951 were continued by its successors well into the 1960s.

Attack from the air has been selected as an appropriate exemplar theme for a number of reasons. Firstly, it was an issue of major concern to the population of the UK throughout a large proportion of the twentieth century. As early as 1932 British Prime Minister Stanley Baldwin had believed, along with a large proportion of his compatriots, that the 'bomber will always get through' (Middlemas and Barnes, 1969, p. 722); this attitude was further reinforced by commercial feature films like Korda's *Things to Come* in 1936, as well as contemporary newsreel footage which showed the devastation wrought by bombers, such as that of Guernica, the sacred Basque city destroyed by the German Condor Legion in April 1937. Fear of attack from the air in Britain soon became the reality of the Blitz of 1940–41 and subsequent raids culminating in the second, almost entirely London-targeted, Blitz of the spring and summer of

1944. This latter offensive was undertaken by missiles, the V1s and V2s,[6] rather than conventional aircraft. Despite the war ending in Europe in May 1945, the ensuing development of the Cold War with the USSR, which lasted until the late 1980s, meant that British citizens continued to live under the threat of aerial attack. Therefore, successive British governments sought to use the medium of film to prepare the civilian population for what might occur should hostilities commence.

In order to appreciate the change effected upon PIFs by the GPOFU and Crown, it is necessary to briefly refer again to *If War Should Come*, a nine-minute short produced by the GPOFU in 1939. It was generally assumed that the German bombers would be quickly unleashed against the UK with devastating results. However, in early September 1939, after the declaration of war, the film was given a new and more immediate title, *Do it Now*, with an exhortation in the title frames that 'the film intended for the future, becomes advice for today. Advice to be heard and taken here and now!' It was rushed onto the national cinema screens with the support of the CEA and was shown in over 2,000 cinemas during the week beginning 18 September 1939 (TNA: INF 6/349). Essentially the film was a set of government instructions illustrated by small cameos interspersed with reassuring stock shots of recognisable sights in the UK set against, initially, a stirring Elgar soundtrack. Much of the poignancy of the film was its naivety in which preparations were being made to counter the aerial threat that, within twelve months, would become all too real.

Reality, however, was somewhat different from expectation in that not only was the aerial bombardment delayed until the summer of 1940 but, when it did occur, despite all the deaths and damage, the majority of British citizens survived. Thus, the key message of subsequent PIFs concerning air attack was one of survivability, and this would last until the early 1960s. This more optimistic approach was quickly incorporated into subsequent PIFs as early as December 1940, with Jennings' *London Can Take It!* (later retitled *Britain Can Take It!*) and other films, such as Holmes and Lee's *Ordinary People*. Not only could life continue during wartime with only minor disruptions, but adequate preparation in terms of bomb shelters and ARP arrangements would ensure that casualties would be limited.

Unfortunately, the cessation of hostilities in 1945 only resulted in a short hiatus in the fear of potential attack from the air. The collapse of the wartime alliance with the Soviet Union and the communist appropriation of many eastern European states created a mutually antagonistic situation with the Western powers, better known as the Cold War. The proxy conflict in Korea, which commenced in 1950, resulted in newsreels again showing scenes of destruction caused by, amongst other things, aerial bombardment. The government's PIF response included Crown's *The Waking Point* with its deeply pessimistic message.

Perhaps more worrying for the general civilian population in Britain was the fact that, although there were conflicts in faraway places, the weaponry and delivery systems available to the principal opponents in the Cold War had become awesome. The dropping of the atomic bombs on Hiroshima on 6 August 1945 and Nagasaki three days later changed the whole paradigm of aerial bombardment. It now meant that one weapon could cause as much damage as a whole fleet of conventional bombers. Alongside this, and from a brutal strategic perspective, it killed, maimed or, perhaps most horrific of all, caused long-term sickness, amongst an enemy population. Although there was some reference to the impact of radiation in the subsequent films, there was little real discussion about it or about the taking of any significant preventive measures.

Amongst several films, which included *Defence Sense* (1956) and *The Warden and the Householder* (1961), distributed in the UK a decade or so after the closure of the Crown, two are worthy of more detailed study, both for the manner in which they address the issue and in their adoption of aspects of previous GPO/CFU productions. The first, *Atomic Attack* (1958), is exceptional in this study as it was not a film but rather a tele-recording made by the BBC for the Belgian television service. To emphasise this point, one of the first scenes included a jeep being driven into shot with a television camera emblazoned with the BBC logo placed in its passenger seat. In one sense, this echoed the early movie cameras being bulky and unwieldy but with the additional disadvantage of being linked umbilically to the recording machines. Apart from the obvious practical disadvantages of filming in this way, the subsequent transfer to cinema-quality 35 mm film significantly reduced the picture quality. However, as the theme is post-nuclear attack, the grainy pictures lend a certain authenticity to the production. The link to the GPOFU/CFU was reinforced as the principal cameraman was, again, Fred Gamage, who had been responsible for several CFU films including *Listen to Britain*, *A Diary for Timothy* and *Daybreak in Udi*.

The first few scenes of *Atomic Attack*, shot at the civil defence training ground at Epsom, were set up to resemble what might occur immediately after a nuclear strike. The camera panned, taking in burning buildings, casualties in the road and even the inside of a telephone box. The audience was unambiguously reminded, not only by the telephone box but also by a postbox and bus stop sign, that these things might and could happen in the UK.

Atomic Attack adopted a common Crown approach of the 1940s in that the action in the film was not undertaken by professional actors but rather, it would seem, the majority, if not all, of the participants were members of the Civil Defence Corps and other volunteer bodies such as the Auxiliary Fire Service. Although, of course, that enabled them to carry out their various tasks competently, the limited dialogue was somewhat forced and stilted. The voiceover narration tended to rescue the coherence and flow of the film by providing the main explanation and linkage between the various scenes. It will always be a moot point as to whether a message is conveyed more authentically by those in reality engaged with the task or actors who understand the demands of the camera and appropriate film direction. As noted earlier, John Mortimer had somewhat caustically recalled that 'It was part of the documentary credo never to use actors: "The Man in the Street" had to be played by the actual man in the street, with results which varied from embarrassing timidity to outrageous over-playing' (Mortimer, 1979, p. 6).

Other Crown employees, such as director Pat Jackson in his BECTU interview in 1991, took the entirely contrary view that the use of non-actors gave the films the hallmark of authenticity, so,

> It was that people had the stamp of the environment and their life and background... not only on their faces but in their physique, which no actor can really give you. It also had the vernacular... their way of speech, their way of phrasing, because they never... even in *Western Approaches* I never asked them to learn lines, so that you get the gist, so that they interpreted the scene and used their own words to describe the content of the scene.

It would therefore seem that the use of an amateur cast, so frequently utilised by the government film units, was continued in some PIFs well after the closure of the unit. There were also other on-screen representations which reflected the films of the 1940s, and the audience would no doubt have appreciated the roles and responsibilities outlined in the main part of *Atomic Attack*. So, for example, the key local role was played by the warden who, as in the Second World War, had the responsibility of reporting local damage and casualties. The principal novelty in the face of the threat of nuclear weapons was that he now carried a Geiger counter to establish local radiation levels. As in *The Waking Point*, the emphasis of the film was that training was essential and that volunteering at the last moment would be totally ineffective.

These post-war films emphasised the survivability assumptions of the earlier films, such as *Ordinary People*. However, by 1958 the situation had dramatically altered, especially in terms of ordnance.[7] The weapons dropped upon Japan were atomic bombs, whereas by the mid-1950s the opposing sides in the Cold War were equipped with hydrogen bombs. Although there is not a direct correlation between the amount of destruction and the power of the device exploded, it is sufficient to be aware that the expected results were many hundreds of times greater than what happened to Hiroshima and Nagasaki. Added to the immense destruction caused by blast and fire would be the inevitable radiation pollution which, depending upon wind direction and other factors, would cause further catastrophic and long-term effects among any surviving population. It was not that the government was unaware of the potential for massive casualties. As early as May 1954, government scientific advisers had pointed out that, depending upon type of weapon used, meteorological conditions and time of day, fatal casualties, either through blast or subsequent radiation poisoning in London (population 8.2 million), for example, could be as high as 4.1 million people (TNA: HO 225/52). Furthermore, in October 1954, following a war game named Exercise Thunder, involving all the armed forces and their civilian counterparts, it was realised, 'It is now clear that an all-out enemy attack would so disrupt the centralised control and reliable and extensive communications upon which the execution of the existing War Deployment Plan

(Xenophon) depends, that it would be impossible to carry it out in practice' (TNA: AIR 20/9115).

Consequently, the assumptions upon which planning in the event of an aerial attack were based were now thought to be redundant. Despite this, in 1958, perhaps to reassure the civilian population, *Atomic Attack* persisted in validating the belief in general survivability.

However, a mere four years later, *Hole in the Ground* (1962) was somewhat different in tone, content and presentation. It marked the beginning of the end of the expectation of survivability and instead a rather cold assumption that many British citizens would become collateral damage in any future nuclear exchange. Gone was the emphasis on casualty recovery and the somewhat enthusiastic amateurism of the civil defence in previous films. Much was still recognisable from previous GPOFU/CFU films – which was hardly surprising as, once again, the chief cameraman was Gamage. The film appeared to have little direct concern for the general populace, who are only shown briefly and in both instances as people running away from the camera to take what little shelter they can in their own homes. Instead, down in the hole of the title – a deep bomb-proof nuclear shelter – the sang-froid and blasé approach of those within towards their compatriots above ground is somewhat surprising to modern audiences. However, it was an attitude which would have been readily recognisable both from earlier Crown wartime films such as *Target for Tonight*, *Coastal Command* and *Western Approaches*, and was also reflected in some of the behaviour seen in the 1950s British war films such as *The Cruel Sea*, *The Dam Busters* and *Ice Cold in Alex* (1958).

The key characters in *Hole in the Ground* were not introduced by name but rather by job title or role. So there was the chief sector warning officer (the only permanent member of staff) and the leading scientist, accompanied by a variety of telephonists and other technical helpers. Consistent with previous CFU films such as *The Magic Touch* or even *Insect Pests in Food*, the scientist had been elevated to hero status and in this film it was his advice which determined the decisions made by the chief sector warning officer. The film detailed the likely sequence of events should the UK be attacked from the air with nuclear weapons. Although the USSR was never mentioned by name, the implicit assumption was always that it would be the aggressor.

The operations room of the Sector Warning and Monitoring Organisation would be readily recognisable to many in the audience as being almost identical to that in *Target for Tonight* and indeed many subsequent films, both documentary and feature, about the air war in the Second World War, where people were earnestly and frantically busy around large maps. *Hole in the Ground* confirmed on screen the government policy of deterrence as it included a series of shots of Vulcan bomber crews enplaning and taking off to attack the enemy. Direct defence of the UK was taken up by Lightning and Buccaneer fighter aircraft scrambling and these, alongside the launching of Bloodhound surface-to-air missiles, were shown engaging and destroying 'enemy planes'. However, the narrator intoned, echoing Baldwin thirty years before, 'it is inevitable that some enemy planes and missiles will get through'.

Amongst the scenes there is a brief homage to earlier CFU films like *Listen to Britain* with a panoramic shot across London, perhaps implying that this was to be the last time it was to be seen this way. Meanwhile, in contrast to the civilians above, those in the Sector Warning and Monitoring Organisation were safely ensconced 120 feet below behind steel doors.

The film also introduced a French liaison officer who advised the chief sector warning officer of potential fallout approaching the English south coast. It was the result of a bomb on Boulogne but, he added, 'only a little one of about 100 kilotons'. This was said in a manner which appeared totally oblivious to the massive destruction and loss of life that even such a 'small' weapon would have caused to his country and countrymen. He does perhaps redeem himself slightly by commenting to his Belgian colleague that the situation '*ce n'est pas joli*'; which was probably the understatement of the film.

All those below ground in the hole carried out their tasks without any show of emotion, despite the fact that, above, families and friends were being slaughtered. There was little hint of the personal impact of what was occurring, except in one screen incident when a female telephonist asked the chief sector warning officer if he was aware of the situation on the south coast. His response was that it was fine, although Southampton had been hit by a bomb. The film cuts to the telephonist's friends who mutter amongst themselves that the young woman's parents lived in that city. Returning to the telephonist, there was a brief lip wobble – but she then took control of herself and returned to her duties. This casualness or sang-froid in the face of what could only be massive devastation persisted throughout the film. Even towards the end the two leading characters were quite cheerful and set about rewarding themselves with chocolate and a smoke. Again, this seems to be more a reflection on the behaviour anticipated and seen in many war films of the 1940s and 1950s. It is not quite as cheerful as the air raid shelter scene in *Ordinary People* but is certainly in the same vein. However, in this case, they are safely in their hole, whereas the majority of the population are on the surface being blasted or irradiated.

This film was produced at a time of heightened tensions between NATO and the Warsaw Pact countries and is contemporaneous with the Cuban Missile Crisis in which a standoff between the USA and the USSR over Soviet deployment of missiles in Cuba almost initiated a global conflict. It was also produced when support for the Campaign for Nuclear Disarmament (CND) was growing in the UK. Although there was much in the film technically and in production values which echoed its government film unit predecessors, its general insensitivity to the civilian population was not a message seen within the earlier productions.

All the films about aerial assault were reflections of the concerns and priorities of the times in which they were produced. In many cases this was overtly demonstrated, normally by the inclusion of appropriate newsreel footage, which contextualised the subsequent action and development within the film. Although not a feature uniquely of government film unit productions it was a device used quite frequently – such films as *Ferry Pilot* and *Coastal Command* included stock footage. In the case of *The Waking Point*, for example, the first scene was set in a cinema where a newsreel was being screened. The newsreel itself showed the deteriorating international situation across the world, culminating with the outbreak of war in Korea. The inclusion of stock shots to emphasise a particular point was used especially by Crown, and *Hole in the Ground* similarly used footage of RAF aircraft and missiles taking off and attacking enemy planes in the middle of the film to establish that retaliation was being undertaken (Figure 10.1).

Figure 10.1 In *Hole in the Ground* (1962) a telephonist is told that, above ground, her family has been obliterated in a Soviet nuclear attack

This tactic reflected the Griersonian dictum that documentary films are 'the creative treatment of actuality' (Grierson, 1933, p. 8) which permeated the approach of many of the government film units' productions and, in turn, the later COI-commissioned PIFs. The drama documentary was seen as a suitable vehicle to convey information even when addressing the ultimate survivability event of a nuclear strike. The narrative aspect of the film provided an easily understandable, direct and, with the use of actors, professional telling of the story. This could either be the intertwining of a number of individual stories relating to the same event as, for example, *Ordinary People* or the interaction of people responding to a possible calamity, as in the case of *Hole in the Ground*. The message becomes personalised but is nonetheless powerful.

Not only were there influences of the GPOFU/CFU in terms of form and approach in the later COI films relating to aerial attack but there are more subtle similarities. As has been noted earlier, the government film units did not challenge the contemporary perspective on social class and this was also to be recognised in the later films. Earlier films tended to conform generally to social class stereotypes. In *Ordinary People*, although the overall message is one of 'we're all in this together', the class stereotypes were plainly evident. Those from the working classes tended to fit into a spectrum, one end of which was stolid and worthy and the other was marked by a mischievous and jokey attitude. In the first category there were Mr and Mrs Payne, the housewife who represented self-sacrifice and neighbourly support and her husband, the worker in an armaments factory who, afterwards, still did his bit as an air raid warden. Similarly, Frank, the GPO telephone engineer, represented diligence and dedication as he continued his repair work even during an air raid. Meanwhile, his mate, Dougie, showed less application but cheerfully eyed up passing women and flicked a V sign at the oncoming German bombers. Not quite in the same category, but still demonstrating humour and cheerfulness throughout the film, was the corpulent taxi driver, Tiny. These working-class stereotypes were replicated in later films as, for example, in *Hole in the Ground*, when the unnamed telephonist stoically composed herself and got on with her duties.

A slight exception to this interpretation of the class stereotypes was that of Joe Mercer, a railway Pullman coach attendant in *The Waking Point*. He was clearly the hero but, in a sense, his heroism was based upon his previous wartime experience in an air raid heavy rescue team and his willingness, eventually, to volunteer once again for civil defence. Furthermore, his commitment was finally rewarded by appointment as one of the few full-time paid officials. Thus, his screen role also chimes with the very early EMB films which often emphasised the dignity of labour. As such he became, through the redemptive process of nearly losing his son in an accident, a stolid and worthy citizen.

In one sense many of Crown's wartime films were exceptional compared to the pre-war productions as, unlike the extreme case of the EMBFU's *One Family*, they reflected a contemporary view that the relationship between the social classes was closer than both pre- and post-war. This was especially true when the on-screen participants were in uniform. In all the films, a uniform confers both respect and responsibility; but it clearly denoted the difference in attitude and behaviour between those officers, normally middle-class, and the other ranks, normally working-class. The individuals who provided the cross-class and cross-rank communication are the non-commissioned officers (NCOs), usually from working-class backgrounds but having been promoted, presumably through their diligence and conscientiousness. The most notable example of this is Bob, the civil defence organiser in *The Waking Point*. Bob's NCO status is emphasised in the film in a number of ways – his uniform and rank badges, his authority demonstrated by his actions during the civil defence exercise and, perhaps most tellingly, by his interaction and deference to Mrs Rankin and the senior regional civil defence officer.

The NCO role is apparent in subsequent films but is less central to the narrative. So, for example, in *Ordinary People* the court usher has the role of both communicating with the judge and the plaintiff, an obviously working-class woman who had fallen in arrears with her rent. Bomb damage to her house had meant that she was unable to take in lodgers. The more formal uniformed NCO role is seen in most of the other films, where military or semi-military figures feature. In *Atomic Attack*, though, the NCO was seen in his traditional role as carrying out the instructions of the officer of the Mobile Defence Corps.[8]

Although the officer role was often depicted and remained very similar across the CFU films, the general depiction of the middle class was quite nuanced. So there were representatives of the professional middle class, such as in the CFU's *Ordinary People* where this role was taken by the judge administering justice at a local level and in a small claims case. He was both the representative of the establishment and the status quo, but also of fairness and understanding. He epitomised a phlegmatic attitude in the face of aerial attack, but also a determination to continue with his duty regardless of any consequences to himself. Similarly, in the later *Hole in the Ground*, the scientific officer also demonstrated his professionalism by his objective assessments and decisions.

The middle-class sense of duty and commitment was a theme running through several of the government units' productions. For example, it had been highlighted early on in such films as

Cavalcanti's *Pett and Pott – A Fairy Story of the Suburbs*. The contrast between the conscientious Pett family and the slovenly Pott family was repeated in *Ordinary People*. The negative representation of the middle class was provided there by an ancillary character, a shopper in the ladieswear department of Bourne & Hollingsworth. This particular store, on the corner of Oxford Street and Berners Street in London, had provided merchandise for middle-class shoppers since the beginning of the twentieth century. Here, in the middle of a major conflict, was an individual who was more concerned about the design of a sweater than an imminent assault by the Luftwaffe. Even when the sirens sounded she had to be shepherded reluctantly down to the shelters. The war, it seemed, had the temerity to interfere with her purchase. Furthermore, her treatment of the shop assistant was also quite dismissive and brusque. This type of characterisation appears in the later films as well. In *Hole in the Ground* both the chief scientific officer and the chief officer, in the middle of a nuclear attack, are dismissive of their more junior colleagues appearing to be more concerned about their chocolate and tobacco fix than the holocaust above.

Revealing what might occur during an air attack is probably the most dramatic subject to be dealt with in a public information film. *Hole in the Ground* can be seen as a direct descendant of those films, such as *If War Should Come* and *The Waking Point*, produced earlier by the GPOFU and Crown. However, a similar argument emphasising the continuity over the years could be made in respect of other areas of national government concern, be they health, road safety or other matters. Public information films in the UK up until the 1970s have generally followed the format pioneered by the earlier government film units. They have tended to reject the 'talking head' expert to concentrate rather on making the point in the form of short drama documentaries. These PIFs produced before 1952 also tended to give prominence to the impression of authenticity, whether, of course, that was created by the use of 'real' people rather than actors or, as was often the case with the GPOFU and Crown, the use of cinematic artifice.

However, most of the films produced by the government film units between 1930 and 1952 were not responses to national emergencies, but rather reflections of the demands of their sponsors.

Before 1939 the EMBFU and the GPOFU produced many films which would now be recognised as exercises in public relations. The fact that they rarely had access to the national commercial cinema circuit meant that exhibition was either determined by the sponsor or through the important loan system which gave access to audiences in a variety of venues such as schools, churches and film clubs. That a small but talented group of filmmakers were able to adapt their skills to the demands of the sponsor was in no small part a result of the support of people such as Stephen Tallents, who saw the advantage of film as a means of conveying a message. Ironically, it was the onset of war in 1939 which released these filmmakers from the restrictions of their GPO sponsor and enabled them to address wider national issues in support of the war effort, which included dabbling in feature-length films. Unfortunately, the end of the war and the ensuing austerity returned the CFU to a pre-war position where it had to seek commissions from individual government departments. Although those departments were more than willing to allow Crown to create and produce films, they often insisted on some editorial control. Thus, Hugh Gaitskell's intervention in the production of *The Cumberland Story* did not redeem a problematic script – and probably made it worse.

It is too simplistic to assert that the government film units just produced public information films. The position was much more nuanced than that. Essentially, a small group of like-minded filmmakers came together to produce films initially in the style of, and encouraged by, John Grierson. Although Grierson departed to Canada, his concept of the creative treatment of actuality underpinned subsequent productions and can be seen in most of the EMBFU, GPOFU and Crown films. Most of these carried a short and usually unambiguous message, be that at the behest of their particular government sponsor or, occasionally, when the situation allowed a more general response to a contemporary anxiety or concern. The instrumentality of these productions should not be seen as a criticism; rather, the men (and women) in red ties were actually pioneering filmic responses to both public relations and public information needs.

Notes

1 All three services maintain strictly segregated messes even today. The importance of command can still be seen in the present army's training methodologies which clearly distinguish between the roles of command, leadership and management (DETS(A), 2015).
2 There is not a great deal in academic discourse about the history and development of schools television in the UK, although the voluminous work by Briggs (1978) has some references, especially vol. IV, *Sound and Vision*.
3 There might have been more television opportunities for CFU films in the late 1940s but these were always blocked by the CEA threatening to cancel the monthly film agreement with the government. See Wildy (1988) for a comprehensive discussion of the negotiations.
4 Human immunodeficiency virus/acquired immune deficiency appeared in the early 1980s and, before treatments were developed, caused significant concern amongst health authorities worldwide.
5 Covid-19 was a coronavirus which caused severe respiratory problems and became a worldwide pandemic from 2020 to 2023, according to the World Health Organization.
6 The V1 (Vergeltungswaffen 1 or Revenge Weapon 1) was a small pilotless jet bomb launched from 'ski-ramps' in France and the Low Countries. Once their fuel was exhausted, they plunged to earth and exploded on impact. Even more frightening were the much larger V2s, which were ballistic missiles. Being supersonic meant that there was no preliminary warning of engine noise before detonation.
7 The weapons dropped upon Japan were 'atomic bombs', which are fission devices where uranium or plutonium is forced into a 'critical mass', causing the atoms of the element to fission or 'split' into the smaller atoms of other elements. When they split, they give off neutrons that split even more of the atoms. Each atom gives off a tremendous amount of energy. The later hydrogen 'H' bombs were fusion devices in which the heat given off by a fission explosion is directed at a container of fusible hydrogen (deuterium). The heat and pressure cause the hydrogen to fuse into helium, the same process that takes place in the sun and stars. This reaction produces an incredible amount of energy, because again a tiny amount of matter from each atom is converted into heat. The destructive output of these weapons is measured in kilotons, equivalent of TNT for the atomic bomb and megatons for the hydrogen bomb. To give some impression of destructive equivalence the bomb which devastated Hiroshima had an explosive power of about 15 kilotons; by the mid-1950s the

arsenals of both the USA and USSR had weapons of 25 megatons and more. By the mid-1950s both the North Atlantic Treaty Organisation (NATO, 1955) and Warsaw Pact (1955) nations were equipped with H bombs. The United States developed its first deployable H bomb in 1954, the USSR in 1955 and the UK in 1957.
8 The Mobile Defence Corps (MDC) was a short-lived (1955–59) army unit designated to assist the civil defence authorities in the event of a nuclear attack.

Appendix: A note on film listing

Film titles

Titles used are those normally applied to a particular film in the UK. Occasionally a film title changed during the production process – for example, *Come Again* started off as *Britain Revisited*. Sometimes a title was changed for the overseas market; thus, *Western Approaches* was released in the USA as *The Raider*. As is explained in the introduction, films which were substantially re-edited and normally reduced in footage for the non-theatrical market are treated as separate entities in the appendices. For example, *Air Operations* (January 1942) was a truncated version of *Target for Tonight* (November 1941).

Possible EMB/GPOFU and Crown titles

There are a few films which were produced during the period 1930–52 that could be reasonably classified as government film unit productions but the evidence is limited and as provenance is questionable they have been excluded. Similarly, films in which production commenced but was not completed, or they were never exhibited, have been excluded. An example of this latter category is the 1944 short *Escort Carrier*.

Release dates

The dates quoted are normally those for theatrical exhibition. It was reasonably common for the films to be available through the

Central Film Library for non-theatrical use two or three months later, often but not always in 16 mm format. However, release dates in both cases must be treated with caution as films were sometimes delayed or pulled at the last minute (for example, *Africa Freed* (1944) was never exhibited as it was thought to be 'too British').

Categories

These are described in detail in the relevant chapters, but in the case of the listing in this appendix, the proportion of films in each category and the abbreviations are as given below.

Empire Marketing Board Film Unit, 1933–36

- Pub – publicity for the Empire Marketing Board (30%)
- Brit – the Best of Britain (45%)
- DA – direct advertising (12%)
- Misc – miscellaneous (12%)

General Post Office Film Unit, 1933–37

- EMB – EMB 'legacy' films (10%)
- General PR – general public relations films for the Post Office (33%)
- Post – public relations films for the postal service (12%)
- Saving – films which emphasised the importance of saving through the Post Office (8%)
- DA – direct advertising (15%)
- Integral – other services which required the involvement of the Post Office (4%)
- Brit – the best of Britain (12%)
- Misc – miscellaneous (4%)

General Post Office Film Unit, 1938–40

- General PR – general public relations films for the Post Office (17%)
- Post – public relations films for the postal service (12%)
- Saving – films which emphasised the importance of saving through the Post Office (5%)
- DA – direct advertising (7%)
- Integral – other services which required the involvement of the Post Office (2%)

- Brit – the best of Britain (22%)
- War prep – preparation for war (10%)
- War – the GPOFU in the first year of the Second World War, 1939–40 (22%)

Crown Film Unit, 1940–45

- Hitting – anti-German/hitting back films (32%)
- Reassurance – reassurance/appeal to patriotism (26%)
- Participation – participation in the war effort (21%)
- Forward – looking forward to peace (19%)
- Misc – miscellaneous (< 4%)

The Crown Film Unit's post-war productions, 1946–52

- Financial problems (4%)
- Unfinished – unfinished business (5%)
- New Jerusalem – new Jerusalem (12%)
- Tech chg – technological changes (14%)
- Social chg – social change (7%)
- Colonies – colonies (11%)
- Red menace – red menace (3%)
- Ed/PR – public education and information (22%)
- Sector sp – specialist audiences (22%)

Screen credits

Many productions do not include any credit references or, if they do, they are very sparse.

Film content

This is a very brief description of the film content. Often a more detailed account may be found in the preceding text or the BFI, TNA or IWM archives.

Feature films

The BFI has defined any film over forty minutes' duration as a feature film and this is the criterion used to identify productions as such.

Table A.1 Government film units' production listing, 1930–52

Film and date	Sponsor	Category allocated	Brief description	Director, etc.
1929				
Drifters			Scottish herring fleet	Grierson
1930				
Conquest	EMB	Pub	Canadian conquest of the forest? Film lost	Wright
Clothes of the Empire	EMB	Pub	Film lost	
One Family	EMB	Pub	Making of the royal Christmas pudding	Creighton
1931				
Plums That Please	Min. Fish. Ag.	DA	National mark for plums	
Furry Folk		Misc	Film lost	
Australian Wine(s)	EMB	Pub	Wine growing	Rotha
People and Products of India	EMB	Pub	Review of products of British India	
Shadow of the Mountains	EMB	Brit	Welsh sheep farming	
Lumber	EMB	Pub	Timber in Canada & New Zealand	

Table A.1 (Cont.)

Film and date	Sponsor	Category allocated	Brief description	Director, etc.
Axes and Elephants	EMB	Pub	Timber in Burma	
A Record of Achievement	Min. Fish. Ag.	DA	Review of National Mark	
1932				
Upstream	EMB	Brit	Salmon fishing	
O'er Hill and Dale	EMB	Brit	Sheep farming in Northumberland	Wright
Erecting Aeroplane Engines	Air M.n.	Misc	Technical description of engines	Elton
Industrial Britain	EMB	Brit	Review of heavy industry in UK	Flaherty
A New Road Transport Train	EMB	Misc	Film lost	
Our Herring Harvest	EMB	Brit	North Sea herring fleet	
Conquest of Natural Barriers	EMB	Pub	Development and opening of new lands	
Canals	EMB	Brit	Film lost	
Irrigation	EMB	Pub	Film lost	

(*continued*)

Table A.1 (Cont.)

Film and date	Sponsor	Category allocated	Brief description	Director, etc.
Mountain Stairway	EMB	Brit	Film lost	
Liquid History	EMB	Brit	Journey down the Thames	Dunstan
The English Potter	EMB	Brit	Probable re-edits from Industrial Britain	
Voice of the World	HMV	DA	Gramophone and radio production	Elton
The Glassmakers of England	EMB	Brit	Probable re-edits from Industrial Britain	
New Generation	EMB	Brit	Education in Chesterfield	Legg
1933				
Spring on the Farm	EMB	Brit	Pastoral scenes	Spice
Windmills in Barbados	EMB	Pub	Sugar growing	Rotha
The Shepherd	EMB	Brit	Recut from O'er Hill, etc.	
The Country Comes to Town	EMB	Brit	Modernisation of farming methods	Wright
Liner Cruising South	Orient Line	DA	SS Orford's journey to Caribbean	Wright
Cargo from Jamaica	EMB	Pub	Traditional v. modern methods	Wright
So This Is London	TIDA	Brit	Travelogue of London sites	Marion Grierson
The Hen Woman		Misc	Film lost	

Table A.1 (Cont.)

Film and date	Sponsor	Category allocated	Brief description	Director, etc.
GPOFU, 1933–40				
1933				
Telephone Workers	GPO	General PR	London's expanding telephone network	Legg
Cable Ship	GPO	General PR	Repair of submarine telephone cable	Legg & Alexander
British Guiana	EMB	EMB	Agriculture and industry	
The Coming of the Dial	GPO	DA	Dial telephone	Legg
Hop Gardens of Kent	TIDA	Brit	From hops to pints	
1934				
Granton Trawler	EMB	EMB	Trawler in North Sea	Grierson
John Atkins Saves Up	GPO	Saving	Romantic comedy supporting PO savings	Elton
Locomotives	GPO	General PR	History of steam locomotives	Jennings
The Glorious Sixth of June	GPO	DA	Reduction in phone charges	Cavalcanti

(*continued*)

Table A.1 (Cont.)

Film and date	Sponsor	Category allocated	Brief description	Director, etc.
Negombo Coast	EMB	EMB	Ceylon fishing industry	Wright
The New Operator	GPO	DA	Recruitment for telephone operators	Legg
Pett and Pott – A Fairy Story of the Suburbs	GPO	DA	Telephone in event of crime	Cavalcanti
Post Haste	GPO	Post	History of Royal Mail	Jennings
St James's Park	TIDA	Brit	St James's Park, London	Marion Grierson
Savings Bank	GPO	Savings	Operation of PO Savings Bank	Legg
Telephone	GPO	General PR	Abstract animation	
Under the City	GPO	General PR	Diverting cables around escalator	Shaw
Weather Forecast	GPO	Integral	Work of Meteorological Office	Spice
6.30 Collection	GPO	Post	Sorting office	Watt & Anstey
The Song of Ceylon	Ceylon Tea Board	EMB	Life of people in Ceylon	Wright
Air Post	GPO	Post	Croydon aerodrome	Clark
Edinburgh	TIDA	Brit	Travelogue	Marion Grierson

Table A.1 (Cont.)

Film and date	Sponsor	Category allocated	Brief description	Director, etc.
Market Place	GPO	Misc/animation	Post office in small town	
Making a Sand Mould and Casting Aluminium Alloy	TIDA	Misc	Casting aluminium	
Britain's Countryside	TIDA	Brit	Travelogue/countryside	Marion Grierson
Conquering Space	GPO	General PR	New communication systems	Legg
Spring Comes to England	Min. Fish. Ag.	EMB	Scilly Island daffodils	Taylor
King Log	EMB	EMB	Recut lumber	Spice
1935				
Banking for Millions	GPO	Savings	PO Savings Bank HQ	Spottiswoode
A Colour Box	GPO	DA	Animation: cheaper rates for parcels	Lye
Introducing the Dial	GPO	DA	Automatic dialling	Legg
BBC The Voice of Britain	GPO	Integral	Tour of BBC	Legg

(*continued*)

Table A.1 (Cont.)

Film and date	Sponsor	Category allocated	Brief description	Director, etc.
CTO: The Story of the Central Telegraph Office	GPO	General PR	Central Telegraph Office	Legg
Droitwich	GPO	General PR	New radio mast	Watt
Rt. Hon. Sir Howard Kingsley Wood MP	GPO	General PR	PMG reviews PO services	
The Story of the Wheel	GPO	Post	Transporting the mail	Jennings
The King's Stamp	GPO	Post	George V's silver jubilee	Coldstream
Coal Face	GPO	Brit	Work of the coal miner	Cavalcanti
Pines and Poles	GPO	General PR	Telephone poles	
1936				
Calendar of the Year	GPO	General PR	GPO during the year	Spice
Gardens of the Orient	Ceylon Tea Board	EMB	Tea gardens	
Message From Geneva	GPO	General PR	Landline to League of Nations	Cavalcanti
Night Mail	GPO	Post	Night services to Scotland	Watt & Wright

Table A.1 (Cont.)

Film and date	Sponsor	Category allocated	Brief description	Director, etc.
Island of Contrast	TIDA	EMB	Ceylon travelogue	
Postmaster General on a Post Office Problem	GPO	Post	Stagger posting	
Rainbow Dance	GPO	Savings	Animation to support PO Savings Bank	Lye
Radio Interference	GPO	General PR	How PO tracks interference	Watt
The Saving of Bill Blewitt	GPO	Savings	Moral tale on need to save	Watt
The Fairy on the Phone	GPO	DA	How to use telephone system	Coldstream
How Stamps are Made	GPO	Post	After death silent version of The King's Stamp	
Simple Magnetism and Electricity	GPO	General PR	Science behind telephone	Bond
How to Tell a Phone	GPO	DA	Shortened version of Fairy	Coldstream
World Exchange	GPO	General PR	International telephone exchange	

(*continued*)

Table A.1 (Cont.)

Film and date	Sponsor	Category allocated	Brief description	Director, etc.
1937				
We Live in Two Worlds	GPO	Misc	J. B. Priestley on international relations	Cavalcanti
North of the Border	GPO	Brit	Film lost	Harvey
Daily Round	GPO	Post	Postman dreams	Massingham
The Copper Web	GPO	General PR	Telephone poles and cables	Harvey
Big Money	GPO	General PR	Finances of Post Office	Watt
Trade Tattoo	GPO	General PR	Post, early animation	Lye
Four Barriers	GPO	General PR	Switzerland developing communications	Cavalcanti
Community Calls	GPO	General PR	New housing development with telephones	
A Job in a Million	GPO	DA	Recruitment	Spice
Letters to Liners	GPO	Post	Mediterranean cruise and ship's mail	
Line to the Tschierva Hut	GPO	General PR	Telephone to Swiss mountain hut	Cavalcanti
Men of the Alps	GPO	General PR	Cables plus Swiss geography and history	Cavalcanti
N or NW	GPO	DA	Importance of postcode	Lye
Roadways	GPO	Integral	Growth of road traffic	Coldstream & Legg

Table A.1 (Cont.)

Film and date	Sponsor	Category allocated	Brief description	Director, etc.
Book Bargain	GPO	DA	Telephone directory	McLaren
How the Dial Works	GPO	General PR	Explanation of automated telephone	
Modern Post Office Methods	GPO	General PR	Modern technology in postal services	
Messenger Boy	GPO	DA	Recruitment	
Farewell Topsails	GPO	Brit	Dufaycolor: last journey of commercial sailing ship	Jennings
1938				
What's on Today	GPO	DA	Help with BBC outside broadcast	McNaughton
On the Fishing Banks of Skye	GPO	Brit	Line fishing off NW Scotland	Grierson (?)
God's Chillun	GPO	Brit	Account of the slave trade	
The Tocher	GPO	Savings	Innovative silhouette animation for savings	Reiniger
Speaking from America	GPO	General PR	Radio telephone links	Jennings
Penny Journey	GPO	Post	Postcard from Manchester to Graffam	Jennings
North Sea	GPO	Integral	Aberdeen trawler in distress	Watt

(*continued*)

Table A.1 (Cont.)

Film and date	Sponsor	Category allocated	Brief description	Director, etc.
News for the Navy	GPO	Post	Letters to the fleet	McLaren
Mony a Pickle	GPO	Savings	Scottish Post Office Savings Bank	
The HPO	GPO	General PR	Angels deliver telegrams	Reiniger
How the Telephone Works	GPO	General PR	Principles of sound transmission	Elton
The Horsey Mail	GPO	Post	Delivery of mail during flooding	Jackson
The Wires Go Underground	GPO	General PR	History of subterranean cables	
Distress Call	GPO	General PR	Shorter version of North Sea	Watt
The Farm	GPO	Brit	Life on the farm - animals etc	Jennings
Making Fashion	GPO	Brit	Norman Hartnell's fashion collection	Jennings
1939				
The First Days	GPO	War	London in September 1939	Jennings
Health of the Nation	GPO	War prep	Changes in social services	Monck
The Chiltern Country	GPO	Brit	Country scenes	Cavalcanti
The City: Talk by Sir Charles Bressey	GPO	Brit	Talk on London and its transport	Elton

Table A.1 (Cont.)

Film and date	Sponsor	Category allocated	Brief description	Director, etc.
If War Should Come/ Do it Now	GPO	War prep	Preparation for war, especially bombing	
The Islanders	GPO	General PR	Communication with GB islands	Harvey
Men in Danger	GPO	War prep	Working conditions in mines and factories	Jackson
Mid-Summer Day's Work	GPO	General PR	Laying cables	
At the Third Stroke	GPO	DA	Speaking clock	Massingham
Spare Time	GPO	Brit	Steel, cotton and coal leisure times	Jennings
Postal Special	GPO	Post	Shortened version of Night Mail	Wright
Oh Whiskers	Min. Health	Misc	Importance of cleanliness	Pickersgill
Nine for Six	GPO	DA	PO telegram service	
SS Ionian	GPO	War prep	Merchant vessel in Mediterranean	Jennings
Love on the Wing	GPO	Post	Airmail service	McLaren
1940				
How the Teleprinter Works	GPO	General PR	How the teleprinter works	Chambers
Health in War	Min. Health	War	Organisation of wartime medical services	Jackson

(*continued*)

Table A.1 (Cont.)

Film and date	Sponsor	Category allocated	Brief description	Director, etc.
French Communiqué	GPO	War	War through French eyes	
Factory Front	MoI	War	Role of factory workers	Elton
La Cause Commune	GPO	War	Britain assisting French war effort	Cavalcanti
London Can Take It	GPO	War	Londoners face Blitz	Jennings
The Story of Cotton	GPO	Brit	Work in a cotton mill	
Squadron 992	MoI	War	Balloon defence	Watt
War and Order	MoI	War	Police in wartime	Hasse
Forty Million People	GPO	War	Shortened version of Health of the Nation	Monck

CFU, 1940–45

1940

Musical Poster No. 1	MoI	Hitting	Animation warning about Nazi sympathisers	Lye
Britain at Bay	MoI	Reassurance	J. B. Priestley draws together images of Britain at war	Watt
Welfare of the Workers	MoI	Participation	New factory and production conditions. Includes speech by Ernest Bevin	Jennings
The Front Line	MoI	Reassurance	Dover during the Battle of Britain	Watt

Table A.1 (Cont.)

Film and date	Sponsor	Category allocated	Brief description	Director, etc.
Men of the Lightship	MoI	Hitting	Dramatisation of sinking of East Dudgeon lightship	MacDonald
Air Communiqué	MoI	Hitting	How statistics for destroyed enemy planes are compiled	Elton
Spring Offensive/ Unrecorded Victory	MoI	Participation	Farming Year/ reclamation of derelict land (GPOFU/CFU)	Jennings
1941				
Britain Can Take It	MoI	Reassurance	Overseas version of London Can Take It	Jennings
Christmas Under Fire	MoI	Reassurance	1940 Christmas: holly and barbed wire	Watt/Hasse
The Heart of Britain	MoI	Reassurance	Tribute to northern and midlands industrial workers	Jennings
India Marches	MoI	Reassurance	Indian soldiers training and at recreation	NK
Lofoten	MoI	Hitting	Commando raid on Norwegian town/ combat film with Army Film Unit	Tennyson d'Eyncourt
Ordinary People	MoI	Reassurance	A day in the life of Londoners during the Blitz	Holmes/ Elton(?)/ Lee

(*continued*)

Table A.1 (Cont.)

Film and date	Sponsor	Category allocated	Brief description	Director, etc.
Merchant Seaman	MoI	Participation	Seaman sunk by U-boat gets revenge	Holmes/Elton
Words for Battle	MoI	Reassurance	Commentary by Laurence Olivier: call to battle, poems etc. over shots of wartime Britain	Jennings
Target for Tonight	MoI	Hitting	Wellington bomber night mission	Watt
Venture Adventure	MoI	Participation	Recruitment film for Air Training Corps	Hasse
The Pilot Is Safe	MoI	Participation	Air Sea Rescue service save downed RAF pilot	Lee
1942				
America Moves Up	MoI	Reassurance	US troops in training	Elton
The Tale of Two Cities	MoI	Reassurance	London and Moscow survive the Blitz	Monck
Air Operations	MoI	Hitting	Abbreviated Target for Tonight	Watt
Ferry Pilot	MoI	Participation	Work of Air Transport Command	Jackson
Wavell's 30000	MoI/AFU	Hitting	Early desert campaign against the Italians	Monck
Listen to Britain	MoI	Reassurance	Sounds of Britain at war	Jennings/McAllister

Table A.1 (Cont.)

Film and date	Sponsor	Category allocated	Brief description	Director, etc.
Builders	MoI	Participation	Emphasises importance of role in wartime and reconstruction.	Jackson
Day that Saved the World	MoI	Hitting	Importance of Battle of Britain	Chambers
United Nations	MoI	Reassurance	Big three powers united against Axis	Dalrymple
Coastal Command	MoI	Hitting	Sunderland Flying Boat on Atlantic patrol	Holmes
1943				
Malta G.C.	MoI	Participation	Siege of Malta tribute	Monck/De Marney/Cekalski
We Sail at Midnight	MoI	Reassurance	Importance of 'lend-lease' to tank building in UK	Spiro/John Ford?
Letter from Ulster	MoI	Reassurance	US troops training in Ulster	Hurst
Fires Were Started/I Was a Fireman	MoI	Participation	The Auxiliary Fire Service (AFS) during the London Blitz	Jennings
The Silent Village	MoI	Hitting	Homage to victims of Lidice massacre	Jennings

(*continued*)

Table A.1 (Cont.)

Film and date	Sponsor	Category allocated	Brief description	Director, etc.
Close Quarters	MoI	Hitting	British submarine operating in North Sea waters	Lee
Before the Raid	MoI	Hitting	Norwegian fishing village under Nazi occupation	Weiss
Workers' Weekend	MoI	Participation	Workers beat record of building Wellington bomber in under 30 hours	Elton
1944				
Come Again	MoI	Participation	Australian, Canadian and New Zealanders on leave in UK	Elton
Up Periscope!	MoI	Hitting	Shortened version of Close Quarters	Lee
South Africa	MoI	Participation	Three races, separate development	
New Zealand	MoI	Participation	Part of Know Your Commonwealth Series No. 2	
Two Fathers	MoI	Hitting	Two fathers, English and French, discover they have children when fighting	Asquith
Africa Freed	MoI	Hitting	Not exhibited as thought too British	Dalrymple/ Boulting

Table A.1 (Cont.)

Film and date	Sponsor	Category allocated	Brief description	Director, etc.
The True Story of Lili Marlene	MoI	Hitting	Song beloved by both Afrika Korps and 8th Army	Jennings
By Sea and Land	MoI	Hitting	Royal Marine Corps in battle for Normandy	Lee
Western Approaches	MoI	Participation	Survivors of torpedoed ship in Atlantic convoy	Jackson
The Eighty Days	MoI	Reassurance	History of V1 attack on southern England	Jennings
Killing Farm Rats	Min. Fish. Ag.	Miscellaneous	Methods of killing by administering poison-bait and poison gas	Wallace
The New School	Min. Ed.	Forward	Encouraging women to train as teachers	Ackland
Transatlantic Airport	MoI	Forward	Urgent medicine flown in from Canada	Gordon
1945				
V1	MoI	Reassurance	Two-reel version of Eighty Days for, mainly, US market	Jennings
The Eighth Plague	MoI	Forward	Locust depredations in East Africa	Lee
Children's Charter	Min. Ed.	Forward	Butler Education Act	Bryant

(*continued*)

Table A.1 (Cont.)

Film and date	Sponsor	Category allocated	Brief description	Director, etc.
Sisal	Col Off	Forward	Growing of sisal in Tanganyika (Tanzania)	Kingsford-Davis
Southern Rhodesia	MoI	Participation	Know the Commonwealth Series No. 5	Wright
Myra Hess	MoI	Miscellaneous	Famous concert pianist	Trumper/Jennings
The Broad Fourteens	MoI	Hitting	Motor torpedo boat (MTB) crew become team	McNaughton
Father & Son	MoI	Participation	Kenyan elderly learning from young man trained by Royal Navy	Schauder
Farm Work	Min. Fish. Ag.	Forward	Post-war opportunities in agriculture	Gordon
This Was Japan	MoI	Hitting	Review of Japanese history, graphic descriptions	Wright
The Channel Islands 1940–45	MoI	Reassurance	Occupation history, re-enactments and newsreel	Bryant
A Diary for Timothy	MoI	Forward	The first year of a baby's life set against final year of the Second World War	Jennings
Australians in London	MoI	Forward	Australians in London; VE parade	Shaw
Picture of Britain	MoI	Forward		Bolton
Canada's North West	MoI	Forward	Canada's plans for development of NW	NK

Table A.1 (Cont.)

Film and date	Sponsor	Category allocated	Brief description	Director, etc.
Unrelenting Struggle	MoI	Reassurance	Wartime speeches of Winston Churchill	NK
Patients Are In	MoI	Miscellaneous	Day to day in a US field hospital in Cirencester	Bolton
Jungle Mariners	MoI	Hitting	Royal Marines jungle fighting	Elton
Johnny Gurkha	MoI	Hitting	Recruitment and training of Gurkha soldiers	NK
1946				
Tea from Nyasaland	Colonial Office	Colonies	Tea growing in Nyasaland	Wright
Fight for Life	Colonial Office	Colonies	Gold Coast, 1 cattle husbandry	
A Defeated People	Control Comm. for Germany	Unfinished	Immediate post-war situation in Germany	Wright
School for Danger	COI	Unfinished	British SOE agents in wartime; also released as Now it Can Be Told	
The Way from Germany	Control Comm. for Germany	Unfinished	Displaced persons camps; Cert. A	Wright
Hausa Village	Colonial Office	Colonies	Life in a village in northern Nigeria	

(*continued*)

Table A.1 (Cont.)

Film and date	Sponsor	Category allocated	Brief description	Director, etc.
The Railwaymen	Min. Trans./Labour	Sector sp	Min. Transport job series	Wallace
Partners	Colonial Office	Colonies	Colonial admin in East Africa partnership	
Indian Background	Foreign Office	Colonies	Changing face of India	
Beginning of History	Min. Ed.	Ed/PR	British life, earliest days to Roman invasion	Wright
Instruments of the Orchestra	Min. Ed	Ed/PR	Instrument by instrument analysis of orchestra	Shaw
Town Meeting of the World	COI	New Jerusalem	Attlee's speech opening of UNO	Wright
The Story of Omolo	Colonial Office	Colonies	Kenyan villager learns science	Wright
Children on Trial	COI	Social chg	Child delinquency	Wright
Mr Jones Takes the Air	ROSPA	Social chg	Driving in the countryside	Wright
It Might Be You	Min. Trans.	Social chg	Road safety	Wright
Minesweeping	Admiralty	Sector sp	Naval instructional film	
The House that Jack Built	Min. of Works	Sector sp	Apprenticeships in building	Shaw

Table A.1 (Cont.)

Film and date	Sponsor	Category allocated	Brief description	Director, etc.
1947				
Moving Millions	London Transport	Ed/PR	London Transport buses and trains	Arthur
Shown By Request	COI	Ed/PR	Central Film Library	Dean
Aircraft Recognition	Army Kinema Corp	Sector sp	Military training film	Arthur
Report on Coal August 1947	Min. Fuel & Power	Sector sp	Durham miners' gala, handed over to NCB	
Mining Review No. 1	Min. Fuel & Power	Sector sp	Cine magazine for coal industry	
Mining Review No. 2	Min. Fuel & Power	Sector sp	Cine magazine for coal industry	
Mining Review No. 3	Min. Fuel & Power	Sector sp	Cine magazine for coal industry	
Mining Review No. 4	Min. Fuel & Power	Sector sp	Cine magazine for coal industry	
Mining Review No. 5	Min. Fuel & Power	Sector sp	Cine magazine for coal industry	Stanford

(*continued*)

Table A.1 (Cont.)

Film and date	Sponsor	Category allocated	Brief description	Director, etc.
Mining Review No. 6	Min. Fuel & Power	Sector sp	Cine magazine for coal industry	
The Charter of the United Nations	COI	New Jerusalem	Formation and structure of UNO	
Breeding for Milk	Min. Fish. Ag.	Sector sp	Breeding improvements for dairy farmers	Gowers
Along the Line	Min. Trans./Labour	Sector sp	Jobs on the railways	McNaughton
Home and School	Min. Ed.	Social chg	Encourage growth of PTAs	Bryant
1948				
The Cumberland Story	Min. Fuel & Power	New Jerusalem	Modernisation of pits	Jennings
Town Rats	Min. Food	Sector sp	Pest control	
Rhondda and Wye	Vis. Aids in Ed.	Ed/PR	Contrast Rhondda with Wye valleys	
Accident Prevention Concerns You	ROSPA	Sector sp	Early H&S film	
KRO Germany 1947	Control Comm. for Germany	Unfinished	Role of Kreis resident officer	Wallace/Borgstadt

Table A.1 (Cont.)

Film and date	Sponsor	Category allocated	Brief description	Director, etc.
Trained to Serve	Control Comm. for Germany	Unfinished	New police force in Germany	Wallace
Furnival and Son	Board of Trade	New Jerusalem	Sheffield steelmaking	Segaller
Postman's Nightmare	GPO	Ed/PR	Post early for Christmas	
Worth the Risk?	Min. Trans.	Social cc=hg	Road safety	
How Townfolk Get Their Water	COI	New Jerusalem	Water supply improvements	
Water Spout	?	New Jerusalem	The construction of two atomic piles in Windscale	
Steps of the Ballet	British Council	Ed/PR	Ballet	Mathieson
School in Cologne	Control Comm. for Germany	Unfinished	Denazification through the school system	Wallace
Patent Ductus Arteriosus	Min. Health	Sector sp	Medical training	
Children of the Ruins	Foreign Office	Unfinished	Post-war life of children in Germany	Jackson
Pop Goes the Weasel	Treasury	Finance	Post-war economic troubles	Jill Craigie
Report on Industrial Scotland	Board of Trade	New Jerusalem	Scottish central belt industry	

(*continued*)

Table A.1 (Cont.)

Film and date	Sponsor	Category allocated	Brief description	Director, etc.
Under New Management	Min. Labour	New Jerusalem	Impact of nationalisation of mines	
Voices of Malaya	COI	Colonies	Malaya in face of communism	
Answer Four Questions	Min. Labour	Sector sp	Civil service training and job opportunities	Freedman/R. Elton
A Yank Comes Back	COI	Finance	Ex-GI telling how GB coping with aftermath of war	Dean
1949				
Queen o' the Border	Board of Trade	Sector sp	Scenes at the annual Hawick Festival	Dean
Early Diagnosis of Acute Anterior Poliomyelitis	Min. Health	Sector sp	Hillingdon Operation	Wilson
Antarctic Lands	Colonial Office	Colonies	British scientists stationed in Falkland Islands	
Cocoa From Nigeria	Colonial Office	Colonies	Cocoa production	
Daybreak at Udi	Colonial Office	Colonies	Development of maternity hospital	Bishop

Table A.1 (Cont.)

Film and date	Sponsor	Category allocated	Brief description	Director, etc.
Dollars and Sense	Economic Information Unit	Finance	Balance of payments issues and devaluation	Pine
Faster than Sound	Min. Supply	Tech chg	Aircraft development	Pine
His Fighting Chance	Min. Health	Ed/PR	Rehabilitation of victims of polio	Innes
Heating Research for Houses	Dept. of Scientific and Industrial Research	Tech chg	Heating improvements	Warren
London Airport	Min. Civil Aviation	Tech Chg	Development of Heathrow	
Inside US Aid				
People of Malaya	Colonial Office	Colonies	Malayan village life	
The People at Number 19	Min. Health	Ed/PR	Venereal disease, cert. A	Holmes
Co-operative Research in Industry	Dept. of Scientific and Industrial Research	Tech chg	Export initiatives	Arthur

(*continued*)

Table A.1 (Cont.)

Film and date	Sponsor	Category allocated	Brief description	Director, etc.
Wonders of the Deep	Admiralty	Tech chg	Frogman and submarine developments	NK
Beet Sugar	Min. Fish. Ag.	Sector sp	Farming advice	Clore
Caring for Children	Min. Labour	Social chg	Youth employment/ girls' careers	
The Good Housewife in Her Kitchen	Min. Food	Ed/PR	Make the most of limited kitchen and larder space	
Pigs on Every Farm	Min. Fish. Ag.	Sector sp	Essentials of pig farming	Warren
The Magic Thread	Board of Trade	Tech chg	The development of rayon	
1950				
The Dancing Fleece	British Council	Ed/PR	Animation showcasing fashion	Wilson/ Reiniger
Atlantic Isles	COI	Ed/PR	Comparing life on Shetland and Channel Islands	
A Family Affair	COI	Social chg	Fostering children	Thomson
Men of the World	COI	Red menace	Tribute to army	Clark
The Magic Touch	Dept. of Scientific and Industrial Research	Tech chg	Make best use of natural resources	

Table A.1 (Cont.)

Film and date	Sponsor	Category allocated	Brief description	Director, etc.
It Need Not Happen	COI	Ed/PR	Road safety	Bryant
Insect Pests in Food	Dept. of Scientifc and Industrial Research	Sector sp	Insect pests in food, crops, storage and means of control	
From the Ground Up	COI	New IJerusalem	Post-war reconstruction	Frankel
Four Men in Prison	Home Office	Social chg	Effect of prison on different offenders	Anderson
Spotlight on the Colonies	COI	Colonies	Helping 40 colonies towards independence	Pine
Trooping the Colour	Foreign Office	Ed/PR	Horse Guards in 1949	Bishop
Into the Blue	Economic Information Unit	Tech chg	BEA and BOAC, Comet, Brabazon, Princess	
Making Engines	Min. Labour	Tech chg	Engineering factory, tractors, heavy goods	
The New Councillor	Min. Health	Ed/PR	New councillor for Luton borough	
Underwater Story	Scottish Office	Sector sp	Scottish fisheries	
The Wonder Jet	Min. Supply	Tech chg	Gas turbine engines & Whittle	

(continued)

Table A.1 (Cont.)

Film and date	Sponsor	Category allocated	Brief description	Director, etc.
Jack of What Trade	Min. Labour	Sector sp	Role of youth employment officer	
Defeat Tuberculosis	Min. Health	Ed/PR	Koch discovery: long cure, mobile X-ray vans	
1951				
Football	COI	Ed/PR	Football every race and colour: Wolves 3: Leicester 1	Frankel
Eagles of the Fleet	COI	Tech chg	Naval aviation	Legg
Industrial Dermatitis	Min. Labour	Sector sp	How to avoid ID	
London Style	Bd. Trade	Tech chg	Rayon manufacture & fashions	Nieter (Seven League)
Surprise Attack	Min. Health	Ed/PR	Smallpox vaccination	
Fire's the Enemy	Home Office	Red menace	Recruitment auxiliary fire service	Frankel
Go Ahead Please	GPO	Finance	GPO film to improve staff productivity	
Mary's Birthday	Min. Health	Ed/PR	How to avoid contamination and spread of disease	
Life in her Hands	Min. Health	Social chg	Widow trains as nurse	
Layout and Handling in Factories		Sector sp	Improved factory layouts	

Table A.1 (Cont.)

Film and date	Sponsor	Category allocated	Brief description	Director, etc.
In on the Beam	Civil Aviation	Tech chg	Air traffic control; use of radar.	
Houses in the Town	Local government	New Jerusalem	Planning laws and changes	Reininger
Prevention of Cross Infection	Min. Health	Sector sp	Gastro-enteritis in infancy	Frankel
Bristol Brabazon – King of the Air	Min. Supply	Tech chg	New airliner development	Leacock
Wing to Wing	Air Ministry	Red menace	Latest RAF aircraft and operations	
The White Continent	Foreign Office	Ed/PR	Record of Norwegian-British-Swedish Expedition to Queen Maud land	
Caribbean	COI	Colonies	Tradition and developments in West Indies	
El Dorado	Colonial Office	Colonies	People, resources and industry of British Guiana	
The Farmer's Horse	Min. Fish. Ag.	Sector sp	Mechanisation on the farm	
Christmas Is Coming	GPO/COI	Ed/PR	Post early for Christmas	Frankel
Post Haste	GPO	Sector sp	Work of the Post Office	Carse?
Out of True	Min. Health	Ed/PR	Nervous breakdown and treatments under NHS	Wallace

(*continued*)

Table A.1 (Cont.)

Film and date	Sponsor	Category allocated	Brief description	Director, etc.
Alien Orders	Colonial & Foreign offices	Red menace	Communist bandit raids in Malaya	Alderson
The Colonies and Britain	Economic Information Unit	Colonies	Relationship between GB and colonies	
Commonwealth of Nations	Commonwealth Rel. Office	Colonies	Story of Commonwealth special relationship	
Festival in London	COI	New Jerusalem	Record of 1951 South Bank Exhibition	
Modern Polar Exploration		New Jerusalem	Research in Antarctic	Leacock
The Waking Point	Home Depts.	Red menace	Civil defence recruitment	
Wanted for Life	Min. Health	Ed/PR	Need for blood donors	Pine
Over to You	Economic Info. Unit	Finance	British productivity in hosiery industry	
The Glassmakers	Board of Trade	Ed/PR	This Is Britain: Glassmaking	Leacock
Man of Fashion	Board of Trade	Ed/PR	Britain's role in men's fashion	Leacock

Table A.1 (Cont.)

Film and date	Sponsor	Category allocated	Brief description	Director, etc.
1952				
A Man on Trial	Colonial Office	Colonies	British judicial procedure	
Royal Scotland	Foreign Office	Ed/PR	Scotland and royal associations	
Atoms at Work	COI	Tech chg	Radioactive isotopes solve problems	
Local Newspapers	Overseas Depts./COI	Ed/PR	Newbury Weekly News	
La Fenêtre Ouverte	Min. Ed.	Ed/PR	Study of landscape painting, in French, CFU edited	Leacock
Electricity Generation and Distribution	Min. Labour	Sector sp	Electricity industry apprenticeships	
Energy Foods	Min. Food	Tech chg	Slice of bread converted to energy	Warren/ Bryant
Light Repetitive Work	Min. Labour	Ed/PR	Mass production: jobs for girls	Pine
Local Handyman	Min. Labour	Ed/PR	Blacksmith and son	
Making Boots and Shoes	Min. Labour	Ed/PR	Old and new methods of shoemaking	Storck
Making of the Soil	Min. Fish. Ag.	Sector sp	Need to preserve soil fertility	

(*continued*)

Table A.1 (Cont.)

Film and date	Sponsor	Category allocated	Brief description	Director, etc.
People's Palace	Colonial Office	Colonies	Tour of Hampton Court	
Protective Foods	Min. Food	Ed/PR	Vitamins and workings of body animation	
There's a Way	Min. Health	Ed/PR	Rehabilitation physio and occupational therapy	Stark
Doctor in Nigeria	COI	Colonies	Medical services in Nigeria	
Lady Returns	Control Comm. (Ger)	Unfinished	Raising 'New York' liner from Kiel Canal	Durden
How the Telephone Works	GPO	Ed/PR	Explanation of telephone	Worth
Harwell Assembly		Tech chg	Restricted audience/ secret footage	Sharples
Radioactive Isotopes		Tech chg	Restricted audience/ secret footage	Bryant
Body Building Foods	Min. Food	Ed/PR	Food maintains body	
The Golden Rule; Careless and Carefree	COI	Social chg	Road safety	

Cinemagazine: This Is Britain Series issue no.

37   Board of Trade

Table A.1 (Cont.)

Film and date	Sponsor	Category allocated	Brief description	Director, etc.
38 General	Board of Trade			
39 General (2)	Board of Trade			
40 Transport	Board of Trade			
41 Agriculture	Board of Trade			
42 Television Looks Ahead	Board of Trade			
43 Accent on Health	Board of Trade			
44 Old Crafts, New Graces	Board of Trade			
45 Britain's New Resources	Board of Trade			
46 Sense of Taste	Board of Trade			
47 Auto Suggestion	Board of Trade			
48	Board of Trade			
49 An Hour from London	Board of Trade			
50 Love of Books	Board of Trade			
51	Board of Trade			

Bibliography

Abel, R. (ed.) (2005) *Encyclopaedia of Early Cinema*. Oxford: Routledge.
Addison, P. (1979) *Home Intelligence Reports on Opinion and Morale 1940–1944*. London: Harvester.
Addison, P. (1994) *Road to 1945*. London: Pimlico.
Ahnert, L. (2013) 'The factual treatment of actuality: The emergence of educational film in the 1920s and its relation to documentary film proper', *Inter Disciplines*, 1, pp. 77–101.
Aitken, I. (1989) 'John Grierson, idealism and the inter-war period', *Historical Journal of Film, Radio and Television*, 9:3, pp. 247–58.
Aitken, I. (1992/2013) *Film and Reform: John Grierson and the Documentary Film Movement*. London: Routledge.
Aitken, I. (ed.) (1998/2020) *The Documentary Film Movement: An Anthology*. Edinburgh: Edinburgh University Press.
Aitken, I. (2000) *Alberto Cavalcanti – Realism, Surrealism and National Cinema*. London: Flicks Books.
Aitken, I. (2006) *Encyclopaedia of Documentary Film*. London: Routledge.
Aldgate, A. (1979) *Cinema and History: British Newsreels and the Spanish Civil War*. London: Scholar Press.
Aldgate, A. and Richards, J (1986/1994/2007) *Britain Can Take It: The British Cinema in World War Two*. Edinburgh: Edinburgh University Press.
Anderson, L (1954) 'Only connect: Some aspects of the work of Humphrey Jennings', *Sight and Sound*, 23:4, pp. 181–86.
Anderson, L. (2009) 'Postcards from the edge: The untidy realities of working with older cinema audiences, distant memories and newsreels', *Participations*, 6:2. www.participations.org./06-02-03-anderson.pdf (accessed 7 May 2024).
Anthony, S. (2018) *Public Relations and the Making of Modern Britain*. Manchester: Manchester University Press.
Anthony, S. and Mansell, J. G. (2011) *The Projection of Britain: A History of the GPO Film Unit*. London: BFI.
Anthony, S. and Russell, P. (2014) 'Postwar documentary: A new way forward (a response to Brian Winston)', *Journal of British Cinema and Television*, 11:2–3, pp. 252–61.

Archibald, D. (2005) 'The Spanish Civil War in the cinema.' Unpublished PhD thesis, University of Glasgow.
Arts Enquiry (1947) *The Factual Film.* London: Oxford University Press.
Ashby, J. and Higson, A. (eds.) (2013) *British Cinema, Past and Present.* London: Routledge.
Atkins, P. (2003) 'Food and the Empire Marketing Board in Britain, 1926–1933,' *8th Symposium of the ICREFH.*
Attridge, S. (1993) 'The soldier in late Victorian Britain: Images and ambiguities.' Unpublished PhD thesis, University of Warwick.
Aveyard, K. (2016) 'Film education, technology and popular culture: Community cinema in rural areas of the UK'. In Thissen, J. and Zimmerman, C. (eds.) *Cinema Beyond the City.* London: BFI/Palgrave, pp. 197–212.
Baird, T. (1938) 'Films and the public service in GB', *Public Opinion Quarterly,* 2:1, pp. 96–99.
Balcon, M. (1952) 'The feature carries on the documentary tradition', *The Quarterly of Film Radio and Television,* 6:4, pp. 351–53.
Balfour, M. (1979) *Propaganda in War, 1939–1945.* London: RKP.
Barefoot, G. (2013) ' "Always a good programme here": The records of the Tudor Cinema, Leicester, 1924–32', *International Journal of Regional and Local History,* 8:1, pp. 26–39.
Barnes, F. (2014). 'Bringing another empire alive? The Empire Marketing Board and the construction of dominion identity, 1926–33', *The Journal of Imperial and Commonwealth History,* 42(1), pp. 61–85.
Barnett, C. (1995) *The Lost Victory.* London: Macmillan.
Barnouw, E. (1993) *Documentary: A History of Non-Fiction Film.* Oxford: Oxford University Press.
Barr, C. (ed.) (1996) *All Our Yesterdays: 90 Years of British Cinema.* London: BFI.
Barthes, R. (1986) 'Leaving the movie theater'. In *The Rustle of Language.* Oxford: Blackwell, pp. 349–54.
Baudrillard, J. (1981/1994) *Simulcra and Simulation.* Ann Arbor: University of Michigan Press.
Beattie, K. (2004) *Documentary Screens – Non-Fiction Film and TV.* London: Palgrave/Macmillan.
BECTU History Project Interviews conducted with a variety of individuals working within the British film industry. Sponsored by Broadcasting, Entertainment, Communications and Theatre Union (BECTU), held by the BFI in London.
Berger, C. R. and Calabrese, R. J. (1975) 'Some exploration in initial interaction and beyond: Toward a developmental theory of communication', *Human Communication Research,* 1, pp. 99–112.
Beveridge, J. (1978) *John Grierson Film Master.* New York: Macmillan.
Bierman, J. and Smith, C. (2003) *El Alamein: War Without Hate.* London: Penguin.
Bingham, A. (2005) 'The British popular press and venereal disease during the Second World War', *Historical Journal,* 48:4, pp. 1055–76.

Bloomfield, V. (1977) 'Caribbean films', *Journal of Librarianship*, 9:4, pp. 278–313.

Bogdanor, V. (2010) *From New Jerusalem to New Labour: British Prime Ministers from Attlee to Blair*. London: Palgrave Macmillan.

Boon, T. (2013) 'British science documentaries: Transitions from film to television', *Journal of British Cinema and Television*, 10, pp. 475–97.

Bottomore, S. (2007) 'Filming, faking and propaganda: The origins of the war film, 1897–1902.' Unpublished master's dissertation, University of Utrecht.

Bourne, J. M. (1989) *Britain and the Great War, 1914–1918*. London: Arnold.

Bower, A. (2019) 'Rebranding empire: Consumers, commodities, and the Empire Marketing Board, 1926–1933.' Unpublished master's dissertation, University of Portland.

Bowles, B. C. (2004) 'La Tragedie de Mers-el-Kebir and the politics of filmed news in France', *Journal of Modern History*, 76:2, pp. 347–88.

Boyd-Carpenter, J. (1980) *Way of Life: Memoirs of John Boyd-Carpenter*. London: Sidgwick & Jackson.

Bradley, K. (2012) 'Juvenile delinquency and the public sphere: Exploring local and national discourses in England, c.1940–1969', *Social History*, 37, pp. 19–35.

Brewer, S. A. (2019). *To Win the Peace: British Propaganda in the United States During World War II*. Ithaca, NY: Cornell University Press.

Brewster, B. and Jacobs, L. (1998) *Theatre to Cinema: Stage Pictorialism and the Early Feature Film*. Oxford: Clarendon.

Briggs, A. (1961–1995) *History of Broadcasting in the United Kingdom*, vols. I–V. Oxford: Oxford University Press.

British Universities Film Council (1973) *Films for Historians*. London: BUFC.

Brode, A. (1977) *The Southampton Blitz*. Winchester: Shurlock.

Brown, G. (2008) 'Land of promise: The British documentary movement', *Journal of Film Preservation*, 78, pp. 127–29.

Brown, S. (2005) 'Coming to a hall near you – Some notes on 16mm road-show distribution in the 1930s,' *Journal of British Cinema and Television*, 2:2, pp. 299–309.

Buchanan, T. (1997) *Britain and the Spanish Civil War*. Cambridge: Cambridge University Press.

Buckman, K. (1997) 'The Royal Air Force film production unit', *Historical Journal of Film, Radio and Television*, 17:2, pp. 219–44.

Bullart, B. J. (1997) *Public Television, Politics and the Battle over the Documentary Film*. New Brunswick: Rutger University Press.

Cairncross, A. (2006) *Years of Recovery: British Economic Policy 1945–51*. London: Routledge.

Calder, A. (1969) *The People's War*. London: Cape.

Calder, A. (1992) *Myth of the Blitz*. London: Pimlico.

Calvocoressi, P. (1978) *The British Experience 1945–75*. London: Bodley Head.
Camplin, R. (1978) *Film* Censorship: The Cinema and the Williams Committee Talk to Cinema Exhibitors' Association. Cinematograph Exhibitors' Association of Great Britain and Ireland. www.infotextmanuscripts.org/webb/webb_film_williams.pdf (accessed 17 August 2013).
Carruthers, S. L. (1990) *Manning the Factories: Propaganda and Policy on the Employment of Women, 1939–1947*. New York: Wiley.
Chan, N. (2013) ' "Remember the Empire – filled with your cousins" Poetic exposition in the documentaries of the Empire Marketing Board', *Studies in Documentary Film*, 7:2, pp. 105–18.
Chapman, J. (1998) *The British at War: Cinema, State and Propaganda, 1939–1945*. London: Tauris.
Chapman, J. (2000) 'The power of propaganda', *Journal of Contemporary History*, 35:4, pp. 679–88.
Chapman, J. (2005) *Past and Present: National Identity and the British Historical Film*. London: Tauris.
Chapman, J. (2013) *Film and History*. London: Palgrave Macmillan.
Chapman, J. (2013) 'The projection of Britain: A history of the GPO Film Unit', *Historical Journal of Film, Radio and Television*, 33:2, pp. 314–17.
Chapman, J. (2015) *A New History of British Documentary*. London: Palgrave Macmillan.
Chapman, J., Glancy, M and Harper, S. (2007) *The New Film History*. London: Palgrave Macmillan.
Chirat, R. (1983) *Le Cinéma français: des Années de Guerre*. Paris: Hatier.
Christie, I. (ed.) (2012) *Audiences: Defining and Researching Screen Entertainment Reception*. Amsterdam: Amsterdam University Press.
Clark, K. (1977) *The Other Half*. London: John Murray.
Colls, R. and Dodd, P. (1985) 'Representing the nation: British documentary film, 1930–1945', *Screen*, 26:1, pp. 21–33.
Cole, S. and Taylor, J. (1990) 'Philip Leacock: A gentleman', *Film and Television Technician*, October, p. 31.
Constantine, S. (2017) 'Bringing the Empire alive'. In MacKenzie, J. (ed.) *Imperialism and Popular Culture*. Manchester: Manchester University Press.
Coultass, C. (1984) 'British feature films and the Second World War', *Journal of Contemporary History*, 19:1, pp. 7–22.
Coultass, C. (1989) *Images for Battle: British Film and the Second World War*. London: Oxford University Press.
Coultass, C. (1998) *The Finest Years: British Cinema of the 1940s*. London: Deutsch.
Coupland, P. (2000) 'H. G. Wells' "liberal fascism"', *Journal of Contemporary History*, 35:4, pp. 541–58.
Crofts, W. (1989) *Coercion or Persuasion? Propaganda in Britain After 1945*. London: Routledge.

Crosby, E. and Kaye, L. (eds.) (2008) *Projecting Britain: The Guide to British Cinemagazines*. London: British Universities Film and Video Council.

Crothall, G. (1999) 'Images of regeneration: Film propaganda and the British slum clearance campaign, 1933–38', *Historical Journal of Film, Radio and Television*, 19:3, pp. 339–58.

Cull, N. (1995) *Selling War*. Oxford: Oxford University Press.

Cull, N., Culbert, D. and Welch, D. (2003) *Propaganda and Mass Persuasion*. California: ABC.

Cunningham, J. (2008) 'The avant-garde, the GPO Film Unit and British documentary in the 1930s', *Journal of English Studies*, VIII, pp. 153–67.

Cunningham, P. (2000) 'Moving images: Propaganda film and British education 1940–45', *Paedagogica Historica*, 36:1, pp. 389–406.

Dalrymple, I. (1982) 'The Crown Film Unit, 1940–43'. In *Propaganda, Politics and Film 1918–45*. London: Macmillan, pp. 209–20.

Davidson, R. and Hall, L. (eds.) (2001) *Sex, Sin and Suffering: Venereal Disease in European Society since 1870*. London: Routledge.

Day, G. (2002) 'A brief history of how culture and commerce were really made for each other', *Critical Quarterly*, 44:3, pp. 37–44.

DeFleur, M. L. (1989) *Theories of Mass Communication*. New York: Longman.

Department of Transport (n.d.) *Reported Road Casualties – Great Britain*. London: HMSO.

DETS(A) (2015) *Command Leadership and Management Policy Handbook*. London: MoD.

Dibbets, K. and Hogenkamp, B. (1995) *Film and the First World War*. Amsterdam: Amsterdam University Press.

Dickinson, M. and Street, S. (1985) *Cinema and State: The Film Industry and the British Government*. London: BFI.

Dixon, W. W. (ed.) (1994) *Re-viewing British Cinema, 1900–1992*. New York: State University of New York.

Docherty, D., Morrison, D., and Tracey, M. (1987) *The Last Picture Show? Britain's Changing Film Audiences*. London: British Film Institute.

Doherty, T. P. (1993) *Projections of War: Hollywood, American Culture and World War*. New York: Columbia University Press.

Drazin, C. (1998) *The Finest Years: British Cinema of the 1940s*. London: Tauris.

Druick, Z. (2007) *Projecting Canada: Government Policy and Documentary Film at the National Film Board*. Montreal: McGill University Press.

Druick, Z. (2012) 'At the margins of cinema history: Mobile cinema in the British empire', *Public*, 40, pp. 118–24.

Druick, Z. and Williams, D. (2014) *The Grierson Effect: Tracing Documentary's International Movement*. London: BFI.

Ducellier, J. P. (2010) *The Amiens Raid: Secrets Revealed*. London: Red Kite.

Dunne, P. (1946) 'The documentary and Hollywood', *Hollywood Quarterly*, 2, pp. 166–72.

Edgerton, D. (1996) *Science, Technology and the British Industrial 'Decline', 1870–1970*. Cambridge: Cambridge University Press.

Ehrlich, E. (1985) *Cinema of Paradox; French Filmmaking under the German Occupation*. New York: Columbia.

Eley, G. (2001) 'Finding the people's war: Film, British collective memory, and World War II', *The American Historical Review*, 106:3, pp. 818–38.

Eliashberg, J. and Shugan, S (1997) 'Film critics, influencers or predictors?', *Journal of Marketing*, 61:2, pp. 66–78.

Ellis, J. (1984) 'The final years of the British documentary movement as the Grierson movement', *Journal of Film and Video*, 36, pp. 41–49.

Ellis, J. (1986) *John Grierson: A Guide to References and Resources*. Boston: Hall.

Ellis, J. C. (2000) *John Grierson: Life, Contributions, Influence*. Illinois: Southern Illinois University Press.

Ellis, J. C. and McLane, B. A. (2005) *A New History of Documentary Film*. New York: Continuum.

Elton, A. (1955) 'The film as source material for history', *Aslib Proceedings*, 7:4, pp. 207–39.

Enticknap, L. (2013) '"This modern age" and the British non-fiction film'. In Ashby, J. and Higson, A. *British Cinema, Past and Present*. Oxford: Routledge, pp. 193–206.

Erickson, P. (2022) 'An empire of "growth and nurture": Agriculture, documentary film and the development of Britain's Empire Marketing Board, 1926–1933', *Contemporary European History*, 32:4, pp 509–24.

Evans, G. (1991) *In the National Interest. A Chronicle of the National Film Board of Canada, 1949–1989*. Toronto: University of Toronto Press.

Evans, G. (2005) *John Grierson: Trailblazer of Documentary*. Montreal: XYZ.

Evans, G. (2014) *Life and Loves of Laurie Lee*. London: Robson.

Eveleigh, D. (2011) *A History of the Kitchen*. Stroud: The History Press.

Farmer, R. (2011) 'A temporarily vanished civilisation: Ice cream, confectionary and wartime cinema going', *Historical Journal of Film, Radio and Television*, 31:4, pp. 479–97.

Flanagan, K. M. (2015) 'The British war film 1939–1980: Culture, history and genre.' Unpublished PhD thesis, University of Pittsburgh.

Forman, D. (1978) *John Grierson: The Man and the Memory*. Stirling: Grierson Archive.

Forman, H. (1982) 'The non-theatrical distribution of films by the Ministry of Information'. In Pronay, N. and Spring, D. W. (eds.) *Propaganda, Politics and Film, 1918–1945*. London: Macmillan.

Fox, J. C. (2005) 'John Grierson: His 'documentary boys' and the British Ministry of Information, 1939–1942', *Historical Journal of Film, Television and Radio*, 23:3, pp. 345–69.

Fox, J. C. (2007) *Film Propaganda in Britain and Nazi Germany: World War II Cinema*. Oxford: Berg.

Fox, J. C. (2012) 'Careless talk: Tensions within British domestic propaganda during the Second World War', *Journal of British Studies*, 51:4, pp. 936–66.
Fox, J. C. (2013) 'From documentary film to television documentaries', *Journal of British Cinema and Television*, 10, pp. 498–523.
Frayling, C. (1995) *Things to Come*. London: BFI.
Fyne, R. (1994) *The Hollywood Propaganda of World War II*. New York: Scarecrow Press.
Garcon, F. (1984) *De Blum à Pétain: Cinema et Societé française, 1936–1944*. Paris: Les éditions du Cerf.
Gardiner, J. (2008) 'Working class heroes', *Sight and Sound*, XVIII:5, p. 92.
Gardiner, J. (2010) *The Blitz: The British Under Attack*. London: Harper.
Geiger, J (2011) *American Documentary Film – Projecting the Nation*. Edinburgh: Edinburgh University Press.
Geraghty, C. (2000) *British Cinema in the Fifties*. London: Routledge.
Gernser, G., Van Oostrum, M. and Leenders, M. (2007) 'The impact of film reviews on the box office performance of art house versus mainstream motion pictures', *Journal of Cultural Economics*, 31:1, pp. 43–63.
Gervereau, L. and Peschanski, D. (eds.) (1990) *La Propaganda sous Vichy, 1940–44*. Paris: Les éditions du Cerf.
Gillett, P. (2003) *The British Working Class in Post-War Film*. Manchester: Manchester University Press.
Gillett, P. (2006) 'Capturing the moment: Realism in British cinema in the late 1940s', *Film International*, IV:24, pp. 50–58.
Gillingham, J. (1991). *Coal, Steel and the Re-birth of Europe, 1945–55*. Cambridge: Cambridge University Press.
Giltrow, D. (1979). Daybreak at Udi: The COI, Crown Film Unit and Terry Bishop, *American Anthropologist*. New York: Wiley.
Glancy, H. M. (1992) 'MGM film grosses, 1924–48: The Eddie Mannix ledger', *Historical Journal of Film, Radio and Television*, 12:2, pp. 127–44.
Glancy, H. M. (1993) 'Warner Bros. Film Grosses 1921–51, The William Schaefer ledger', *Historical Journal of Film, Radio and Television*, 15:1, pp. 53–73.
Glancy, H. M. (1998) 'Hollywood and Britain: The case of MGM-British'. In Richards, J. (ed.) *The Unknown 1930s: An Alternative History of the British Cinema*. London: Tauris, pp. 57–74.
Glancy, M. (2010) 'Going to the pictures: British cinema and the Second World War', *Past and Present*, 8, pp. 7–9.
Glancy, M. (2011) 'Picturegoer: The fan magazine and popular film culture in Britain during WW2', *Historical Journal of Film, Radio and Television*, 31:4, pp. 453–78.
Gold, J. and Ward, S. (2005) 'Of plans and planners'. In Clark, D. (ed.) *The Cinematic City*. London: Routledge.
Goldsworthy, D. (1971) *Colonial Issues in British Politics 1945–1961: From 'Colonial Development' to 'Wind of Change'*. Oxford: Clarendon.

Grant, B. K. and Sloniowski, J. (1998) *Documenting the Documentary: Close Readings of Documentary Film*. Detroit: Wayne State.

Grant, M. (1994) *Propaganda and the Role of the State in Interwar Britain*. Oxford: Clarendon.

Grant, M. (1999) 'Towards a Central Office of Information: Continuity and change in British government information policy, 1939–51', *Journal of Contemporary History*, 34:1, pp. 49–67.

Grant, M. (2010) *After the Bomb: Civil Defence and Nuclear War 1945–1968*. London: Palgrave.

Grierson, J. (1932) 'The first principles of documentary cinema'. Reprinted in Grierson, J. (1946) *Grierson on Documentary*. London: Collins.

Grierson, J. (1933) 'The documentary producer', *Cinema Quarterly*, 2:1, pp. 7–9.

Grierson, J (1946) *Grierson on Documentary*. London: Collins.

Grierson, J. (1952) 'The front page – Dissolution of the Crown Film Unit', *Sight and Sound*, XX1:4, pp. 142–43.

Grieveson, L. and McCabe, C (eds.) (2011) *Film and Empire*. London, BFI.

Grove, V. (2000) *Laurie Lee: The Well-Loved Stranger*. London: Penguin.

Haggith, T. (1998) ' "Castles in the air": British film and the reconstruction of the built environment, 1939–51.' Unpublished PhD thesis, University of Warwick.

Haggith, T. (2021) 'Women documentary film-makers and the British housing movement, 1930 – 1945', *Journal of British Cinema and Television*, 18:4, pp. 478–97.

Hammond, M. (2001) 'The big show: Cinema exhibition and reception in Britain in the Great War.' Unpublished PhD thesis, Nottingham Trent University.

Hanson, J. (1992) 'Boyhood in wartime Cumnor'. Cumnor Parish Records. www.bodley.ox.ac.uk/external/cumnor/recollections/boyhood.htm (accessed 26 October 2014).

Hanson, J. (1992) *The Development of Modern Farmoor, 1900–1974*. Oxford (private publication).

Harding, A. (2004) 'The closure of the Crown Film Unit in 1952: Artistic decline or political machinations?', *Journal of Contemporary British History*, 18:4, pp. 22–51.

Hardy, F. (ed.) (1966) *Grierson on Documentary*. London: Faber.

Harper, S. (2004) 'A lower middle-class taste-community in the 1930s: Admissions figures at the Regent Cinema, Portsmouth, UK', *Historical Journal of Film, Radio and Television*, 24:4, pp. 565–87.

Harper, S. (2006) 'Fragmentation and crisis: 1940s admissions figures at the Regent Cinema, Portsmouth, UK', *Historical Journal of Film, Radio and Television*, 26:3, pp. 361–94.

Harper, S. (2010) 'The ownership of woods and water: Landscapes in British cinema'. In Harper, G. and Rayner J. (eds.) *Cinema and Landscape*. Bristol: Intellect, pp. 147–60.

Harper, S. and Porter, V. (2003) *British Cinema of the 1950s*. Oxford: Oxford University Press.

Harrison, R. (2014) 'Inside the cinema train: Britain, empire and modernity in the twentieth century', *Film History*, 26:4, pp. 32–57.

Harrisson, T. (1976) *Living Through the Blitz*. London: Collins.

Hartley, J. (2007) 'The best propaganda: Humphrey Jennings's *The Silent Village* (1943)'. In McKee, A. (ed.), *Beautiful Things in Popular Culture*. London: Blackwell, pp. 144–63.

Havardi, J. (2014) *Projecting Britain at War: The National Character in British World War II Films*. Jefferson, NC: McFarland.

Henley, P. (1985) 'British ethnographic film: Recent developments anthropology', *Today*, 1:1, pp. 5–17.

Hennessy, P. (1992) *Never Again: Britain 1945–51*. London: Cape.

Hennessy, P. (2003) *Secret State: Whitehall and the Cold War*. London: Allen Lane.

Hennessy, P. (2007) *Cabinets and the Bomb*. London: Oxford University Press.

Higson, A. (1998) *Waving the Flag: Constructing a National Cinema in Britain*. Oxford: Clarendon.

Hildenbrand, K. and Hugues, G. (eds.) (2008) *Images of War and War of Images*. Newcastle: Cambridge Scholars.

Hiley, N. (1993) 'Hilton DeWitt Girdwood and the origins of British official filming', *Historical Journal of Film, Radio and Television*, 13:2, pp. 129–48.

Hiley, N. (1995) 'The British cinema auditorium'. In Dibbets, K. and Hogenkamp, B. (eds.) *Film and the First World War*. Amsterdam: Amsterdam University Press, pp. 160–68.

Hiley, N. (2012) ' "At the picture palace": British cinema audiences, 1895–1920'. In Christie, I. (ed.) *Audiences: Defining and Researching Screen Entertainment Reception*. Amsterdam: Amsterdam University Press, pp. 39–53.

Hillier, J. and Grant, B. K. (2009) *100 Documentary Films*. London: BFI.

Hinton, D. (1991) *The Films of Leni Riefenstahl*. New York: Scarecrow Press.

Historical Journal of Radio Film and Television (2011) British Cinema and the Second World War, 31:4, special edition.

HMSO (1939) *Schedule of Reserved Occupations*. London: The Stationery Office (Cmd 5936).

HMSO (1946) *Strength and Casualties of the Armed Forces and Auxiliary Services of the United Kingdom 1939–1945*. London: The Stationery Office (Cmd 6832).

HMSO (1946) *Report on War Casualties. London*: The Stationery Office (Cmd 6832).

Hoare, J. G. (2010) 'Imperialism and "alternative" film culture. The Empire Marketing Board 1926–1933.' Unpublished PhD thesis, University of Kingston.

Hoffman, H. (1996) *The Triumph of Propaganda: Film and National Socialism*. Oxford: Berghahn.
Hogenkamp, A. P. (1991) 'The British documentary movement and the 1945–51 Labour governments.' Unpublished PhD thesis, CNAA Westminster College, Oxford.
Hogg, J. (2016) *British Nuclear Culture: Official and Unofficial Narratives*. London: Bloomsbury.
Holbrook, M. and Addis, M. (2008) 'Art versus commerce in the movie industry: A two-path model of motion picture success', *Journal of Cultural Economics*, 32:2, pp. 87–107.
Hollins, T. J. (1981) 'The Conservative Party and film propaganda between the wars', *English Historical Review*, 96:379, pp. 359–69.
Holly, M. (2013) 'Local authorities and film censorship: An historical account of the 'naughty pictures committees' in Sale and Manchester', *Entertainment and Sports Law Journal*, 11. Available at www2.warwick.ac.uk/fac/soc/law/elj/eslj/issues/volume11/hally/#a7 (accessed 17 August 2013).
Hooley, T. (2002) 'Visions of a new Jerusalem: Predictive fiction in the Second World War.' Unpublished PhD thesis, University of Leicester.
Houston, P. (1955) 'The undiscovered country', *Sight and Sound*, 25:1, pp. 10–14.
Houston, P. (2002) 'The nature of evidence'. In McKernan, L. (ed.) *Yesterday's News: The British Cinema Newsreel Reader*. London: BUVC, pp. 290–99.
Hurd, G. (2008) *National Fictions: World War Two in British Film and Television*. London: BFI.
Izod, J., Kilburn, T., and Hibbard, M. (2000) *From Grierson to Docu-Soap: Breaking the Boundaries*. Luton: University of Luton Press.
Jackson, A. (2010) 'The colonial film archive and the British empire at war, 1939–1945'. Research paper No. 1, The British Empire at War Research Group. London: King's College.
Jackson, K. (ed.) (1993) *The Humphrey Jennings Film Reader*. Manchester: Carcanet.
Jackson, K. (2004) *Humphrey Jennings*. London: Picador.
Jackson, P. (1999) *A Retake Please! Night Mail to Western Approaches*. Liverpool: Liverpool University Press.
Jacobs, L. (ed.) (1979) *The Documentary Tradition*. New York: Norton.
James, R. (2006) '*Kinematograph Weekly* in the 1930s: Trade attitudes towards audience taste', *Journal of British Cinema and Television*, 3:2, pp. 229–43.
James, R. (2007) 'A very profitable enterprise: South Wales Miners' Institute cinemas in the 1930s', *Historical Journal of Film, Television and Radio*, 27:1, pp. 27–61.
James, R. (2011) 'Popular film-going in Britain in the early 1930s', *Journal of Contemporary History*, 46:2, pp. 271–87.

Jarvie, I. (1986) 'British trade policy versus Hollywood, 1947–8: "Food before flicks"?', *Historical Journal of Film, Radio and Television*, 6:1, pp. 19–41.

Jeacle, I. (2009) ' "Going to the movies": Accounting and twentieth century cinema', *Accounting, Auditing & Accountability Journal*, 22:5, pp. 667–708.

Jennings, M.-L. (ed.) (1982) *Humphrey Jennings: Film-Maker, Painter, Poet*. London: BFI.

Jerslev, A. (2002) *Realism and Reality in Film and Media*. Denmark: Museum Tusculanum Press.

Johnson, T. (1997) *Censored Screams: The British Ban on Hollywood Horror in the Thirties*. North Carolina: McFarlane.

Jones, K., Aucott, P. and Southall, H. (2013) *Bomb Sight: Mapping WW2 Bomb Census*. Portsmouth: University of Portsmouth.

Jones, R. (1997) 'The boffin: A stereotype of scientists in post-war British films, 1945–1970', *Journal of the Public Understanding of Science*, 6, pp. 31–48.

Jones, S. (2018) *The British Labour Movement and Film, 1918–1939*. London: Routledge.

Kandiah, M. D. (1995) 'Television enters politics: The Conservative Party's central office and political broadcasting, 1945–55', *Historical Journal of Film, Radio and Television*, 15:2, p. 265.

Katz, E. and Lazarsfeld, P. (1955) *Personal Influence*. New York: The Free Press.

Kingston Bagpuize Local History Society (n.d.) Village Stories. http://www.kbsonline.org.uk/history (accessed 5 May 2024).

Kirkpatrick, B. J. (1965) *A Bibliography of E. M. Forster*. London: Hart Davis.

Klinger, B. (1994) *Melodrama and Meaning: History, Culture and the Films of Douglas Sirk*. Bloomington: Indiana University Press.

Kothari, U. (2014) 'Trade, consumption and development alliances: The historical legacy of the Empire Marketing Board poster campaign', *Third World Quarterly*, 35:1, pp. 43–64.

Kreimeier, K. (1999) *The Ufa Story*. Los Angeles: University of California Press.

Kuhn, A. (1999) 'Cinema-going in Britain in the 1930s: Report of a questionnaire survey', *Historical Journal of Film, Radio and Television*, 19:4, pp. 531–43.

Kuhn, A. (2002) 'Children, horrific films and censorship in the 1930s', *Historical Journal of Film, Radio and Television*, 22:2, pp. 197–202.

Kynaston, D. (2007) *Austerity Britain 1945–1951 (Tales of New Jerusalem)*. London: Bloomsbury.

Lago, M. and Furbank, P. (1983) *E. M. Forster – A Life*. London: Collins.

Lasswell, H. (1927) 'The theory of political propaganda', *American Political Science Review*, 21:3, pp. 627–31.

Lay, S. (2002) *British Social Realism – From Documentary to Brit Grit*. London: Wallflower.
Lazarsfeld, P. and Merton, R. (1948) 'Mass communications, popular taste, and organized social action'. In Schramm, W. and Roberts, D. (eds.) (1971) *Process and Effects of Mass Communications*. Urbana: University of Illinois Press, pp. 554–78.
Lee, J. (1972) 'The dissolution of the Empire Marketing Board, 1933', *Journal of Imperial and Commonwealth History*, 1:1, pp. 49–57.
Lee, J. M. (1977) *Reviewing the Machinery of Government, 1942–1952*. Plymouth (private publication).
Legard, J. (1994) Interview with Nora Lee. London: British Entertainment History Project. https://historyproject.org.uk/interview/nora-lee-nee-blackburne (accessed 7 May 2024).
Logan, P. C. (2011) *Humphrey Jennings and the British Documentary: A Reassessment*. London: Ashgate.
Lord, G. (2005) *John Mortimer: The Devil's Advocate*. London: Orion.
Lovell, A. and Hillier, J. (1972) *Studies in Documentary*. London: Secker.
Low, R. (1979) *The History of British Film 1929–39*. London: GAU.
Mackay, R. (2002) *Half the Battle: Civilians in Britain During the Second World War*. Manchester: Manchester University Press.
MacKenzie, N. (1983) 'Film propaganda and the audience, examples of Britain's official films in World War One', *Journal of Contemporary History*, 18:3, pp. 463–94.
MacKenzie, S. P. (1992) *Politics and Military Morale*. Oxford: Clarendon.
MacKenzie, S. P. (2001) *British War Films, 1939–45: The Cinema and the Services*. London: Hambledon.
MacKillop, I. and Sinyard, N. (eds.). (2003) *British Cinema of the 1950s: A Celebration*. Manchester: Manchester University Press.
Marcus, L. (2009) 'The creative treatment of actuality: John Grierson, documentary cinema and "fact" in the 1930s'. In Bluemel, K. (ed.) *Intermodernism – Literary Culture in Mid-Twentieth Century Britain*. Edinburgh: Edinburgh University Press, pp. 189–207.
Marwick, A. (1974) *War and Social Change in the Twentieth Century*. London: Macmillan.
Mathieson, M. (1948) 'Music for Crown', *Hollywood Quarterly*, 3:3, pp. 323–26.
Mayer, J. P. (1948) *British Cinemas and Their Audiences*. London: Dennis Dobson.
McCluskey, M. (2016) 'Humphrey Jennings in the East End: *Fires Were Started* and local geographies', *The London Journal*, 41:2, pp. 170–89.
McGlade, F. (2010) *History of the British Army Film and Photographic Unit in the Second World War*. Solihull: Helion.
McKee, A. (ed.) (2007) *Beautiful Things in Popular Culture*. London: Blackwell.
McKernan, L. (ed.) (2002) *Yesterday's News: The British Cinema Newsreel Reader*. London: British Universities Film and Video Council.

McLaine, I. (1979) *Ministry of Morale*. London: GAU.
McLane, B. A. (2012) *A New History of Documentary Film (2nd Edition)*. New York: Continuum.
McQuail, D. (1997) *Audience Analysis*. New York: Sage.
Mellor, L. (2020) 'It's only chance that you're safe and sound': Meanings of the body in Humphrey Jennings' *A Diary for Timothy*,' *Journal of War & Culture Studies*, 13:2. pp. 163–78.
Merle, K. (2010) 'British cinema and the manipulation of public opinion during the inter-war years.' Unpublished master's dissertation, Rhode Island College.
Messinger, G. S. (1993). 'An inheritance worth remembering: The British approach to official propaganda during the First World War', *Historical Journal of Film, Radio and Television*, 13:2, pp. 117–27.
Middlemas, K. and Barnes, J. (1969) *Baldwin: A Biography*. London: Weidenfeld and Nicolson.
Miles, P. and Smith, M. (2013) *Cinema, Literature & Society: Elite and Mass Culture in Interwar Britain*. London: Routledge.
Monger, D. (2012) *Patriotism and Propaganda in First World War Britain: The National War Aims Committee and Civilian Morale*. Liverpool: Liverpool University Press.
Moore, M. (2004) 'Development of communication between the government, media and people of Great Britain, 1945–1951.' Unpublished PhD thesis, University of London (LSE).
Morgan, K. O. (1984) *Labour in Power 1945–1951*. Oxford: Oxford University Press.
Mortimer, J. (1979) 'Valiant for truth', *The New Statesman*, 4 May, p. 6.
Mortimer, J. (1982) *Clinging to the Wreckage*. London: Weidenfeld and Nicolson.
Mortimer, J. (1994) *Murderers and Other Friends*. London: Viking.
Murphy, R. (1992) *Realism and Tinsel: Cinema and Society in Britain 1939–1948*. London: Routledge.
Murphy, R. (2005) *British Cinema and the Second World War*. London: Continuum.
Murphy, R. (ed.) (2006) *Directors in British and Irish Cinema – A Reference Companion*. London: BFI.
Murphy, W. T. (1972) 'The method of *Why We Fight*', *Journal of Popular Film*, summer, p. 185.
Murray, A. (2010) *Framing the Nation – Documentary Film in Inter-War France*. London: Continuum.
Neild, A. (2011) The COI Collection Five: Portrait of a People. London: BFI.
Newton, M. (2013) 'Strategic news management in the Iraq war: How were US and UK media organisations utilised by coalition forces to instigate information and psychological operations against domestic audiences?' Unpublished master's dissertation, University of Aberystwyth.
Nowell-Smith, G. (1990) 'On history and the cinema', *Screen*, 31:2, pp. 160–71.

O'Brien, H. (2004) *The Real Ireland – The Evolution of Ireland in the Documentary Film*. Manchester: Manchester University Press.

O'Neil, E. (2006) 'British World War Two films, 1945–65: Catharsis or national regeneration.' Unpublished PhD thesis, University of Central Lancashire.

Orr, J. (1932) 'The cinema and the empire', *Sight and Sound*, 1(1), p. 19.

Oswell, D. (2002) *Television, Childhood and the Home: A History of the Making of the Child Television Audience in Britain*. Oxford: Oxford University Press.

Page, B. (2014) 'And the Oscar goes to... *Daybreak in Udi*. Understanding late colonial community development and its legacy through film', *Development and Change*, 45, pp. 838–68.

Palmer, G. (1990) 'Basil Wright: Definitions of documentary.' Unpublished PhD thesis, University of Stirling.

Paris, M. (2005) 'Promoting British aviation in the 1950s cinema', *History of Technology*, 26, pp. 63–78.

Pelling, H. (1970) *Britain and the Second World War*. London: Collins.

Philo, G. (2002) 'Television news and audience understanding of war, conflict and disaster', *Journalism Studies*, 3:2, pp. 173–86.

Pilard, P. (2011) 'Londres brûle-t-il?', *Positif* (Paris), December, pp. 109–11.

Poole, J (1987) 'British cinema attendance in wartime: Audience preference at the Majestic, Macclesfield, 1939–46', *Historical Journal of Film, Radio and Television*, 7:1, pp. 15–34.

Popple, S. (1996) 'Group Three: A lesson in state intervention', *Film History*, 8:2, pp. 131–42.

Powell, D. (1947) *Films Since 1939*. London: British Council.

Preston, P. (1978) *The Coming of the Spanish Civil War*. London: Macmillan.

Pronay, N. and Spring, D. (1982) *Propaganda, Politics and Film*. London: Macmillan.

Pronay, N. (1983) "The land of promise": The projection of peace aims in Britain'. In Short, K. R. M. (ed.) *Film and Radio Propaganda in World War Two*. New York: Croom Helm, pp. 51–77.

Pronay, N. (1988) 'The British post-bellum cinema: A survey of films relating to World War II made in Britain between 1945 and 1960', *Historical Journal of Film, Radio and Television*, 8:1, pp. 39–54.

Pronay, N. (1989) 'John Grierson and the documentary – 60 years on', *Historical Journal of Film, Radio and Television*, 9:3, pp. 227–46.

Pronay, N. (1993) 'British film sources for the Cold War – The disappearance of the cinema going public', *Historical Journal of Film, Radio and Television*, 13:1, pp. 7–17.

Proud, J. (1995) *Children and Propaganda: Il etait une fois...: Fiction and Fairy Tale in Vichy France*. Oxford: Intellect.

Public Health England (2012) *Acute Poliomyelitis: Annual Corrected Notifications & Deaths, England & Wales 1912–2007*. London: HMSO.

Purcell, H. (1995) 'Glory traps', *New Statesman & Society*, 12 May.

Ramsden, J. (1978) *The Age of Balfour and Baldwin*. London: Longman.

Ramsden, J. (1998) 'Refocusing the people's war: British war films of the 1950s', *Journal of Contemporary History*, 33:1, pp. 35–63.
Ramsden, J. (2003) *The Dam Busters*. London: BFI.
Rattigan, N. (1994) 'Last gasp of the middle classes'. In Dixon, W. (ed.) *Re-Viewing British Cinema, 1900–1992*. New York: State University of New York, pp. 143–52.
Rattigan, N. (2001) *This Is England: British Film and the People's War, 1939–1945*. London and Ontario: Associated University Press.
Reeves, N. (1986) *Official British Film Propaganda during the First World War*. London: Croom Helm.
Reeves, N. (1993) 'Film propaganda and its audience', *Journal of Contemporary History*, 13, pp. 463–93.
Reeves, N. (1997) 'Cinema spectatorship and propaganda: 'Battle of the Somme' and its contemporary audience', *Historical Journal of Film Radio and Television*, 17:1, pp. 5–28.
Reeves, N. (1999) *The Power of Film Propaganda: Myth or Reality*. London: Cassell.
Reimer, R. C. (ed.) (2000) *Cultural History Through the National Socialist Lens*. London: Camden House.
Reith, J. (1949) *Into the Wind*. London: Hodder.
Renov, M. (1993) *Theorizing Documentary*. New York: Routledge.
Rice, T. (2011) 'From the inside: The Colonial Film Unit and the beginning of the end'. In Grieveson, L. and MacCabe, C. (eds.) *Film and the End of Empire*. London: BFI., pp. 135–53.
Richards, J. (1987) 'Wartime British cinema audiences and the class system: The case of *Ships with Wings* (1941)', *Historical Journal of Film, Radio and Television*, 7:2, pp. 129–41.
Richards, J. (1992) 'New waves and old myths: British cinema in the 1960s'. In Moore-Gilbert, B. and Seed, J. (eds.) *Cultural Revolution*. London: Routledge. pp. 171–85.
Richards, J. (1994) 'Cinemagoing in Worktown: regional film audiences in 1930s Britain', *Historical Journal of Film, Radio and Television*, 14:2, pp. 147–66.
Richards, J. (ed.) (1998) *The Unknown 1930s: An Alternative History of the British Cinema*. London: Tauris.
Riefenstahl, L. (1992) *Leni Riefenstahl: A Memoir*. New York: St Martins.
Rist, P. R. (2014) *Historical Dictionary of South American Cinema*. Maryland: Rowman & Littlefield.
Roads, C. H. (1965) 'Film as historical evidence', *Journal of the Society of Archivists*, 3, pp. 183–91.
Roberston, J. (1992) *The Hidden Cinema: British Film Censorship in Action 1913–1972*. London: Routledge.
Robertson, J. C. (1982) 'British film censorship goes to war', *Historical Journal of Film, Radio and Television*, 2:1, pp. 49–64.
Roeder, G. (1993) *The Censored War: American Visual Experience During World War II*. New Haven: Yale University Press.

Rogers, E. (1995) *Diffusion of Innovations*. New York: Simon & Schuster.
Rose, S. O. (2003) *Which People's War; National Identity and Citizenship in Wartime Britain, 1939–1945*. Oxford: Oxford University Press.
Rosenthal. A. (1972) *The New Documentary in Action*. Los Angeles: University of California Press.
Rosenthal, A. and Corner, A. (eds.) (2005) *New Challenges for Documentaries*. Manchester: Manchester University Press.
Rotha, P. (1973) *Documentary Diary*. London: Secker.
Rotha, P. (1999) *A Paul Rotha Reader*. Exeter: University of Exeter Press.
Rothman, W. (1997) *Documentary Film Classics*. Cambridge: Cambridge University Press.
Rüffert, C. (2019) 'Film as an instrument of social enquiry: The British documentary film movement of the 1930s', *Research in Film and History*, 2. https://mediarep.org/server/api/core/bitstreams/37e643fb-782f-4199-aea5-d3851659abcc/content (accessed 15 January 2019).
Russell, P. (2013) 'Dust and shadows: A progress report', *Journal of British Cinema and Television*, 10:3, pp. 415–29.
Russell, P. and Piers Taylor, J. (2010) *Shadows of Progress: Documentary Film in Post-War Britain*. London: BFI/Palgrave Macmillan.
Ryan, T. (1986) 'Labour and the media in Britain, 1929–1939.' Unpublished PhD thesis, University of Leeds.
Salkeld, A. (1996) *A Portrait of Leni Riefenstahl*. London: Pimlico.
Sanders, M. L. (1983) 'British film propaganda in Russia 1916–1919', *Historical Journal of Film, Radio and Television*, 3:2, pp. 117–29.
Sedgwick, J. (2000) *Popular Filmgoing in 1930s Britain: A Choice of Pleasures*. Exeter: University of Exeter Press.
Seino, T. (2010) 'Realism and representations of the working class in contemporary British cinema.' Unpublished MPhil thesis, De Montfort University, Leicester.
Shaka, F. O. (1999) 'Instructional cinema in colonial Africa: An historical reappraisal', *Ufahamu, Journal of African Studies*, 27, pp. 1–21.
Shapiro, J. (2002) *Atomic Bomb Cinema: The Apocalyptic Imagination on Film*. London: Routledge.
Shaw, T. (2001) *British Cinema and the Cold War*. London: I.B. Tauris.
Short, K. R. M. (ed.) (1983) *Film and Radio Propaganda in World War Two*. New York: Croom Helm.
Short, K. R. M. (1997) 'RAF Bomber Command's *Target for Tonight*', *Historical Journal of Film, Radio and Television*, 17:2, pp. 181–200.
Short, K. R. M. (1997) *Screening the Propaganda of British Air Power: From 'R.A.F.' (1935) to 'The Lion Has Wings' (1939)*, Studies in War & Film, 6. Trowbridge: Flicks Books.
Short, K. R. M. and Dolezal, S. (eds.) (1988) *Hitler's Fall: The Newsreel Witness*. New York: Croom Helm.
Sinyard, N. (2014) *British Film in the 1950s*. BFI ScreenOnline. www.screenonline.org.uk/film/id/1147086 (accessed 26 January 2016).
Slater, J. (2009) *Under Fire: A Century of War Movies*. London: Ian Allen.

Smith, A. (2003) 'Humphrey Jennings' 'Heart of Britain' (1941): A reassessment', *Historical Journal of Film, Radio and Television*, 23:2, pp. 133–51.
Smith, A. (2012) *Public Relations and the Making of Modern Britain*. Manchester: Manchester University Press.
Smith, H. (1996) *Britain in the Second World War: A Social History*. Manchester: Manchester University Press.
Smith, M. (2000) *Britain and 1940: History, Myth and Popular Memory*. London: Routledge.
Smith, P. (ed.) (1976) *The Historian and Film*. London: Cambridge University Press.
Smith, R. (2013) 'Grierson, the British documentary movement and colonial cinema', *Film History*, 25:4, pp. 82–113.
Smyth, R. (1979) 'The development of British Colonial Film Policy, 1927–1939, with special reference to East and Central Africa', *Journal of African History*, 20:3, pp. 437–50.
Smyth, R. (1988) 'The British Colonial Film Unit and sub-Saharan Africa, 1939–1945', *Historical Journal of Film, Radio and Television*, 8:4, pp. 285–98.
Smyth, R. (1992) 'The post-war career of the Colonial Film Unit 1946–1955', *Historical Journal of Film, Radio and Television*, 12:2, pp. 163–77.
Smyth, R. (2013) 'Grierson, the British Documentary movement and colonial cinema', *Film History*, 25:4, pp. 82–113.
Sohn, T. W. (1977) *An Historical and Descriptive Analysis of the 'Why We Fight' Series*. New York: Arno Press.
Sparrow, J. H. A. (1949) *Morale*. London: HMSO.
Spicer, A. (2003) 'Extending people's minds for a brief time every day: The wartime propaganda short', *Journal of Media Practice*, 4:2, pp. 105–12.
Staiger, J. (1990) 'Announcing wares, winning patrons, voicing ideals: Thinking about the history and theory of film advertising', *Cinema Journal*, 29:3, pp. 3–31.
Staiger, J. (1992) *Interpreting Films: Studies in the Historical Reception of American Cinema*. Princeton: Princeton University Press.
Staiger, J. (2005) *Media Reception Studies*. New York: New York University Press.
Stollery, M. (2011) 'The Crown Film Unit and the challenge of representing the empire war effort'. In Grieveson, L. and MacCabe, C. (eds.) *Film and the End of Empire*. London: BFI, pp. 35–53.
Stollery, M. (2013) 'Canonising Humphrey Jennings/conceptualising British documentary film', *Journal of British Cinema and Television*, 10, pp. 395–414.
Stollery, M. (2015) 'Biography, craft, creative labour: The timeliness of Dai Vaughan's *Portrait of an Invisible Man*: The working life of Stewart McAllister, film editor', *Journal of British Cinema and Television*, 12:3, pp. 277–99.

Street, S. (1985) 'The Hays Office and the defence of the British market in the 1930', *Historical Journal of Film, Radio and Television*, 5:1, pp. 37–55.
Sussex, E. (1975) *The Rise and Fall of the British Documentary*. Los Angeles: University of California Press.
Swann, P. (1983) 'The selling of the empire: The Imperial Film Unit 1926–1933', *Studies in Visual Communication*, 9:3, pp. 15–24.
Swann, P. (1983) 'John Grierson and the GPO Film Unit', *Historical Journal of Film, Radio and Television*, 3:1, pp. 19–34.
Swann, P. (1989) *The British Documentary Film Movement, 1926–46*. London: Cambridge University Press.
Tallents, S. (1932) *The Projection of England*. London: Faber.
Taylor, A. J. P. (1972) *Beaverbrook*. London: Hamish Hamilton.
Taylor, H. (1998) 'The politics of the rising crime statistics of England and Wales, 1914–1960', *Crime, Histoire & Sociétés / Crime, History & Societies*, 2:1, pp. 5–28.
Taylor, P. (1981) '*If War Should Come:* Preparing the fifth arm for total war, 1935–1939,' *Journal of Contemporary History*, 16:1, pp. 27–51.
Taylor, P. M. (ed.) (1988) *Britain and the Cinema in the Second World War*. London: St Martin's Press.
Taylor, P. M. (1999) *British Propaganda in the Twentieth Century: Selling Democracy*. Edinburgh: Edinburgh University Press.
Taylor, R. (1998) *Film Propaganda – Soviet Russia and Nazi Germany*. London: I. B. Tauris.
Temple, M. and Witt, M. (eds.) (2004) *The French Cinema Book*. London: BFI.
Theuerkauf, H. (1998) *Goebbels' Filmerbe*. Berlin: Ullstein.
Thomson, D. (1994) *A Biographical Dictionary of Film*. London: Deutsch.
Thorpe, F. and Pronay, N. (1980) *British Official Films in the Second World War*. Oxford: Clio.
Toffell, G. (2011) 'Cinema-going from below: The Jewish film audience in inter-war Britain', *Participations*, 8:2, pp. 522–38.
Toulmin, V., Popple, S. and Russell, P. (eds.) (2005) *The Lost World of Mitchell and Kenyon: Edwardian Britain on Film*. London: BFI.
Trench, C. (2012) 'Terry Trench: Documentary film maker.' http://callytrench.co.uk/terry-trench.html (accessed 3 February 2014).
Upchurch, A. R. (2013) 'Missing from policy history: Dartington Hall Arts Enquiry, 1941–1947', *International Journal of Cultural Policy*, 19:5, pp. 610–22.
Van Gorp, A. (2017) ' "Springing from a sense of wonder": Classroom film and cultural learning in the 1930s', *Paedagogica Historica*, 53:3, pp. 285–99.
Van de Winkel, R. (2004) 'Nazi newsreels in Europe 1939–45: The many faces of Ufa's foreign weekly newsreel versus German's weekly newsreel', *Historical Journal of Film, Radio and Television*, 24:1, pp. 5–34.

Vaughan, D. (2011) 'Portrait of an invisible man: The working life of Stewart McAllister, film editor'. In Anthony, S and Mansell, J (eds.) *A Projection of Britain: A History of the GPO Film Unit*. London: BFI, pp. 72–79.
Von Feilitzen, C. (1998) 'Media violence: Four research perspectives'. In Dickinson, R., Harindranath, R. and Linne, O. (eds.) *Approaches to Audiences: A Reader*. London: Arnold, pp. 88–103.
Von Kassel-Siambani, E. (2008) *Humphrey Jennings*. Paris: L'Harmatton.
Ward, K. (1977) 'British documentaries of the 1930s', *History*, 62:206, pp. 426–31.
Ward, P. (2005) *Documentary – Margins of Reality*. London: Wallflower Press.
Watt, H. (1974) *Don't Look at the Camera*. New York: St Martins.
Welch, D. (1999) 'Powers of Persuasion', *History Today*, 49:8, pp. 24–26.
Welch, D. (2001) *Propaganda and the German Cinema*. London: Tauris.
Whiteley, N. (1994) 'High art and high street, the commerce versus culture debate'. In Keat, R., Whiteley, N. and Abercrombie, N. (eds.) *The Authority of the Consumer*. London: Routledge.
Wilcox, T. (1983) 'Projection or publicity: Rival concepts in the pre-war planning of the Ministry of Information', *Journal of Contemporary History*, 18:1. pp. 97–116.
Wildy, T. (1986) 'From the MOI to the COI – Publicity and propaganda in Britain, 1945–51: the National Health and Insurance campaigns', *Historical Journal of Film, Radio and Television*, 6:1, pp. 3–17.
Wildy, T. (1988) 'British television and official film, 1946–51', *Historical Journal of Film, Radio and Television*, 8:2, pp. 195–202.
Williams, D. (2008) *Australian Post-War Documentary Film – An Arc of Mirrors*. Bristol: Intellect.
Winston, B. (1995) *Claiming the Real – Griersonian Documentary and its Legitimations*. London: BFI.
Winston, B. (1999) *Fires Were Started*. London: BFI.
Winston, B. (2000) *Lies, Damned Lies and Documentaries*. London: BFI.
Winston, B. (2008) *Claiming the Real II – Grierson and Beyond*. London: BFI.
Winston, B. (2014) 'The Griersonian tradition postwar: Decline or transition?', *Journal of British Cinema and Television*, 11:1, pp. 101–15.
Wood, L. (1986) *British Films 1927–1939*. London: BFI.
Wood, L. (2006) 'Jack Lee'. In Murphy, R. (ed.), *Directors in British and Irish Cinema*. London: BFI, pp. 365–67.
Woodruff, D. (1933) 'The Empire Marketing Board'. *Fortnightly Review*, 135, pp. 208–16.
Woods, D. (1971) 'John Grierson: Documentary film pioneer', *Quarterly Journal of Speech*, 57:2. pp. 221–8.
Wright, B. (1976) *The Long View*. London: Secker & Warburg.

Index

6.30 Collection 81

Admiralty 53, 176
Air Ministry 53, 245
Air Post 81
Aircraft Recognition 21, 176, 195
Aitken, Ian 11–12
Alien Orders 20, 170, 244
Along the Line 176
Amery, Leo 45
Anstey, Edgar 56, 95, 123, 241
Anvil Productions 241
Appointment in London 109, 243
At the Third Stroke 93
Atomic Attack 252–55, 260
Attlee, Clement 44, 141, 147, 156, 232–33
Australian Wines 54
Axes and Elephants 55

Baldwin, Stanley 44, 250
Ball, Joseph 43, 99–100
Banking for Millions 83
Battle of the Ancre and the Advance of the Tanks, The 34
Battle of the Somme 33–34
Beddington, Jack 105, 109
Blitz 112, 115, 120, 123, 129, 214–15, 245, 250
Boer War 28–31
Book Bargain 72, 84

Boxall Report 105–07, 228
Boyd-Carpenter, John 1, 5, 221–22, 224, 234–36
Breeding for Milk 2, 149
Brief Encounter 13, 136, 217
Britain Prepared 32–33
Britain's Countryside 21, 88
British Board of Film Censors (BBFC) 41, 203
British Council 126, 176–77
British Film Institute (BFI) 4, 7, 8, 15, 22, 24, 113
British Guiana 74
Broad Fourteens 119
Broadcasting, Entertainment, Communications and Theatre Union (BECTU) 14–15, 25
Builders 3, 129–30, 147, 210, 242
By Sea and Land 118

Cable Ship 75, 192
Calendar of the Year 76–77, 192
Cameron, Ken 238, 240, 249
Cargo from Jamaica 55
Caring for Children 166
Cause Commune, La 104
Cavalcanti, Alberto 82, 84, 87, 91, 95, 107, 111, 113, 196, 239, 260–61
Central Film Library 110, 175, 189, 266

Central Office of Information (COI) closure of CFU 1, 5, 142, 152, 222, 228–30, 232, 234–38
and film 2, 17, 23, 143–44, 156, 160, 175, 185, 193, 196–97, 205, 212, 227, 234, 240, 248–49, 258
library 51, 177, 181, 183, 190, 235, 248
Chamberlain, Neville 97, 102, 105, 184
Chapman, James 17, 25, 99, 138
Children of the Empire 52
Children of the Ruins 166
Children on Trial 166
Children's Charter 137, 165
Chiltern Country, The 95, 196
Christmas Is Coming 149
Christmas Under Fire 23, 38
Cinema Exhibitors Association (CEA) 6, 110, 109, 149, 156, 187, 205, 224–27, 251
Cinema Quarterly 10
cinema vans 5, 15, 44, 75, 99, 110, 184–91, 192, 194, 198, 219
Cinematograph Act (1909) 41
Cinematograph Films Act (1927) 66, 201
City, The 95
Clark, Kenneth 14, 16, 100, 102, 105
Close Quarters 64, 65, 118
Coal Face 87
Coastal Command 115, 118, 212, 214, 220, 255, 257
Cocoa from Nigeria 167, 169, 240
Collis, A. G. D. 228–30
Colonial Film Unit 167, 197, 240
Coming of the Dial, The 75
Committee of Imperial Defence 90
Conservative Party 43–44, 99, 184, 224, 230–37
Copper Web, The 75
Country Comes to Town, The 200
Crazy Gang 20, 37
Creighton, Walter 46–48

CTO – *The Central Telephone Exchange* 75
Cumberland Story, The 157, 158, 161, 218, 222, 262
Cushing, Peter 164, 233

Daily Express 116–17, 214–15, 231
Daily Mail 60
Daily Mirror 60, 193–94, 210–11, 214, 215
Daily Round 81
Dalrymple, Ian 3, 9, 107
Dam Busters, The 12, 115, 243–46, 255
Dancing Fleece, The 210–11
Dartington Hall Trust 5
Day the Earth Stood Still, The 162, 243
Daybreak in Udi 1, 144, 169, 220, 240, 253
Defeated People, A 152–55
Desert Victory 218
Diary for Timothy, A 8, 39, 121, 131, 135–36, 138, 139, 151, 217, 222, 241, 253
documentary movement 2, 3, 6, 8–12, 45, 46, 79, 222, 232, 244
Documentary News Letter 8, 24, 105, 185–86
Dollars and Sense 150
Drifters 10, 46–47, 51, 56
Droitwich 75, 86
Duck and Cover 173

Eagles of the Fleet 162
Early Diagnosis of Acute Anterior Poliomyelitis 176, 193, 221
Edinburgh 88
Eighth Plague, The 197
Eisenstein, Sergei 10, 49
El Dorado 169, 240
Elton, Arthur 62, 82
Empire Marketing Board 2, 6, 11, 21, 182
English Potter, The 57

Enquiry on Publicity (1943) 40
Erecting Aeroplane Engines 62

Factory Front 111
Factual Film, The 5, 182, 206, 218
Family Affair, A 166, 211
Farewell Topsails 201
Farm, The 95
Faster than Sound 162
Ferry Pilot 111, 126–28, 139, 244, 246, 257
Festival in London 2
Fight for Life 169
Films Division 91, 99–101, 105, 106, 117, 142, 152, 185, 190, 197, 204
Fire's the Enemy 149
Fires were Started 2, 3, 7, 8, 12, 128, 214–15, 220, 246
First Days, The 102, 104
Flaherty, Robert 9, 10, 56–57
Football 174
Foreign Office 33, 174, 196
Forster, E. M. 133, 135, 136
Four Barriers 88
Fowle, H. E. (Chick) 64, 79, 238, 239
Fox, Jo 17
French Communiqué 104
From the Ground Up 159, 160
Front Line, The 107
Furry Folk 62

Gamage, Fred 64, 132, 247–49, 253, 255
Gardens of the Orient 73
Gaumont-British Pictures 56–57, 65, 200
German Retreat and the Battle of Arras, The 34
Gielgud, John 217
Glancy, Mark 25, 179
Glassmakers of England 57
Glorious Sixth of June, The 84
God's Chillun 21, 95
Goebbels, Joseph 18, 181

Golden Rule 164
Good Housewife in Her Kitchen, The 223
Granton Trawler 87
Grierson, John
  EMBFU 21, 45–47, 49, 51–52, 54, 56, 59, 60, 64, 69, 185, 189
  GPOFU 70–71, 74–75, 77, 79, 87–89, 95, 192
  ideas 9–11, 21, 24, 33, 45, 63–64, 87, 100, 182, 188–89, 200, 226–27, 231–33, 242, 258, 262
  later career 223–23, 237
  pre-EMBFU 2, 4, 8–9, 13
Grierson, Marion 59–60, 88, 248

Harper, Sue 15, 25, 26
Hartnell, William 153
Harwell Assembly 21, 194
Health in War 101
Heart of Britain 8
Heating Research for Houses 223
Hess, Myra 34, 134
Hiley, Nicholas 31, 33, 180
His Fighting Chance 174
Hitchcock, Alfred 114, 218
Hole in the Ground 255–61
Hollins, T. J. 17
Holmes, Jack 2, 89, 107, 145, 214, 242
Horsey Mail 92
Houses in Town 248
Housing Problems 95
How the Dial Works 91
How the Teleprinter Works 21, 91

If War Should Come/Do It Now 97–98, 122, 251, 261
Imperial Institute 21, 51, 67, 189
imperial preference 44–46, 49, 50, 62, 69, 74
Imperial Six 57, 65, 74, 200
Imperial War Museum 7, 22, 32
In Which We Serve 13

India Marches 124
Industrial Britain 2, 56–57, 182, 200
Insect Pests in Food 40, 255
Into the Blue 248
Introducing the Dial 2
Is This the Job for Me? 195, 247
It Might Be You 164, 173, 233, 249

Jackson, Pat 2, 14, 92, 126, 129, 139, 216, 240, 242, 253
Jennings, Humphrey
  attitudes and philosophy 8, 13, 39, 132–34, 136, 154–55, 158, 161, 238, 241–42
  CFU post-war 152, 154, 157–59, 217–18, 222
  CFU wartime 2–3, 7, 22, 37, 119, 121, 123, 125, 128, 131–33, 136, 138–39, 202, 204, 214–15, 217, 246, 251
  GPOFU 63, 71, 76–78, 81, 84, 91–92, 94, 96–97, 102–04
  post-CFU 222
John Atkins Saves Up 82–83
John Bull's Animated Sketchbook 37, 38
Jones, Frank (Jonah) 3, 24, 64, 65, 79, 102, 107, 245, 248

Kinematograph Renters Society 6
Kinematograph Weekly 6, 10, 24, 100–01, 105, 109, 110, 187, 202, 204, 218, 225–27, 23
King George VI 6, 235
King Log 74, 200
King's Stamp, The/How Stamps are Made 80
Kingsley Wood, Howard 69, 74
Korda, Alexander 90, 100, 250
KRO Germany 155

Labour Party 156, 227
Layout and Handling in Factories 248
Leacock, Philip 2, 109, 243
League of Nations 78, 88

Lee, Jack 2, 65, 109, 120, 243
Lee, Nora 15, 24
Legard, John 238, 241
Legg, Stuart 53, 63, 65, 85
Leopard's Spots, The 39, 111, 113
Letter from Ulster 124
Letters to Liners 81
Light Repetitive Work 247
Line to the Tschierva Hut 46, 88
Liner Cruising South 62
Lion Has Wings, The 100, 115
Listen to Britain 34, 37, 125, 134, 138, 151, 154, 253, 256
Local Newspapers 174–75
Locomotives 76
Lofoten 204
London Airport 162, 233
London (Britain) Can Take It 12, 123, 251
Love of Books 174
Love on the Wing 92
Lumber 55, 74, 200
Lye, Len 77–78, 83

Magic Touch 160, 161, 162, 243, 255
Making Boots and Shoes 247
Making Engines 195
Malta G.C. 2, 245
Man in the White Suit, The 162, 243
Manchester Guardian 5, 45, 182, 188, 192, 234
Mass Observation 24, 99, 203, 205
McAllister, Stewart 241
McLaine, Ian 17, 109
Men of the Alps 88
Men of the Lightship 20, 23, 111, 113–15, 121, 128, 213, 218
Merchant Seamen 128, 218
Meredith, Burgess 150–52
Message from Geneva 78
Messenger Boy 192
Midsummer Day's Work 91
Miles, Bernard 20, 217
Minesweeping 176, 195
Mining Reviews 146, 175, 193

Ministry of Agriculture 53, 65
Ministry of Information (MoI)
  attitudes towards 5, 44, 99,
    100, 112, 205–08, 210
  dissolution 142–43, 204, 208,
    212, 220, 225–26, 234
  First World War 34–36, 38, 40
  re-establishment 14, 23, 72,
    90–91, 202–03
  Second World War 2, 16–17,
    23, 100–01, 104–05, 107,
    109–10, 112, 113–14, 117,
    185–86, 188, 196–97,
    203–05, 218–19, 220
Mitchell and Kenyon archive 29–30
Moana 9, 56
mobile cinema vans 5, 110,
  184–91, 192, 194, 219
Mony a Pickle 93
Morrison, Herbert 143, 187, 219,
  230, 234
Mortimer, John 2, 4, 216, 253
Mr Jones Takes the Air 164–65
Movietone 16

N or NW 85
Nanook of the North 10, 56
National Film 35
National Mark 60–61
National Savings 190
National War Aims Committee 35
Navy, Army and Air Force Institutes
  (NAAFI) 15, 110, 194
Negombo Coast 73
New Road Transport Train, A 62
New York Times 168–69
News for the Navy 92
Night Mail 2, 64, 71, 79–80,
  132, 192
Nine for Six 93
North Sea 94
Now You're Talking 101

O Cangaceiro 239
O'er Hill and Dale 57–58, 200
Olivier, Laurence 139, 217
On the Fishing Banks of Skye 95

One Family 47–49, 51, 69,
  200, 259
Operation Jericho 118
Ordinary People 120–22, 123,
  246, 251, 254, 257–61
Oscar committee 169
Other Half of the World, The 200
Our Herring Harvest 258
Over to You 150

Patent Ductus Arteriosus 176,
  193, 247
Pathé 16
Patients Are In 219
Penny Journey 92
People and Products of India 54
People at Number 19, The 145,
  242–43
People's Palace, The 176
*Pett and Pott – A Fairy Story of the
  Suburbs* 84, 261
Pigs on Every Farm 223, 247
Pilot Is Safe, The 38, 128
Plums That Please 60–61
Pop Goes the Weasel 39, 150
Port of London 52
Post Haste 3, 81
Postman's Nightmare 21, 173
Priestley, J. B. 88–89
Projection of England, The 49–50
Pronay, Nicholas 12, 17, 208, 231
propaganda
  attitudes towards 16, 18, 35,
    99, 100–01, 143, 213
  First World War 31–35, 37–38,
    41, 111, 113
  general and studies of 6,
    17–20, 72
  post-war 134, 154, 157, 198,
    202, 204–05, 207, 211,
    225–26
  Second World War 90, 97, 100,
    109, 112, 114, 130, 181,
    215, 218
  uses of 16–17, 43–44, 48, 50,
    90–91, 93, 101, 120, 184,
    187, 197, 233–34

Railwaymen, The 175
Rainbow Dance 83
Ramsden, John 13, 243–46
Realist Films 223, 241
Reclamation 132
Redgrave, Michael 133, 134, 139, 243
Reeves, Nicholas 17, 31, 33–34, 40, 112
Rhondda and Wye 149
Richards, Jeffery 12
Roadways 3, 85, 86
Rotha, Paul 54, 182, 233
Royal Scotland 248

Saving of Bill Blewitt, The 39, 82, 192
Savings Bank 83
Shadow on the Mountain 57
Shepherd, The 59
Shown by Request 185
Silent Village, The 3, 8, 20, 119, 139, 204, 214–16
Sisal 137, 167, 197, 226
So This Is London 59, 248
Song of Ceylon 72–73
Spare Time 71, 96
Speaking from America 91
Spice (Cherry), Evelyn 60, 74, 76, 77, 85
Spring on the Farm 60
Spring Offensive 22
Squadron 992 102–03, 111, 113
SS Ionian 97
St James's Park 88
Staiger, Janet 26, 180, 208
Steps of the Ballet 21, 176
Stollery, Martin 13–14
Story of the Bristol Brabazon, The 162
Story of Omolo, The 197
Strand Films 110, 187, 205
Sunday Times 158, 213
Surprise Attack 174, 222, 250
Sussex, Elizabeth 9, 159
Swann, Paul 11, 21, 66, 70–71

Tale of Two Cities, The 123–24, 139, 170
Tallents, Stephen 11, 45–46, 49–50, 54, 63, 64, 70, 71, 74, 89, 90, 99, 262
Target for Tonight 2, 3, 7, 12, 13, 15, 26, 64, 115–18, 204, 209, 213–14, 218, 220, 244–46, 255–56, 265
Tea from Nyasaland 167, 226
Technicolor 78, 216
Telephone 75
Things to Come 90, 250
This Is Britain 146
This Was Japan 14
Times, The 211, 213, 215–17, 236
Tocher, The 93
Topical Film Company 36
Town Meeting of the World, The 233
Trade Tattoo 78
Trained to Serve 155
Transatlantic Airport 137, 147
Travel and Industrial Development Association (TIDA) 59, 195, 196
Treasury 52, 63, 79, 94, 105, 150, 223–24, 228–30, 236, 238
Trench, Terry 14
Tritton, Ronald 152, 222
Triumph of the Will 16
Trooping the Colour 248
True Story of Lili Marlene, The 14, 39, 119
Trumper, John 138
Twelve O'Clock High 116
Two Fathers 217

Undefeated, The 220
Under the City 75
United Nations 125
Universum Film Aktien Gesellschaft (UFa) 181
Upstream 58, 200

Index

Venture Adventure 125, 128
Voice of Britain 85–86
Voice of the World 62
Voices of Malaya 170–71, 198

Waking Point, The 20 171–73, 252, 254, 257, 259–60, 261
Watt, Harry 2, 7, 13, 22, 79, 82, 102, 107, 115, 159, 213, 214, 222, 245
Way from Germany, The 14, 155
We Live in Two Worlds 88, 201
We Sail at Midnight 128
Weather Forecast 85
Welch, David 18–19
Wellington House 32, 34
Western Approaches 12, 15, 128, 139, 204, 216, 220, 246, 253, 255, 265

What's on Today? 93
Whittle, Frank 162–63
Windmill in Barbados 54
Wildy, Tom 17, 142
Winston, Brian 3, 7–8, 13–14, 45, 128
Woman's Portion, The 38
Wonder Jet, The 162–63
Wooden Horse, The 109, 243
Words for Battle 125, 139, 217, 241
Workers' Weekend 111, 210
World Film News 10
Worth the Risk? 164, 211, 249
Wright, Basil 14, 53, 55, 57, 62, 72, 74, 79, 131, 133, 174, 223, 231, 241

Yank Comes Back, A 150, 151, 222